F V

# Show Business Law

# *SHOW BUSINESS* LAW

## Motion Pictures, Television, Video

**PETER MULLER**

**Quorum Books**
New York • Westport, Connecticut • London

The information in this book is meant for reference only. Please consult with an attorney and certified public accountant of your own choice prior to finalizing any agreements and contracts based on the information you have received in *Show Business Law.*

**Library of Congress Cataloging-in-Publication Data**

Muller, Peter.
   Show business law : motion pictures, television, video / Peter Muller.
      p.   cm.
   Includes bibliographical references and index.
   ISBN 0-89930-493-1 (lib. bdg. : alk. paper)
   1. Motion pictures—Law and legislation—United States.
   2. Television—Law and legislation—United States.   3. Video recordings—Law and legislation—United States.   4. Performing arts—Law and legislation—United States.   I. Title.
   KF4298.M85   1991
   344.73'097—dc20
   [347.30497]      90-40699

British Library Cataloguing in Publication Data is available.

Library of Congress Catalog Card Number: 90-40699
ISBN: 0-89930-493-1

First published in 1991

Quorum Books, 88 Post Road West, Westport, CT 06881
An imprint of Greenwood Publishing Group, Inc.

Printed in the United States of America

The paper used in this book complies with the Permanent Paper Standard issued by the National Information Standards Organization (Z39.48-1984).

10  9  8  7  6  5  4  3  2  1

To my wife and best friend,
Esther.
To my parents,
Dr. Alexander and Elizabeth Muller.

# Contents

|    | Acknowledgments | ix |
|----|------------------|-----|
| 1. | The Acquisition of Motion Picture Rights by Option | 1 |
| 2. | The Personal Manager Agreement | 10 |
| 3. | The Agent Agreement | 21 |
| 4. | The Actor Agreement | 33 |
| 5. | The Screen Writer Agreement | 52 |
| 6. | The Producer Agreement | 64 |
| 7. | The Director Agreement | 82 |
| 8. | Master Recording Use for a Motion Picture and Synchronization Rights | 100 |
| 9. | The Motion Picture Distribution Agreement: The Worldwide Pick-Up Deal | 106 |
| 10. | The Pay-Per-View Agreement | 115 |
| 11. | Licensing Feature Films for Television Syndication | 127 |
| 12. | International Coproductions | 137 |
| 13. | The Home Video License Agreement | 146 |
| 14. | Endorsements | 157 |
| 15. | Independent Production Financing | 172 |

16. The Attorney and the Accountant                                    183

    Appendix A: Copyright Registration Forms                           187

    Appendix B: Labor Organizations and Associations                   245

    Notes                                                              249

    Bibliography                                                       257

    Index                                                             259

# ACKNOWLEDGMENTS

The compilation of a book as comprehensive as *Show Business Law* could not be the job of one person. Jim Sabin of Greenwood Press immediately recognized the need for a book that would present the major contracts utilized in the motion picture business in a manner that is readable and understandable by all who could benefit from such a book – artists, producers, writers, directors, and the many other members of the entertainment community nationwide. What I attempt to achieve in *Show Business Law* is a book that strips the contracts down to their bare essentials and explains, in an understandable manner, what goes into the provisions that are the blood, bones, and sinews of an entertainment agreement.

Steven M. Schiffman, Esq., deserves special thanks for his assistance. He helped with the book from its inception, researching and assisting in the editing of the chapters. I would especially like to thank Steve for his extensive contribution in the preparation and final editing of the chapters "Licensing Feature Film for Television Syndication," and "International Coproductions."

Thanks also goes to Robert Greco. While assisting in the research for *Show Business Law,* he was completing law school and saddled with studying for his bar exam. Michael McHugh and Michael Manarel also contributed to the final effort.

Most of all, I would like to thank all the invaluable clients and friends I have made in the entertainment and communications industry.

The entertainment business is a most democratic business. Anyone, from any walk of life, has an even chance of succeeding in the entertainment industry. Talent, ability, and drive are central to an individual's success. However, an individual's talent must be backed up with knowledge. *Show Business Law* cannot supply the talent, ability, or drive, but it can be used as a reference tool that will help to provide the knowledge requisite to finalizing an equitable agreement. Armed with this knowledge, the dreamers, dream makers, and dream weavers can better face each other on an even playing field. Ultimately, it is this knowledge, coupled with talent, that affords everyone a fair chance of being a hit in show business.

# Show Business
# Law

# 1

# THE ACQUISITION OF MOTION PICTURE RIGHTS BY OPTION

The most fundamental element of any motion picture or telecast is its story line or plot. Whether the production is based on an original screenplay, novel, play, or short story, the process required to convert that written word to a motion picture or television project is complex, requiring the producer to obtain the necessary clearance rights. Generally, the first step is to obtain the motion picture rights relating to the underlying literary property. Those motion picture rights, as well as any rights inherent in a work, are property rights that are granted, or held back, at the owner's discretion and will.[1]

## ACQUISITION OF RIGHTS

The producer, the purchaser of the rights, can acquire the rights to a motion picture in various legal forms or entities: as an individual, corporation, or partnership. Given the economy of scale and the high cost of production, the producer seeking a literary property tends to negotiate for the acquisition of all media rights from the owner. Those underlying rights are typically acquired, during the preliminary stage of preproduction, in the form of an option agreement. In this manner, the producer may be able to develop the project, cast it, and seek potential investors to determine whether such a project is economically feasible and, if so, obtain the necessary capital to create the movie.

In addition to offering the work to potential financiers, the producer may also attempt to interest a major Hollywood motion picture studio into financing the project. If interest exists, either from investors or the major studios, the producer will then generally exercise the option to purchase the motion picture rights. In holding this option, it would be difficult to be circumvented by those who would rather not deal with the producer, who would possess, for the term of the agreement, ownership rights in the work for the rights optioned.

The agreement held by the producer typically stipulates to the underlying rights holder that while the producer will use his or her "best efforts" to produce a movie or television show based on the plot or story line, the producer is under no legal obligation to produce, distribute, release, perform, or exhibit any motion picture, television, theatrical, or other production based upon, adapted from, or suggested by the literary property. The option to acquire the motion picture rights, as described, grants to the producer the right to produce a motion picture without a binding guarantee. The option is, in a sense, a leveraged approach to acquiring the underlying movie rights of a literary property.

## WARRANTIES AND REPRESENTATIONS

Depending upon the complexity of the proposed motion picture agreement, the option contract may in itself be as complex as an actual literary purchase contract. Within the option agreement, the owner of the literary work will generally represent and warrant that the literary property is truly his or her work and, if a published novel, was published on a certain date by a certain publisher.

## COPYRIGHT REGISTRATION

The owner of the work, or the publisher if applicable, will usually be required to stipulate that the literary work has been filed and registered in the copyright office of the Library of Congress in Washington, D.C.

If the material was not already published, it is generally agreed in the contract that the owner will register the work with the copyright office on a "time is of the essence" basis.

## SOLE AND EXCLUSIVE USE OF BOOK

If the literary property is a published novel, the rights owner is typically required to affirm that no other motion picture or dramatic version of the literary property has been manufactured, produced, presented, or authorized by the owner and that no motion picture, radio, or television agreement or development deal based on the optioned works is presently in effect. If, on the other hand, the literary property had been optioned or developed on a prior occasion, the owner generally attests that all rights had reverted to him or her and that he or she has the complete unencumbered right to enter this option agreement. Generally, the owner further states that no oral or written agreement was made and executed with respect to the literary work, except those provisions stipulated in the agreement.

## ORIGINAL SOURCE OF MATERIAL

Clarifying the rights of original ownership in a literary property is of primary importance in acquiring the rights. In that regard, the contract will generally state that the owner did not base his or her literary work on any literary, dramatic, or other material of any description. An exception to this hard rule would be if the owner of the work based its creation upon a work within the public domain. Under those circumstances, the right of ownership by copyright is generally considered waived by the original owner, who had permitted the work to lapse into the public domain and thereby loses statutory protection.[2] A work in the public domain may include the written work itself as well as the plot, scenes, sequences, musical elements, or story line.

### Privacy

The owner of the rights to the work is generally asked to warrant that the story does not violate the privacy of others and that the material is not libelous or defamatory.

### Exclusive Ownership of the Literary Property

The owner of the literary rights typically warrants and guarantees that, throughout the world, he or she is the exclusive owner of such rights detailed in the agreement. The owner, in addition, may stipulate that he or she has not encumbered, diminished, or impaired those rights nor assigned them to a third party.[3]

Because this agreement is often an option agreement based on predefined criteria, the fee received at the signing of the agreement may be the sole expenditure towards acquiring the rights to the work until the actual acquisition is completed. Should this clause, or any other clause regarding the owner's true ownership rights in the work, prove to be defective, the only funds at risk are those options monies.

## IN CASE OF DISPUTES

The option agreement could provide that in the event litigation does arise, the term of the agreement would be extended for a period of time equal to the length of the controversy. Under those circumstances, the option period will be extended until there is no challenge or litigation regarding the ownership of the literary work.

## EXERCISE OF AN OPTION

The contract may stipulate exactly how notice of the acceptance of the option will be performed. The agreement may provide for the producer to notify the owner of the literary work in writing by verifiable mail (e.g., certified mail, return receipt requested, Federal Express, messenger with a signed receipt), and that such a receipt would constitute the exercise of such an option.

The contract should also contain the general provision that oral statements or conducts will not be considered a valid means to indicate acceptance of the option, be it by the producer or the producer's agents or representatives.

## DEPOSIT OF MATERIALS

The agreement may include a provision close in context to an escrow agreement. Under this provision, the parties agree that, at the signing of the option agreement, all necessary papers are to be deposited with an attorney or representative acceptable to both parties. That attorney or representative could be required, if agreed upon in the agreement, to turn over all documents to the producer in the event that the option is exercised. On the other hand, if the option is declined or expires, all documents signed and deposited with the attorney or representative would be returned to the owner of the literary works. Such documents could include copyright registration, powers of attorney, warranties, and representations.

## POWER OF ATTORNEY

The contract may grant to the producer the power of attorney should the option agreement be exercised but the necessary documentation not followed through. For example, if the work was never registered with the copyright office, this agreement could provide the producer with the authority both to register it and to name the producer as holder of the copyright.[4]

## RIGHT TO COMMENCE PRODUCTION

Even though the option is not fully effective until notice has been properly made, the option agreement typically allows, during the period of the option, for the producer to engage at his or her expense in the preproduction of a movie based on the literary work, including preparing a screen play. Generally, the only restriction is that the producer not publish or produce the screenplay until the option is completely exercised.

## PREJUDICIAL ACTIONS

A clause stipulating that the owner may not take any action during the effectiveness of the option period that will prejudice the rights optioned for against the producer can also be provided in this agreement.

## THIRD PARTY NEGOTIATIONS

During the option period, the owner can be enjoined from negotiating with a third party regarding future ownership of the option, unless such negotiations are granted by the producer and would not conflict with the option rights granted. This can be an important provision, especially if the producer is attempting to obtain financing or other means of support and it is learned that a competing production team is negotiating for the same literary property. Such a situation may damage the producer's chances for finalizing the financing and production of the motion picture.

In the event of a breach of any of these conditions by the owner or publisher of the literary work, and depending on the bargaining strength of the parties, the producer will generally have the alternative of either permitting the owner to cure the defect, thereby allowing the option to continue uninterrupted, or to completely nullify and void the option agreement in its entirety. In the latter case, the funds advanced to the owner could be returned to the producer.

## ASSIGNMENT

The owner may try to limit the assignability of the option, which prevents the producer from assigning the rights in the work, thereby "flipping the rights."[5] The right to assign the work lessens the owner's ability to maintain control over the producer and the work.

When, however, the option is executed and the literary property is acquired by the producer, the right to assignment could become absolute in the producer's favor. Provisions that would avoid such an eventuality can be included in the agreement. A "turnaround" clause would enable the owner to reacquire the rights in the event the producer fails to proceed with the film project.[6]

## RIGHTS AVAILABLE

The agreement generally outlines in detail what rights are available under the agreement as well as those typically reserved to the owner. The rights the producer normally attempts to acquire are as broad as possible, including the right to produce, exhibit, and broadcast the work, be it in the form of motion pictures, remakes, sequels, theater, television, radio, music, video cassettes, or any other media format now known or to be developed.

### Ancillary Rights

In addition, the producer usually negotiates for the right to novelize a motion picture, to record its soundtrack, and to merchandize all products derived from it—clothing, accessories, toys, dolls, products, and so forth. These rights can represent a substantial amount of revenue.

The producer may also attempt to secure a percentage of the revenues earned from the republication of the work, if the original work appeared as a novel, in the event of a successful response by the audience to the picture at the box office.

### Additional Rights

All rights granted to the producer should be clearly defined in the agreement, including the right to use, in other formats, the characters, story, plot, and setting incidental to the work. For example, the right to take the characters and plots from a popular film or television show and use them as the basis for an animation series is a separate right that can represent a substantial amount of additional revenues.

### Retained Rights by the Owner

The owner may wish to retain several categories of rights, including the rights for live stage presentations, publication, and, at times, motion picture sequels that feature the same characters and settings as those in the rights acquired by the producer. For example, where the owner retains the right to use a character in a motion picture for additional works, written or filmed, such rights fall outside those purchased by the producer. If the producer cannot acquire those rights, he or she may request that the owner hold back using or granting those rights for a period of time after the release of the motion picture, arguing that the exploitation of those rights would lessen the appeal for the motion picture audience, thereby critically damaging the rights obtained by the producer and representing a substantial loss of revenue.

### Creative Control and Editing

An important right is that of total and unlimited discretion by the producer to edit, vary, change, alter, modify, add to, and delete from the property, to rearrange and transpose, change the sequence, and alter the characters and descriptions of the characters, and use a portion or portions of the property, characters, plots, or theme in conjunction with any literary, dramatic, or other material.[7] The ownership of creative control can shape the whole look, feel, and tone of the work. Generally, the party with the stronger track record and industry clout maintains creative control.

### Moral Rights

Since the acquisition is typically for both domestic and international use, it is important that the contract contain a waiver of "droit moral" (moral rights). In some countries, such as France, the moral right of author is not generally waived. Under those conditions, even if the contract provides that the producer may change the story any way he or she wishes, it may not have any legal standing in France.[8]

## COMPENSATION

The producer will usually pay the owner an agreed sum when exercising the option agreement. In some instances, that initial payment is credited against payment for all the rights upon the timely exercise of the option. Additional payments are usually made upon renewal of the option. As an added means of compensation, the owner may negotiate for a percentage of the gross or net earnings generated from the exploitation of the motion picture.[9] The stronger the original work and the more successful the owner, the more chance he or she has for securing an equity percentage in the motion picture based on it.

The owner may also negotiate for additional payments for the productions of sequels, remakes, miniseries, or television serializations based on the characters in a motion picture. If agreed, the size and schedule of those payments are usually negotiated with the purchase of the original option.

### Compensation Factors

The amount of compensation is often based on several factors, including the age of the property, its popularity while in print (if a novel), the actual subject matter, the reputation of the owner, to name just a few. Also determining the price is the length of the option. If the owner's works are desirable, or if the work is considered highly commercial, the option may be made even prior to the actual writing or publication of the story. Option payments may be credited towards the eventual purchase price (a hybrid lease/purchase option) of the literary property, if negotiated.

## OWNER'S NAME, LIKENESS, AND BIOGRAPHY

The agreement generally establishes whether the producer has the right to publish, advertise, announce, or use the name, biography, and photographs or other likenesses of the owner.[10] The agreement also typically includes a provision that should the owner of the literary project not be the original creator of the work, then the owner has received permission to use the name, likeness, and biography of the creator. The means for establishing the validity of such a permission is typically stated within the contract. In the event that the owner has not secured such rights, the agreement could provide for a suspension of services and obligations as required by the acquisition of rights by option contract until a separate agreement can be reached by the creator, owner, or producer.

## SCREEN CREDITS

The contract provides that the writer receive credit on the screen in a manner agreed upon by the parties.[11] The credit may read: "Based on the novel by. . . ." or "Based on an original story by. . . ."

Aside from minimum guarantees, the contract usually states the size of the owner's name on the screen, the conditions under which it may appear, and how the size, placement, and wording relates to other screen credits. In the event of an editing or other error regarding the credits, this clause may also stipulate that such an omission is not to be construed as a material breach of the contract, thereby forestalling equitable suits as a result of the failure.[12]

## PRODUCER'S ACTIVITIES DURING THE OPTION PERIOD

The producer should use the option period to gather all the elements necessary – screenwriter, director, actors, and crew – to make the production a success. Locations can be scouted and financing finalized. The producer may try to insure that no obligation to exercise the option will exist until the budget has been raised and the principal photography is ready to commence.

## REVERSION OF RIGHTS TO OWNER

A reversion clause in the agreement typically provides that, if the option is not exercised in a timely fashion, or if material provisions of the option agreement are not fulfilled, the option terminates and all rights in the work revert to the owner.[13] Generally, monies advanced to the owner are not refundable.

## COPYRIGHT

The contract typically contains a clause in which the rights owner grants and assigns to the producer all of the owner's rights and titles to and interest in any and all copyrights to the work. It may also provide the producer with all the remedies associated with copyright infringement, including damages and share of profits.[14]

Since the value of the work is based on the protection afforded the producer by the copyright, the owner in this clause generally agrees to prevent the work from falling into the public domain. In this connection, the owner agrees to affix, or require any publisher of the property to affix, to each copy of the writing offered for sale or publication a complete notice of copyright complying in all respects to the U.S. copyright law and the Universal Copyright Convention.

Under most circumstances, the producer may want to defend his or her interest in the literary work. The contract may stipulate that the owner agrees to appoint the producer as the owner's attorney-in-fact, with the right, but not the obligation, for the sole benefit of the producer and at producer's expense, to bring, prosecute, defend, and appear in suits, actions, and proceedings of any nature under or concerning all copyrights to the writings. This provision generally permits the owner and producer to file as party plaintiffs or defendants in any suit arising from any infringement of such rights.

## DOCUMENTS

Since the ownership of the literary property is protected primarily by copyright, it is important that the contract provides for the exchange of all appropriate and required documents. Under this clause, the owner stipulates that he or she acknowledges and will execute and deliver to the producer any and all documents, assignments, releases, and other legal instruments necessary to expeditiously carry out the purposes of the contract.

# 2

---

# The Personal Manager Agreement

A personal manager's key responsibility is to advise and counsel the talent on how best to establish, further, and maintain the talent's career in the entertainment industry. The personal manager should know the agents specializing in the motion picture business and be familiar with the executives who oversee the production of motion pictures, the producers who are making movies, and the directors who can bring out the best in the talent. The personal manager must keep up with trends in the movie industry and know what motion pictures are being developed and filmed. Also, the personal manager should have the negotiating skills necessary to secure the most favorable agreements for clients, considering their present bargaining positions, skills, and recognized potentials.

The areas that typically generate much of the negotiation between the personal manager and the talent relates to such issues as the length of the management agreement, the gross percentage the manager will receive from the income earned by the talent during the agreement, the percentage received by the manager from a negotiated deal after the agreement has lapsed, the responsibilities of the manager, and which ancillary activities performed by the talent, if any, are exempt from the agreement and therefore not commissionable by the manager.

A problem may arise if the personal manager, in order to generate income for the talent and help further his or her career at the outset, secured employment for the talent at such venues as licensed clubs and theme parks. In some states, the personal manager has, by virtue of securing bookings, assumed the role of agent, an individual generally licensed by the state to perform the services of a talent agency. The personal manager, if unlicensed, may have stepped over the boundary of propriety and actually breached fiduciary duties and obligations to the talent. Such a breach may prove to be grounds for costly litigation at a later date.[1]

The relationship between the talent and personal manager is a close one. If successful, they cultivate their careers together. The talent's stage and cinematic persona often relies on the manager's experience and abilities as advisor and negotiator. But, as the talent develops and grows, becoming more successful and recognized, the personal manager's influence may wane.

The talent/personal manager agreement should make both parties feel that they are using the abilities of the other to the fullest, with the aim of enhancing each individual's potential. Basically, the talent/personal manager agreement is an employment agreement that should be drafted taking into consideration each party's unique requirements and needs. It must be remembered, though, that the personal manager is employed by the talent.

The management contract is often drawn by the personal manager and presented to the talent for negotiation and approval. There are several key elements to each contract that must be understood and agreed upon by both parties. In order for each party to be counseled correctly and to avoid the possibility of a deal-breaking conflict of interest at a later date, the talent and personal manager should employ independent counsel familiar with the customs and practices of the entertainment industry to negotiate on their behalf.

## THE PARTIES

The contract generally spells out clearly the parties to the agreement. The personal manager, as an individual or member of a personal management firm, is one party. The talent is the other. If the talent is an acting group, it may be considered in the dual capacity of the group as a whole, including the new members who join the group after the contract is signed, and as an individual who is also a member of the represented group. In the more common case, the talent is considered an individual irrespective of any acting group or company which retains his or her acting ability. This chapter will deal with the talent as an individual.

### Key Person Clause

If the talent feels that a particular manager is critical to success, the manager and the talent insert a "key person" clause into their agreement. The key person clause creates a contractual bond between the talent and the personal manager that will survive the agreement. If the manager leaves his or her present employ and goes to work for another manager or

establishes his or her own management company, or if the agreement is
assigned to another management company, the key person clause assures
that the talent and the manager's creative relationship will continue uninterrupted.

## MANAGER'S DUTIES

The personal manager is generally required to clarify his or her duties.
Of primary importance is the continuing obligation to give advice, guidance, and counsel to the talent at reasonable times.

An area that should be carefully drafted relates to the precise areas that
are commissionable to the manager and the duties that fall under his or
her jurisdiction. The agreement may be broad and all inclusive, calling
for the personal manager to receive an agreed upon percentage of all income and revenues earned from the talent's activities in the entertainment industry as a whole.

The term entertainment should be carefully defined. Without a precise
definition, the commissions earned by the manager may cover areas not
anticipated by the talent. Therefore, when drafting the agreement, special care should be taken to note that the legal bond created between the
talent and the personal manager is strictly limited to the entertainment
industry as defined in detail in the contract. The talent's nonentertain-
ment employment is generally excluded from the definition of entertainment. Ancillary activities, such as the talent's career in the music
industry or as an author, may be excluded from the agreement if specifically agreed.

The duties of the manager generally includes advising the talent on
such issues as employment offers, public relations strategy, scripts, commercial and advertising opportunities, literary offers, performing offers,
and appointing booking agents, personal business managers, and
accountants.

The personal manager is called upon to advise and consult with the
talent regarding the packaging of the talent to the public through films,
well-timed publicity jaunts, and live performances. The objective is to
control overexposure and limit negative experiences. This area can be
very important but highly subjective. The contract may stipulate that the
manager will give advice, with the talent's artistic limitations and best
interests in mind.

Moreover, the agreement usually states specifically that the personal
manager will provide expert advice related to whether compensation
offers should be accepted or rejected by the talent. This role must be
carefully delineated in order to assure that the role of the agent and personal manager do not become intertwined.

In most cases, the role of the manager is to advise the talent on the amount of the compensation to be demanded or accepted, considering the talent's position within the industry. Industry standards, the actual roles offered, and the long-term goals of the talent must also be considered. While the agent may do the actual booking and on-premise negotiations, the manager usually counsels the agent as to the overall career potentials of job offers. Based on the talent's career objectives, the manager and the talent decide together whether an offer will be accepted or rejected.

While the role of the publicist or public relations agency is to promote the image of the talent, the manager usually works with the talent to decide whether the advice suggested by the public relations firm is acceptable. In addition, this clause typically establishes that the services of the personal manager will be made available to the talent at all "reasonable" times. If the relationship with the talent is on an "as needed" basis, such a relationship should be stated clearly in the agreement to prevent any doubt of the manager's obligations during future discussions.

## MANAGER VERSUS AGENT

The contract should clearly state that the role of the personal manager is distinct, separate, and apart from that of the booking agent. In most of the fifty states, agents must be licensed by a governing authority while managers are at present virtually unregulated.[2] The manager is not an agent and should not let the talent believe that he or she can act as an employment agency. The effect of this law may cause some misunderstanding, for example, the talent may not comprehend why the manager is not booking clubs. Therefore, the contract should state that the personal manager, in most jurisdictions, cannot by law secure employment for the talent in such venues as clubs or arenas.[3] The agreement should state in clear and unambiguous language that the personal manager is not acting as an agent or employment agency, will not seek or procure employment or engagements for the talent, and is not obligated, authorized, licensed, or expected to do so.[4]

The contract also typically states that the talent is obligated to seek and retain an employment agent or booking agency. Generally, the manager requires the talent to consult him or her before deciding on an agent.

### Talent's Duties

The talent's duty is, simply, full devotion to career. In so doing, the talent fulfills his or her professional obligations to the personal manager. The talent's failure to pursue a career in a reasonable manner can result in a breach of the contract, relinquishing the personal manager from all duties to the talent without fear of liability or legal recrimination.

The manager usually maintains control over the creative decisions affecting the talent's public look, sound, and persona. Creative control can include final say over publicity, marketing, and the physical look and dress of the talent. The manager may claim that all aspects of the talent's creative components are part of the package that must be controlled to achieve success. The manager and the talent generally decide between themselves who has ultimate control on all creative decisions.

### Exclusivity

The talent is, under most circumstances, signed exclusively to the personal manager. The manager, on the other hand, may represent many individuals or performers. The talent, when signing with a manager, should evaluate the manager's background, reputation, and history in the industry. He or she should consider the number and performance styles of other talents represented by the personal manager.

### Term

An important aspect of the talent/personal manager contract is the duration of the agreement, usually defined as a term of years. The rationale for a term to extend over several years (e.g., two years with three one-year options) is that a certain amount of preliminary ground work is required to carry out the strategy that will establish the name and reputation of the talent. It takes time to break the talent into the entertainment field.

An initial term that is considered excessively lengthy, eight or ten years for example, may be ruled unconscionable, and therefore unenforceable, by the courts.

There are times when the talent may not wish to employ a personal manager for an extended period of time. This typically takes place when the manager is new to the industry and has not firmly established a track record. The personal manager, on the other hand, sees the client from a long-term perspective. Proper representation that satisfies the objectives of both talent and personal manager is the best way for both to achieve mutually successful careers.

### Options for Renewal

The initial term may be extended for a predetermined time period by granting the personal manager the option to renew the term of the agreement. This clause establishes the limits of the relationship that binds the parties and generally can not be severed unilaterally without showing undue influence, fraud, misrepresentation, or unconscionability.[5]

The talent may be concerned about whether the personal manager can actually secure employment as intended. The manager, on the other hand, may wish to test the entertainment waters without unnecessary and lengthy obligations. The agreement, therefore, may consist of an option, which can be self-executing or based on the attainment of yearly performance levels. The right to exercise the option may be granted to the talent. Conversely, the option may be subject to the manager's prerogative.

The talent may request performance-level based options – option renewals based on the attainment of certain performance plateaus, such as securing a motion picture contract to act in a picture release by a major studio, or receiving a stipulated amount of gross annual earnings before the obligation to renew the contract for additional years becomes self-executing.

In order to extend the term of the agreement, and thereby exercise the option, the agreement generally states that the party exercising the option must notify the other, within a specified number of days, of the intent to exercise the option.

Also subject to negotiation are self-executing based options. The option to accept continuing management functions will be self-executing, whereby, without a written communication to the contrary, the manager or the talent automatically renews the option for the specified period of time.

## Territory

The territory over which the personal manager guides and advises the talent should be clearly established in the contract. Under most circumstances, the personal manager is granted worldwide rights. But, the territory agreed upon in the agreement can be as limited, or expansive, as mutually agreed.

The personal manager may demand the right to assign a portion of his or her territorial rights to other, equally competent, managers, if in his or her sole judgment such an assignment is in the best interest of the talent.

## POWER OF ATTORNEY

Three words can sign away many of the individual rights a talent has in his or her work and career, and, like a term of endearment, are often used indiscriminately to entice, control, and manipulate. They are power of attorney.

A power of attorney is the grant of legal authority from one person to another, in this case, from the talent to the personal manager, authorizing the one to whom the power is granted, the personal manager, to act for the other, the talent. The attorney-in-fact is empowered to represent and act for the talent, and to legally bind the talent to the terms of an agreement of which he or she may not even be aware.

The law places upon the attorney-in-fact an obligation to uphold a standard of fiduciary care above that normally required of one individual when dealing with another.[6]

Personal managers, attorneys, business managers, and agents often request that a talent grant them a broad power of attorney, giving them the right to execute agreements, enforce the collection of revenues, make investments, and perform any other act the manager or attorney believes should be performed on the talent's behalf. Under the general heading of this last grant, the attorney-in-fact generally has the freedom to sign for the talent on a wide range of topics. Certainly, the attorney-in-fact is held to a high standard of fiduciary care, but to prove a standard that is less than acceptable, the talent will usually be forced into an expensive and lengthy legal quarrel.

Powers of attorney can be drafted limiting the power to specific tasks required of the talent's representative, such as signing agreements pertaining to advertisers, press agents, unions, publicity, limited personal appearances, accounting, and so forth without risking major legal battles in the future.

This clause may also grant the personal manager the authority to do such things as approve and permit any and all advertising of the talent; grant permission to use the talent's name, likeness, voice, sound effects, caricatures, writings, and musical materials for promotion and advertising; sign agreements on contracts for services in the event the talent is unavailable to sign but fully apprised of the agreements. Moreover, power of attorney may permit the manager to sign checks in the name of the talent and receive monies and endorse the talent's name to all checks payable to the talent. In addition, the manager can be entitled to hold such monies received owed to the manager.

This agreement may be subject to intense negotiations between the parties, certainly if the talent already has or plans to have a business manager. Often, the business manager prefers to be granted authority in matters relating to business and financing.

## COMPENSATION

The personal manager often receives a fee equal to a percentage of the talent's gross income. Gross revenue is usually defined as all monies, sums, fees, bonuses, royalties, personal or real property, or any form of compensation received without any deductions, and in any manner, means, or form as a result of all entertainment and career-related endeavors earned by the talent during the term of the management agreement. The term "the entertainment industry" is broad and should be spelled out. It usually includes the following fields: music, recording, publishing, motion pictures, television (pay and free), video cassettes, cable, radio, live performances, merchandising, advertising, and any and all other forms of media or distribution now known or to be devised at any future time. The talent's compensation is generally described as all sums of money, revenues, royalties, advances, bonuses, stock options, and fees earned in any manner or form, including real or personal property, bonuses, shares of stock, or in any other form or manner of compensation. The definition of gross in the agreement should be detailed and well defined. If any exceptions are to be made to this definition, they should be made and executed prior to signing the agreement.

The actual percentage commissionable by the manager is usually decided based on both parties' respective strengths within the entertainment business. An unknown talent is generally less empowered to make compensatory demands on a manager than a successful talent with a string of successful box office hits.

The contract should clearly establish which employment performances executed by the talent are commissionable to the manager and which are not. Typically, the manager receives a percentage only of the gross revenues, based on the monies actually received by the talent and not on collectibles. For example, if the talent is due compensation after winning a breach of contract suit, the manager would not normally receive a portion of that sum until the talent is actually compensated.

Managers may take on roles as producers or packagers of projects, packaging their various clients for a particular motion picture, program, or television special. At times, the producer pays the manager a fee for the role of "packaging entity." The compensation clause, within the talent/personal management agreement, should reflect such a possibility. Depending on the strength of the parties, a typical agreement usually stipulates that the personal manager must receive the talent's written permission to accept a fee as "packaging entity." It is thought that such notice will prevent the possibility of a conflict of interest on the personal manager's part when suggesting particular assignments to clients.

## Annuity Clause

Under the annuity clause, the personal manager is entitled to compensation during the term of the agreement for any extensions to the agreement (options or modifications) and, after the termination of the agreement, for any revenue earned from agreements entered into or performed totally or partially during the term of the agreement. The talent may attempt to diminish the manager's financial percentage over a fixed period of years after the termination of the agreement.

The agreement should also establish clearly that any income received subsequent to the departure of the manager, but earned during the manager's tenure of employment, would also be deemed commissionable.

The issue becomes thorny when, for example, the talent is involved in a long-term employment contract with a television program with several built-in options, resulting in the talent being granted the option to continue to perform or to cease performing. As long as the manager continues to function as manager, there is little contractual dispute as to his or her rights to compensation. A problem may arise when the manager is replaced by another, and the talent exercises the option to renew his or her contract with the television program. For example, if a studio signs up an actor or director for one movie with the option to perform in or direct several others, the options are typically different and newly negotiated contracts with respect to terms, salary, and the like. The issue boils down to whether the manager should receive a full commission on the options, presuming of course that the execution of such options takes place subsequent to the dismissal or resignation of the personal manager. Under such a possible scenario, the employment agreement between the talent and manager might provide the manager with a declining commission on any work obtained as a result of such options or long-term commitments. Unless a compromise is reached, the talent may find him or herself in the unenviable position of paying double commission, one to the original manager and one to the new manager, since both may insist on being commissioned for such work.

The management agreement should take into account any subsequent improvements made by the talent in an employment agreement following the term of the talent/personal management relationship. If the talent, therefore, is able to significantly increase the compensation for appearing in a previously contracted television program subsequent to the departure of the personal manager, then the original manager typically does not receive a commission based on that additional sum. However, if the increase is part of a previously negotiated option, then the manager may be entitled to a commission on the difference.

## Expenses

The talent is usually responsible for all expenses incurred by the manager on his or her behalf. Those expenses should be detailed and accountable. Depending on the relationship of the talent and the manager as well as the stature of both parties, the provision regarding expenses can be all-encompassing or restrictive.

The detailed approach to expenses stipulates that the talent is obligated to reimburse all reasonable expenses incurred by the manager in furthering the talent's career. The contract may list examples of such expenses, including postal correspondence, long distance telephone calls, facsimiles, business lunches, publicity materials, and travel expenses.

The more restrictive approach is to establish a threshold amount that can be expended by the personal manager without specific approval. Greater expenses must be authorized in writing by the talent prior to the outlay of funds by the manager. For example, the manager may be able to advance up to $250 per item without receiving prior approval. Once that sum is spent, written approval for more is required.

## SUSPENSION CLAUSE

If the talent fails to meet his or her obligations under the requirements of the agreement by reason of gross negligence, malicious intent or willful failure, the personal manager usually has the right, under the suspension clause to extend the term of the agreement for a period of time equal to the duration of such failure. This assures the personal manager that the talent stays under contract for the agreed period of time, instead of avoiding obligations by simply letting the term run out.

## AUDITING THE BOOKS

Both the talent and the personal manager should retain the right to audit the books and records of the other party by employing independent, certified public accountants of their choice to determine whether the accounting statements rendered by each are accurate. This is an important function whereby either party can be assured of receiving the revenues due them based on the terms of the agreement. A statute of limitations defines the period during which parties can file complaints over alleged inaccuracies.

## FAILURE TO PERFORM

If either talent or personal manager fails to fulfill obligations and responsibilities under the agreement, the wronged party could be required, under this provision, to bring that failure to the attention of the other in writing. This puts the parties on notice that the defaulting party has a reasonable period of time to right the wrong. If after that period the wrong has not been cured, the agreement may be severed without liability if the wrong is considered a material breach and if the agreement calls for such a severe penalty.

## UNENFORCEABILITY

In the event a single condition of the agreement is ruled to be unenforceable by a change in the law or an interpretation of the courts, the parties can agree that the rest of the contract will remain in full force and effect. This will insure consistency in performing the terms of the contract without fear that one error could void the whole agreement and years of labor.

## INCORPORATION BY TALENT

In the event the talent forms a corporation, the personal manager may request the assurance that the new corporation will enter into an identical agreement with the manager. The manager and talent, by agreeing to this clause, will usually be able to continue their working relationship, no matter what business format their organizations take in the future.

## LIMITATION OF LIABILITIES

In order to limit the liabilities, remedies, and rights of each party, both could agree that the agreement they are entering is not a joint venture or partnership. The manager, by this clause, is generally considered to be an independent contractor.

## JURISDICTION

The agreement clarifies which state has jurisdiction over disputes. The most convenient state is the one where both maintain their businesses, which lessens expenses in the event of litigation.

## ARBITRATION

The parties may agree to settle their disputes by arbitration, regulated by the rules of the American Arbitration Association (AAA). Arbitration proceedings are less formal than civil proceedings. The decision of the arbitrator is final and enforceable by the courts. Resolving a dispute through arbitration is often a less lengthy, and thereby less costly, process than litigation. There is more leniency in the arbitration proceeding, and the arbitrators are often peers in the music industry.[7]

# 3

---

# THE AGENT AGREEMENT

The agent has earned a special niche in the entertainment business. The link between the creative talent and the employer, the agent evaluates scripts; refers manuscripts to producers, actors, directors, writers, and publishers; and discovers and recruits unknown talent in search of tomorrow's stars.

The agent usually grows in strength and clout in the entertainment industry by the success of his or her clients. If the agent does not procure work for clients, the talent may understandably search elsewhere for the service.

## LICENSE

In most states, the talent agent must be licensed by the appropriate state department.[1] By regulating the agent, the state is attempting to reassure the talent of the agent's credibility. The agent's license may be revoked if he or she oversteps the bounds of the agreement to the detriment of the talent.

The agency agreement typically states that the agent retained by the talent is licensed within the state of his or her principal business operations to engage in offering, promising, procuring, or attempting to procure employment for the talent. There are, however, substantial legal differences between major entertainment industry states, such as New York and California. The talent should review the laws related to agencies in his or her state of residence.

The regulatory control the state has over the agent is one of the major differences between a personal manager and an agent. Consequently, unless a personal manager is also licensed as an agent, managers are generally prohibited by law from obtaining employment for talent. Since the agent is regulated, often the ceiling on what an agent may charge is also regulated by law.[2]

## DUTIES

The agency agreement clarifies the agent's duties, which typically include the use of all reasonable efforts to procure employment for clients, be they writers, directors, authors, lyricists, actors, or performers, in all aspects of the entertainment industry, including motion pictures, advertising, radio, television, recording, publishing, and live stage performances.

### Scope of Representation

Many agency agreements grant the agent responsibility over all the entertainment activities of a talent. The contract typically states that the talent engages and employs, on a sole and exclusive basis, the agent to represent him or her in procuring employment in all aspects of the entertainment, publishing, advertising, merchandizing, and communication industries throughout the world.

If, however, the talent is already well established in one specific area, the agreement could be negotiated to remove certain services from the responsibility of the general agency agreement. In addition, the scope of the agent's duty can be limited to a specific field if the agent's strength is so limited. The talent may agree to an agency agreement specifically geared to commercials for example, thereby excluding motion pictures, television series, and live stage performances from the agent's duties.

## TERM

The talent is generally required to retain the agency for a fixed period of time. An option to renew the employment agency agreement may be added to the original agreement, if negotiated. Generally, the greater the stature of the talent, the more negotiating strength he or she has with regard to the length of the term and the grounds upon which he or she can sever the agency agreement without incurring liability.

### Performance Criteria Requirement

Depending on his or her bargaining strength, the talent may require certain guarantees from the agent. One of those guarantees may regard the agent's efforts in finding employment for the talent. While the term "reasonable efforts to attempt to procure employment" is sufficient for the beginner, the more established talent may require that the agency meet certain performance minimums during the period of representation for the agreement to remain in full force and for options, if included, to take force.

Such a guarantee may require that a specific number of engagements be offered to the talent. Alternatively, the talent may require a minimum income within a defined period of time. Most commonly, the terms of the agency agreement, if the agreement is to be conditioned by performance criteria, extends to the point of making such work available. If the talent, for no extraordinary reason, declines to accept employment procured and offered by the agent, the value of such an offering may be included in the minimum.

## REQUIREMENT TO JOIN A GUILD

Usually included is a clause stipulating that if the talent is not, upon signing with the agency, a member of a trade union or guild, and if the talent subsequently joins a sanctioned union or guild with an industry-wide agency agreement, then the agency agreement becomes secondary with respect to the union requirements pertaining to agency agreements.

## NONEXCLUSIVITY OF AN AGENT'S SERVICES

The agency agreement generally requires that the talent acknowledge and approve the fact that the agent represents other clients, in addition to him- or herself, in a similar business. Even though the talent is under an exclusive representation deal with the agent, the agent in general is not exclusive to the talent.

## KEY PERSON CLAUSE

The "key person" provision is an important negotiated element of the agreement generally demanded by the talent. Under the terms of the key person clause, the talent can insist that a specific person within an agency be, and remain, his or her agent.

Under such an arrangement, if the key person decides to change agencies or ceases to perform agent services to the talent, the talent is entitled to unilaterally terminate the agreement with the agency.

## DOUBLE COMMISSIONS

The agency agreement usually addresses the issue of double commissions and subsidiaries.

Many major talent agencies have foreign-based branches and subsidiaries. Current business practices dictate that each of these offices or subsidiaries become profit centers on its own behalf. Therefore, foreign subsidiary agencies may charge a commission for their services to American performers. Without a clause to the contrary, an agency in the United States may charge the talent a commission for work done in Europe, notwithstanding the fact that its foreign subsidiary or branch had already charged the talent.

The talent generally negotiates that the agency be able to appoint others, including the agent's subsidiary or affiliated corporations, to aid in securing employment for the talent, with the added caveat that the talent has no obligation to pay any sums beyond those specified in the original agency agreement for the services of anyone the agency appoints.

The issue of double commissions also develops when the talent is a member of an ensemble group, and the agency books engagements for both the performer as an individual and as part of a group or team. For such situations, the contract may spell out that the commissions are paid solely on the earnings of the group, unless the talent was booked separately from the group.

## AGENCY COMPENSATION AND COMMISSIONS

This section of the agency agreement establishes what commission fee will be due the agent in exchange for his or her services. In some jurisdictions, the maximum amount of commission is regulated by the state. Basically, commissions can be divided into three groups: statutorily permitted commissions, union negotiated ceilings, and free competitive market rates.

### Commission Rates

Generally, the agency rate of 10 percent covers entertainment-related work, including acting, writing, directing, and so forth. Higher commission rates may be negotiated for nonacting, ancillary income sources, including lecturing and merchandising. If both the agency and the talent anticipate a variety of income sources, the contract should assign each activity with a separate commission schedule.

### Pay or Play

The agency agreement generally provides that the agent is commissioned for work contracted but not necessarily carried out by the talent. A typical example is a pay or play agreement.[3] A talent may have an agreement with an advertising agency to appear in a promotional advertising campaign that is canceled at the last moment. Under the pay or play provision, the talent is paid in full, or at a negotiated rate, even though he or she did not provide any service to the advertiser. Under such a situation, the agency generally insists that income is likewise commissionable.

In this regard, the agency agreement typically states that a contract may be defined as any agreement, oral or written, directly or indirectly relating to the talent's rendition of services or refraining from the rendition of services.

## Renewals, Extensions, Options, and Future Income Considerations

The agent usually continues to receive compensation beyond the term of the agreement if the talent continues to earn fees, royalties, and revenues from employment opportunities entered into during the term of the agreement.

In general, the difficulty of this clause, and the aspect that may lead to lengthy litigation, is determining what exactly constitutes employment opportunities negotiated or entered into during the life of the agency agreement. This is especially true when the talent contract has a clause regarding extensions, options, or renewals. Generally, the agent demands a commission on any employment opportunity predicated on an employment contract negotiated and entered into during the term of the original agreement.

In addition, the agency agreement often provides that, if a production company or other contracted party changes ownership or is merged, or in the event the original contracting party changes positions is no longer employed by the original contracting party or production company, the commissions are still to be paid to the agent based on the original agreement.

## Status Reports on Agency Negotiations

With the objective of eliminating disputes regarding the deals or agreements, whether oral or written, which were in the making at the time of the expiration or termination of the agency agreement, this clause should address itself to the requirement that the agency submit to the talent monthly or periodic reports indicating the status of such contacts and negotiations. By inserting such a clause in the agreement, potential problems regarding what was commissioned and what was only nominally discussed may be alleviated. Clarification and specification are often methods of mitigating disputes.

### Future Earnings of the Talent

Generally, the agency contract also states that, in the event the agent is no longer employed by the talent but is claiming a commission based on employment to be performed by the talent following the termination of the agency agreement, the agency agrees to service that commissioned account for the duration, since the new agency could argue that it should not have to service a particular job assignment if it is not receiving a commission. It should be noted that even if such an acknowledgment is not stipulated in this agreement, conventional contract law may require the agency to fulfill its obligations to be entitled to its commission.

There is an exception to the servicing provision in which the agency could be entitled to compensation without performing additional work, namely royalty payments and profit sharing earned by the talent from previously performed work. For example, the agency agreement typically states that any proceeds received as a result of a royalty-based endeavor, such as a motion picture, home video program, television syndication series, or ongoing advertising campaign, would be commissioned even if the agent does not currently represent the performer.

Of course, should the employment agreement involve options, such a contingency would be determined by what is detailed in the contract.

## PREVIOUSLY NEGOTIATED AGREEMENTS

When a talent retains a new agent who is negotiating an extension of an employment agreement negotiated by a prior agent, the basis for calculating the commissions due to the new agent should be stipulated clearly in this agreement.

A point of negotiation and contention usually is: At what income basis does the commission take place? For example, if the new agency negotiates an increase of 30 percent over the original contract, does the agency get its commission based on the additional income only or on the total new amount?

### Pending Agreements at Time of Departure

Within this same context, the agreement may deal with the situation in which an agent has negotiated an employment agreement for the talent that the talent did not accept or reject during the term of the agreement.

These concerns may be mitigated by inserting a provision that any agreement pending at the time the agency agreement expires will be commissioned to the agent if the talent accepts the employment offer.

## Determining Bona Fide Offers

A means to determine whether a bona fide offer is made and commissionable is as follows: (a) define a bona fide offer as one in which all material terms of the employment offer have been substantially negotiated, and (b) if this requirement is met, the agreement is to be considered bona fide and therefore commissionable.

## Prior Offers Accepted After Termination of Agreement

The agreement also typically covers situations in which the talent rejects an offer generated by the agency, but accepts the offer at a later date under the auspices of a new agent. The agreement may stipulate that if negotiations are at any time terminated but thereafter revived, and if the terms ultimately agreed upon between the third party and the talent are substantially no less favorable than those negotiated at the time of the termination, the agreement will be considered negotiated by and therefore commissioned to the original agent.

## DEFINITION OF COMPENSATION

Since the agency receives its commission based on the gross income or compensation of the talent, it is important to specify precisely what is meant as income or compensation within the provisions of the agency agreement. While compensation or payment is routinely defined as money, that may not always be the case. This clause generally defines, clearly and concisely, exactly what is meant by compensation and how the agent defines terms of art, including net or gross compensation. The definition may state, as an example, that gross compensation means all monies, properties, and considerations of any kind or character, including but not limited to salaries, earnings, fees, royalties, rents, bonuses, real or personal property, gifts, proceeds, stock, and profit and stock options, without deductions of any kind, except as expressly provided for in the agreement.

## Nonmonetary Income of the Talent

Since the compensation to which the agent is entitled may include nonmonetary funds, the contract should state whether the talent has the option to give the agency a proportion of the actual consideration (a nonmonetary means of compensation) or to give the agent money instead. Moreover, the method of appraising the value of other forms of consideration should be addressed or negotiated in this section of the contract. If a talent is given stock options in lieu of cash payment, for example, what is the market value of that option? Does the agency base its appraisal on the day the option was granted to the talent, or does the agency base its commission on the value of the stock option on the day it is executed? What happens if the stock option is not executed due to the underlying stock plummeting in price to a value well below the option price in the agreement? Does the agency lose its entire commission?

### Recovering Monies Due the Talent

The agency agreement may state that, in the event the talent is required to spend out-of-pocket expenses to hire a lawyer to recover outstanding fees, or to pay an auditor or CPA to go over the books in a dispute over ticket receipts or profit participation, a direct proportion of that cost will be paid by the agent. The agent may negotiate to pay an amount equal to its commission percentage for any such expenses.

### Distinguishing Compensation from Expenses

A point to be negotiated in defining expenses granted to the talent, is whether such expenses are deemed to be reasonable and commissionable as compensation. For example, if the talent is offered additional compensation specifically for first class air transport, is the price of the ticket commissionable, or is the difference in cost between an economy seat and a first class seat deemed income that is commissioned to the agency?

### THE OPTION CLAUSE

The talent may have concerns as to whether the agent can actually secure employment opportunities as promised and, more importantly, whether there exists a good, long-term working relationship between the talent and the agent. The agent may feel that, for a talent just beginning a career, it is in the best interest of both parties to test the market as to the talent's potential. However, if the talent is relatively well established, a long-term contract may be preferred from the agent's perspective. Therefore, the contract may consist of an option to renew based on performance. The option may be granted to the performer or, conversely, subject to the agency's prerogative. In other cases, the option may be based upon a mutual decision.

With respect to the option being granted solely to the talent, the talent may demand that option renewals be based on the attainment of performance plateaus. For example, securing an acting role in a major film or receiving a stipulated amount of gross annual earnings may be necessary before the obligation to renew the contract for additional years can be self-executing. Such a gross amount reflects the status and experience of both the agent and the talent. In this case, the option provision typically states that the talent has a specified number of days to notify the agent in writing of the talent's intention to exercise the option.

The talent is generally required to submit to the agent a full and accurate accounting statement of all gross monies earned from the direct efforts of the agent during an agreed upon time period. In addition to gross income, which is usually defined as monies or other forms of consideration received without any deductions, as a result of all personal appearances, movie assignments, and other entertainment and career-related endeavors, the accounting could also indicate monies that could have been earned by the talent for work he or she was offered but declined to accept without good cause.

Depending on the experience and stature of both talent and agent, an option agreement may be drafted so that the agent has the option to not continue with the agreement or continue at his or her sole discretion. This clause typically requires that the agent notify the talent in advance of the decision to discontinue representing him or her.

Also subject to negotiation, this clause could provide that the option to accept continuing agency functions is self-executing. Without a written communication to the contrary, the agent will thereby automatically renew the agency agreement for the specified period.

## THE ESCAPE CLAUSE

Many agency agreements include an "out" clause, which grants the talent the right to sever the contractual relationship without liability should the talent not receive within an agreed period of time an offer of legitimate employment from a bona fide employer in the fields specified. Certain guilds and unions have determined the specific number of consecutive days that is considered ample time for the agent to secure employment for the talent. The talent relies on the agent for employment. If the agent is unable to procure employment for the talent, the relationship is less than successful, and it is best for both parties to go their separate ways. Yet, even if the talent takes advantage of the out clause, the agency is not precluded from receiving its compensation after termination for work performed during the term of the agreement.

Out clauses vary according to type of contract. In a general services agreement, the provision for an escape clause can be negotiated on an individual basis. However, if the agreement is a union sanctioned contract, the escape clause could be structured differently, and may be based on what concessions the guilds received when negotiating with the major talent agencies.

Since the typical contract states that the escape clause is applicable if the agency cannot obtain bona fide employment for its client within a designated period, the agreement generally stipulates that the employment offered and accepted must be of a stature related to the reputation of the talent. Therefore, an agent would not be able to avoid losing a major client simply by offering him or her a one-day appearance in an unacceptable, remote regional theater every four months.

## SUSPENSION CLAUSE

In the event the talent fails to meet his or her obligations under the requirements of the agreement by reason of gross negligence, malicious intent, or willful failure, the agent generally has the right under the suspension clause to extend the term of the agreement for a period of time equal to the duration of such failure. This assures the agent that the talent will be under contract for the agreed period of time, instead of avoiding obligations by simply letting the term run out.

## AUDITING THE BOOKS

Both the talent and the agent have the right to audit the books and records of the other party by independent, certified public accountants of their choice in order to determine whether the accounting statements rendered by each are accurate. This is an important business function whereby either party can be assured of receiving the revenues due them based on the terms of the agreement. A statute of limitations defines the period in which one party can file a complaint over an alleged inaccuracy in the books and records submitted by the other.

## FAILURE TO PERFORM

A provision may be negotiated stipulating that if either the talent or agent does not fulfill the obligations and responsibilities under the agreement, the wronged party must bring that failure to the attention of the other in writing. This puts the parties on notice that the defaulting party has a reasonable period of time within which to right the wrong. If after that period the wrong has not been corrected, the agreement may be severed without liability, if the wrong is considered a major breach.

## UNENFORCEABILITY

In the event one condition is ruled to be unenforceable by a change in the law or an interpretation by the courts, the parties can agree that the remainder of the contract will remain in full force and effect. This will insure consistency in the performance of the terms of the contracts without the fear that one error could void the whole agreement and years of labor.

## INCORPORATION BY TALENT

If the talent incorporates, the agent may request the assurance that the new corporation will enter into an identical agreement with the agency. The agent and talent, by agreeing to this clause, will usually be able to continue their working relationship no matter what business format their organizations take in the future.

## POWER OF ATTORNEY

A power of attorney grants legal authority from one person to another, authorizing the one to whom the power is granted to act for the other. The attorney-in-fact, in this case the agent, is usually empowered to represent and act for the talent, and to bind the talent legally to the terms of an agreement of which he or she may not even be aware.

The law places upon the attorney-in-fact an obligation to uphold a standard of fiduciary care above that normally required of one individual when dealing with another. The agency agreement often stipulates that such a legal capacity be granted to the agent, especially in collecting fees for work negotiated by the agency and carried out by the talent.

Powers of attorney can be drafted limiting the power to specific tasks required of the performer's representative, such as signing agreements with advertisers, press agents, and unions; publicity; limited personal appearances; the right to demand an accounting on the performer's behalf; and so forth without risking a legal battle in the future.

The power of attorney clause may also grant the agency the authority to do such things as approve and permit any and all advertising of the talent; provide permission to use the name, likeness, voice, sound effects, caricatures, writings, and musical materials for promotion and advertising; and sign agreements or contracts for services committing the talent if the talent is unavailable to sign but has been fully appraised of the agreement. Moreover, power of attorney may permit the agency to receive monies payable to the talent and to endorse the talent's name to all checks payable to the talent. In addition, the agency under this clause is typically entitled to hold such monies owed to them.

## UNCONSCIONABILITY

The term, commission fees, and obligations stipulated in the agreement should not be excessively overbearing or overly imposing on the talent, or the whole agreement risks being overturned in a court proceeding based on unconscionability.[4]

## LIMITATION OF LIABILITIES

In order to limit the liabilities, remedies, and rights of each party, both could agree that the agreement they are entering is not a joint venture or partnership. The agent is generally considered an independent contractor.

## JURISDICTION

The agreement clarifies which state has jurisdiction over disputes. The most convenient state is the one where both maintain their businesses, which lessens expenses in the event of litigation.

## DISPUTE RESOLUTION

The agreement may specify that the parties agree to take all disputes to the AAA and abide by its decisions. Since the rules governing arbitration are more lenient than those governing litigation, with easier rules of discovery and evidence, arbitration often costs less than litigation. The arbitrators, appointed by the AAA, are usually members of the entertainment profession and therefore peers of the contending parties. Often, the feeling is that arbitration is a more appropriate means of resolving disputes than litigation because the arbitrators have a personal understanding of the quirks peculiar to the entertainment profession.

# 4

# THE ACTOR AGREEMENT

The actor may very well be the most visible and susceptible member of the show business community. The actor's position often seems to be securely cemented in the American landscape, an impregnable icon of the cinematic culture. Yet, few actors remain steady wage earners.

The vulnerability of the actor in the entertainment community, his or her reliance, initially, on being cast for the part from the hundreds, even thousands, of hopefuls auditioning for the same role, usually places the actor in an uneven bargaining position with the seemingly more powerful producer.

The agreement the actor enters into with the producer can often dictate the development of his or her career. The agreement will generally spell out the length of the actor's commitment to a motion picture, the credits received, compensations, and other conditions necessary to insure the actor's career has a chance of survival.

The actor's agreement is generally either a personal services agreement or a loan-out agreement. The loan-out agreement is usually between the producer and a business entity with the exclusive rights to the services of the actor. This method is typically based on tax considerations rather than creative purposes. This chapter will deal with a typical personal service agreement.

## DUTIES AND SERVICES

The actor usually agrees to portray an agreed role in a contracted motion picture. The actor should understand that during the term of the agreement his or her services may be exclusive to the producer, unless the producer agrees otherwise in signed document. The producer usually requires the actor's exclusive services in order to insure that these services will be delivered unencumbered from other obligations that may conflict with or detract from actor's complete committment to the motion picture.

The producer, in general, demands to be apprised of the actor's whereabouts during the term of the agreement. Film schedules depend upon changing weather conditions and fluctuating scheduling and may require the availability of the actor on short notice. Furthermore, the actor's services may be required for night or holiday filming during the term.

The actor also agrees to perform all reasonable services required by the motion picture, including a voice recording for sound effects in connection with the film, advertising, and publicity. In addition, the actor is often obliged to film retakes, additional scenes and close-ups; record his or her voice on the sound track; and be available for dubbing (laying voices over the dramatic action) and filming scenes for trailers (promotional shorts), advertising, and publicity shots. Unless agreed to otherwise, these services are usually rendered at no additional compensation, if performed during the contracted term.

The actor is available to perform services in studios and locations selected by the producer and generally demands round trip plane tickets to the designated location if it is more than a stipulated distance from the actor's residence. In addition, the actor will generally negotiate for a daily expense account for day-to-day living expenses.

Since the international distribution rights of movies are growing in importance, the contract may also provide that the producer retains the right to substitute the voice of another performer for the actor's voice under agreed upon conditions, including the following:

1. When necessary to expeditiously meet the requirements of foreign exhibition;
2. When necessary to expeditiously meet censorship requirements both foreign and domestic;
3. When the actor is not available, despite advance notice;
4. When the actor is unable to meet certain requirements of the role, such as singing or other similar or comparable services requiring special talents or abilities other than those possessed by the actor.

Moreover, the actor's agreement may also grant the producer the express right to use a double in filming the movie if it is deemed in the best interest of the project. Generally, the actor insists on retaining a veto right over who is selected as a double. However, the actor is not generally allowed to unreasonably withhold permission.

## Guaranteed Period of Services

This provision spells out the conditions that must be adhered to in order for the actor to receive the contracted compensation. The actor's commitment generally encompasses the preproduction (also known as principal photography) and postproduction phases of the motion picture production schedule.

The actor with a busy schedule will generally agree to remain exclusive to the production during the actual filming of the motion picture, and for a limited period during the preproduction and postproduction phases. During the latter phase, the actor will be available for reshoots, dubbing, and other production requirements.

## COMPENSATION

The actor may receive a flat fee, payable according to an agreed upon schedule, as full payment for his services. The actor is usually paid a percentage of his or her fee upon signing the contract, with the remaining payable, on an agreed schedule during principal photography. It is also generally agreed that, in the event the actor's services are required following the termination of the designated production and post-production schedule, the actor will receive additional compensation.

Moreover, the agreement generally stipulates that, in addition to the guaranteed period of services, the actor be available for an additional number of free days that need not necessarily be consecutive. The purpose behind these free days is to provide for contingency plans in the event the director requires the actor's services to dub, loop, or edit out wild lines, or reshoot a particular scene.

The agreement may state that the producer endeavor to make the free days consecutive in order to ease the burden on the actor. The amount of actual free days stipulated in the agreement is negotiable.

Although an actor may have a specific number of working weeks guaranteed in the contract, various contingencies may arise where an actor only works for part of the schedule. In such an event, a well negotiated contract provides the basis upon which the performer gets paid. In addition, the contract generally distinguishes between studio weeks and location work weeks.

For example, in terms of a studio work week, if the agreement states that the work week consists of five shooting days, each day of work is deemed one-fifth of a week, with weekly compensation pro rated at 20 percent.

With respect to on-location shooting, where time and expenses are at a premium and thereby more work may be required of the actor, the work week may be deemed to be longer than five days. Based on a six-day work week, working just one day would equal one-sixth of a week, with compensation being 16.7 percent of the week's salary or income.

The agreement generally defines which shooting sites are considered on-location weeks and which are deemed studio weeks. For example, if the script calls for exterior shots within the boundaries of the city where the studio is situated, the agreement may classify those locations as studio rather than location shots.

### Pay or Play

One area generally negotiated between actor and producer is the "pay or play" clause.[1] Without such a clause, if the producer decides not to follow through with the planned use of the actor in the part agreed to in the contract, the producer may be free to disregard the entire work product and pay the talent only for work actually completed.

Under most definitions of the pay or play clause, the talent is guaranteed full payment for the contract whether or not the actor's services are actually used in the filming of the motion picture. Under the pay or play provision, it is generally to the advantage of the producer to exploit the work of the actor, since the production will have to pay the entire contract anyway. The inclusion of such a clause in the agreement often depends on the bargaining strength and market demand of the actor.

### Percentage of Net or Gross Profits

In addition to the actor's flat fee, the producer may agree to pay the actor a percentage of the net (or gross) profits generated from exploiting the motion picture in the agreed territory. This contingent compensation is based on the premise that the movie will generate a profit. The exact percentage agreed upon by the actor and producer usually varies according to the stature, defined in most cases as the box office draw, of the actor.

The agreement may be negotiated on a graduated basis, where the actor's percentage of profit varies depending on the gross receipts earned by exploiting the motion picture. As an example, the actor may agree to receive 5 percent of the gross proceeds in excess of the full amount required to recoup the production, printing, and advertising costs of the motion picture, and as additional thresholds are met, a higher or lower percentage.

The compensation clauses should be drafted very carefully and defined in detail since the words may have specific meanings. The term gross proceeds may not be deemed gross in the ordinary sense, but only after certain expenses, such as taxes, guild payments, conversion, lab costs, and so forth, have been deducted.

If the actor performs additional duties in the motion picture, such as singing a song, and if the song appears on a soundtrack of the motion picture, the actor may be entitled to receive an additional royalty from the exploitation of the soundtrack album in the agreed territory.

### Retakes

Even if the actor was available for the guaranteed term of the contract, conditions may have existed whereby the producer could not complete principal photography according to the production schedule. Such circumstances may have been due to errors or omissions made by the director of photography or director that were not apparent until well into the editorial or postproduction stage. On other occasions, the producer may have found the need to add or change scenes following the end of the production phase of the motion picture. These eventualities may require retakes, additional scenes, script changes, or even special shooting in order to film a trailer.

If the delay is not a result of the actor's behavior, the agreement may state that the actor will receive additional income for services rendered during such additional periods. The added income may be a flat fee or based on a contracted formula, depending on whether the additional shoots are considered studio shoots or on-location shoots. Moreover, the agreement may state that this additional income is not connected in any way with contingency compensation based on profits. Alternatively, if the delays were the result of the actor's behavior, the extra time required to replace the time lost may not be compensated.

Due to the nature of filmmaking, some problems requiring retakes may not be discovered until well into the postproduction stage, which can be as long as three or four months subsequent to the termination of principal photography. Without agreeing to compensations and schedules at the formation of the agreement, the producer may be required to negotiate additional compensation and work dates for the actor, who may have other commitments. The purpose of this clause is to bind the actor at the outset to the extent that he or she agrees to be available for such contingencies within a certain period of time after the guaranteed period of services has expired. The actor may agree to accept a salary that is in proportion to the payscale he or she had earned during the shooting. The added compensation may also be based on whether the additional acting work will be performed in a studio or on location. The actor would agree to be available for such additional work at the location required by the producer, as long as the actor does not have a conflicting commitment. Where there is a conflict, the actor may agree to be available at the earliest possible date thereafter.

## BREACH OF CONTRACT, DEFAULTS, INJUNCTION

The actor generally agrees that his or her services are unique and irreplaceable, and that the producer has the right to seek an injunction and other equitable relief to prevent a breach of this agreement, since the loss of the actor's services would cause the producer a loss that could not be adequately compensated in a legal action.

If the actor fails or refuses to comply with any of the material terms or conditions of the contract as a whole, the producer may reserve the right to terminate the contract and replace the actor, provided that advance written notice is received by the talent. If the actor has enough bargaining strength, he or she may insist on including a subclause requiring the producer to allow the actor a reasonable period of time to remedy the breach.

The term material breach is contrasted to harmless breach. What may be characterized by this clause as a harmless breach of some technical aspect of the contract would normally not be used as a pretense for terminating the services of the actor.

As an alternative to termination, the contract may provide for the temporary suspension of the actor's services. The contract typically states that any incapacity or default of the performer would be deemed to continue until the producer receives a written notice that the actor is ready, willing, and able to perform his or her services as required under the contract.

Since the primary responsibility of the actor is to carry out his or her commitment to the producer, this clause may also stipulate that the actor will not render services for any other producer until his or her total commitment is completed under the terms of this agreement.

The agreement may also state that in the event the actor is suspended without pay and subsequently reinstated, the term of the entire contract would be extended the same amount as was the suspension. For example, if the contract for a guaranteed period of services were to run eighteen months from the inception to the completed release of the movie, and if the actor was suspended for six of those months, then the contract would be extended for six months.

If the actor is of sufficient caliber and stature, he or she may insist on inserting a clause stating that the actor has the right to render services to another producer during any period of suspension. However, the actor would be required to return to the producer's set upon ample notice.

## PREPRODUCTION AVAILABILITIES

The making of a motion picture requires an extraordinary amount of preparation, including rehearsals, wardrobe fittings, tests, publicity interviews, production conferences, promotions, and so forth. The producer may require the nonexclusive services of the actor during the preproduction period as part of the actor's contractual obligation. Should additional services be required subsequent to the expiration of actor's guaranteed period of services, the actor usually agrees to be available.

If the producer agrees not to bind the actor to an exclusive agreement during the preproduction period the producer will generally use his or her best efforts to work around the existing commitments of the actor.

In the event the actor is required to perform musical numbers, and the producer decides that the recording of those musical numbers will take place prior to the actual shooting of the movie, the actor is generally compensated for the preproduction work. In that situation the producer understands that the prerecording work is not considered part of the guaranteed period of services.

## CREDITS

The placement of an actor's credits establishes his or her acceptance in the public eye. The star actor generally requests that his or her credit be in the first position above the entire cast and title, of an appropriate size, and on a separate frame or card. The star actor usually requires that the credits prominently display his or her name on all prints of the motion picture, and in all advertising and promotional trailers. The star actor generally requires that his or her name and likeness appear prominently on all soundtrack album covers. Naturally, a developing actor with less box office clout can make fewer demands regarding the placement and size of his or her credits, which generally grow in size in direct relationship to the actor's growth in stature.

## RIGHTS GRANTED

The actor generally grants to the producer the exclusive rights to use his or her services in the motion picture specified in the agreement and to all the results and proceeds of those services. Typically, the producer requests the right to photograph and reproduce the actor's performances, acts, poses, and appearances in connection to the motion picture, and demands the right to record, reproduce, and transmit the actor's voice, with or without musical instruments and accompaniment, in connection with the motion picture. The actor usually grants the producer the right to exhibit and exploit the motion picture bearing his likeness, voice, and name in perpetuity.

The actor generally also grants to the producer the right in perpetuity to advertise and publicize his or her motion picture performance on television, radio, in print, and other forms of advertising and promotion. The producer may use the actor's name, voice, likeness, sound, and image in any reasonable capacity to that end. The producer usually requires that the actor submit an up-to-date biography, which generally requires the approval of the producer prior to being released publicly by the actor or his or her publicist.

### Copyrights

One of the key elements of the contract with the actor is the provision that clearly details the fact that the producer retains all rights accruing from the actor's output, including such things as all copyrights, patents, trademarks, and other rights relating to, and emanating from, the work. Such other rights include incidents, plots, dialogue, characters, action, and titles.

### Moral Rights

The agreement may deny the actor any artistic rights, which many European countries call *droit moral,* or moral rights. By retaining all moral rights in the motion picture, the producer also has retained the exclusive right to subtract from, change, arrange, revise, adapt, rearrange, make variations, translate the motion picture title into any and all languages, or change the sequence or characters. By denying the actor any moral rights, the producer generally avoids any subsequent claims that the actor's rights have been violated and his or her creative work has been improperly altered.

In the United States, the producer generally requests that the actor waive his or her moral rights. In much of Europe, the *droit moral* is a right inherent to any artistic or creative work. It is not a recognized right in the United States, unless specifically agreed upon.

By inserting a clause such as this into the agreement, the producer may be protected in the event that moral rights are adopted in the future by an amendment to the U.S. copyright laws.

### RIGHTS SECURED

The rights secured by the producer usually include, but are often not limited to, motion pictures, sequels, television, video cassettes, music, publishing, radio, merchandising, advertising, and all other rights that are attached to the motion picture in any and all media. This is a broad clause, but its inclusion in one form or another in virtually all entertainment contracts is based on the realization that the entertainment industry is a rapidly changing business. The failure to include such a broad sweeping clause into the contracts entered into by actors of the 1930s,

1940s, 1950s, and even 1960s resulted in many entertainers not receiving revenue from the highly profitable video cassette industry, a form of media unknown in the early days of motion picture.

Under the rights clause, the actor usually agrees that all material, work, and ideas used by the actor in the motion picture become in perpetuity the property of the producer. The actor also usually agrees that the name of the character, as well as the characterization of that character in the motion picture, are and will remain the property of the producer. Furthermore, the actor may agree to forfeit for all time any rights, title, interest in, or use of the characters, story, or title of the motion picture.

## FORCE MAJEURE

Since this contract is for a specific performance, where time is of the essence, it is important to provide a clause that establishes what will happen if events external to the control of the talent makes the performance impossible or impractical. The *force majeure* clause accommodates the unforeseen events imposed on the producer or actor by outside forces, that require the postponement of the performance obligation.[2]

The practical effect of this clause is to avoid a breach of contract and provide for a cure. This typically provides for the resumption of the obligation as soon as the event that triggered the clause is declared over. While many contracts mention *force majeure,* it is imperative to enumerate possible events that would create this status, since there are unique aspects of the film industry.

Aside from routine disclaimers, such as by reason of fire, earthquake, labor dispute, act of God or public enemy, municipal ordinances, state or federal laws, or governmental orders or regulations, there should be wording that covers the suspension of the producer's business or the death, illness, or incapacity of a principal cast member, director, or producer.

This clause should include a termination provision that is mutually beneficial. Such a clause should have the effect of avoiding an indefinite suspension of the agreement. If the wording of the clause is to the benefit of one party over another, it is likely that the courts or arbitrators will void or amend this clause to balance the protected interests.

## TERMINATION

The producer generally indicates that he or she may terminate the agreement at any time after the occurrence of the actor's disability and his or her inability to perform. The actor generally has the right to terminate the agreement if the producer's disability results in a suspension of compensation for a specified period of time. Naturally, the amount of time is to be negotiated between the parties prior to the signing of the agreement with a stipulation on how such written notice is to be delivered.

## WARRANTIES AND PERFORMANCE DUTIES

The agreement will often state that the actor is ready, willing, and able to perform the contract, which includes following the instructions of the director, producer, and others granted such rights by the agreement. In addition, the actor may indicate that he or she is subject to the producer's or director's reasonable approval, direction, and control at all times. The actor may also warrant to do the work expected in a professional and artistic manner to the best of his or her ability.

## INCORPORATION BY THE ACTOR

In the event the actor incorporates, the producer may request the assurance that the new corporation will enter into an agreement with provisions identical to the original agreement. The producer and the actor, by agreeing to this clause, will usually continue their working relationship in a manner that is comfortable and secure, no matter what business format their organizations take in the future.

## JURISDICTION

The agreement clarifies which state has jurisdiction over disputes. In most circumstances, the most convenient state is the one where both parties maintain their businesses, lessening expenses in the event of litigation.

## ARBITRATION

The parties may agree to settle their disputes by arbitration, understanding that they will be bound by the regulations and rules of the AAA.[3] Arbitration proceedings are less formal than civil proceedings and the decision of the arbitrator is final and enforceable by the courts. Resolving a dispute through arbitration is often a less lengthy, and thereby less costly, process than litigation. There is generally more leniency in the arbitration proceeding, and the arbitrators are usually peers in the industry, rather than judges.

## NEGATIVE COVENANTS

The producer may wish to control the dissemination of news items to the press in order to time the release of information with the theatrical presentation of the motion picture. The actor is usually restricted from issuing news stories or publicity relating to the film or television program unless directed to do so by the producer or until such time as the producer decides to initiate the planned release of publicity.

## EXPENSES

Since many motion picture projects are produced on location, the agreement generally covers the payment of expenses to the actor while on the film set. The producer typically furnishes and pays for, or reimburses, the actor for reasonable living and traveling expenses incurred. The contract may provide for a guaranteed weekly draw. Moreover, the agreement may also provide for any savings below such a draw to revert to the producer.

What is considered to be reasonable expenses is generally subject to negotiation. Usually, the expenses allowed the actor is based on the stature of the actor and the location of the filming.

## NAME AND LIKENESS

Since the producer must accord credits to the actor in certain promotional materials such as posters, marquee displays, newspaper advertisements, and other means of promotion, the producer typically secures the right to use the actor's name and likeness for such purposes. The actor usually grants the producer the right to use his or her name and likeness in all advertising and in any manner or form of exploitation of the picture under industry standards.

To protect the exploitation value of the actor's reputation, the clause may also include a limitation on the producer. It may state that such advertising does not include the direct endorsement of any product other than the movie in question without prior consent from the actor.

## SEQUELS, SPIN-OFFS

Ordinarily, the producer is not obligated to use the services of the actor for any sequels, serializations, or spin-offs.[4] The producer usually frees him- or herself from being tied in to the actor's services in the future. The actor, on the other hand, may prefer the opportunity to develop the characters and story he or she originated in the original motion picture, or be compensated for his or her inability to appear in sequels using the same character the actor developed.

## GROSS OR NET PROFITS

Since the star actor's agreement may call for compensation of a percentage of the royalties or profits from the motion picture, it is important to define clearly and concisely the term net proceeds as it is used in this specific agreement. In addition, it would be advisable to define gross profits, if the term is used in the agreement.

The terms are nebulous concepts that must be defined in each separate agreement. For example, gross profits can be defined as all monies and receipts earned from the exploitation of the motion picture, without any deductions whatsoever, or it may mean all monies and receipts earned less specified deductions. The definition used depends on the explanation of the term in the body of the specific contract.

The deductions referred to in the above definition must be clarified in order to lessen the possibility of protracted litigation or arbitration at a later date. Clearly, the definition of gross as used in a particular agreement can be the difference between a sizeable earning and a minimal earning for the actor.

The stronger the producer's bargaining position, the more the producer can dictate the definition of gross profits. In the case of a producer and distributor of the stature of Paramount Pictures, Twentieth Century Fox, or Warner Brothers, for example, gross profits may mean receipts generated from the distribution of the motion picture from all parties exhibiting the motion picture in theater and on television, all receipts received by the producer from the licensing or granting of distribution rights, including video cassettes, pay-per-view, pay television and satellite, as well as all earnings received by the producer from the sale and license of advertising accessories and merchandising.

Deductions from the gross profits entitled to the producers may include certain expenses, including all taxes; duties; customs; and imports; the costs of acquiring permits, and any other costs necessary to secure the entry, licensing, exhibition, performance, use, and television play within any country; the expenses required to transmit any funds accruing to the producer from any country to the United States and any discounts taken to convert such funds into U.S. currency; the cost of litigation or arbitration required to contest any of the matters agreed to in the agreement; and all payments due to actors, writers, directors, unions, guilds, pension funds, or other participants based on contractual agreements entitling those persons or entities to gross or net profit participation in the earnings generated from the exploitation of the motion picture.

## STATEMENTS AND RECORDS

The producer will typically agree to furnish the actor, who has negotiated a profit-sharing agreement, with an accounting at regular intervals of the gross receipts earned from the exploitation of the motion picture.

## MONIES HELD IN TRUST

Funds held in trust by the producer for the benefit of the actor represent a fiduciary obligation of the highest degree, comparable to the fiduciary obligation a bank has to its depositors. The producer may prefer to limit liability by clearly specifying that he or she may co-mingle the funds owed to the actor, and that such funds are not held in trust for the actor.

## NO GUARANTEE OF SUCCESS

The producer usually warrants that he or she has not made any representations regarding the gross receipts the motion picture will generate.

## UNIONS AND GUILDS

The producer generally warrants that he or she is a signatory to the Screen Actors Guild's pension, health, and welfare plan and will make all appropriate contributions, as outlined in the guild agreements.

The actor usually warrants that he or she is a member in good standing of all unions and guilds, as required, including the Screen Actors Guild and the American Federation of Musicians (AFM), if applicable.

## WARDROBE AND HAIRDRESSER

In order to insure the general look of the actor as portrayed in the motion picture, the producer usually furnishes the actor's wardrobe and often requires the right to approve all wardrobe, hair, and make-up personnel for the actor, unless the actor maintains the ability to make and receive such demands.

## PUBLICITY

Often, the actor is one of the elements of a motion picture that induces the audience to see the motion picture. The actor is generally required to cooperate with the producer for the purpose of advertising and exploiting the motion picture through public relations and advertising campaigns. The producer usually requires the actor to avail his or her voice, likeness, name, and photograph to better exploit the motion picture. If the physical presence of the actor is required, the producer's request for such presence is usually subject to the actor's prior approval, which should not be unreasonably withheld.

## STANDARD OF LIVING

An actor may be able to request a limousine, private dressing trailer, special diet, or other amenities during the term of the agreement and during all additional periods when the actor's services are required, including personal appearances, dubbing dates, and retakes.

## MERCHANDISING

Revenues received from the merchandising of characters portrayed by the actor in the motion pictures may generate a source of revenue beyond the compensation agreed upon in the employment agreement. The actor generally grants to the producer the right to the perpetual use of the actor's name, picture, photograph, likeness in connection with the motion picture role to merchandise posters, novelty items, and objects, including toys, clothes, accessories, and so forth. With respect to actual compensation, the producer generally agrees to pay the actor an agreed percentage of the producer's net merchandising receipts.

## INSURANCE

The production of a motion picture is a costly venture that often relies on the health and well-being of a few key individuals. A star performer's sudden illness can cost the production company hundreds of thousands of dollars, depending on the urgency of the film and how it relates to the general marketing campaign. The producer, in order to insure investment interests, will often require that the actor submit to the necessary and required examinations and obligations required by an insurer. The beneficiary of such insurance is usually the distributor, production company or the producer, who often consider this clause to be essential and may require the termination of the actor's agreement if the actor is unable to obtain insurance at reasonable rates.

However, the actor may mitigate that problem by inserting a clause requiring the actor, if able to find proper insurance at a premium higher than the one authorized by the producer, to reimburse the producer the amount of the premium that the producer would ordinarily pay, providing the actor pays the balance and adheres to the conditions spelled out in the insurance policy. If the actor refuses to cooperate with the underwriter, then he or she may be liable for termination with notice by the producer.

## ASSIGNMENT

The producer generally has the right to assign the agreement to any responsible production company that will assume all of the producer's obligations. The filming of the motion picture, with the attached actors, directors, and distribution agreements in place, may be an incentive for the producer to assign rights. The producer generally demands those rights of unhindered transferability.

## NO OBLIGATION TO PRODUCE

Even though the producer generally uses his or her best efforts to produce the motion picture, the producer is normally not obligated to produce the motion picture but is obligated to pay to the actor the agreed upon compensation if a pay or play provision has been included in the agreement.

# THE ACTOR IN A TELEVISION SERIES

The actor in a television series faces clauses, provisions, terms, and conditions unique to that medium. Several of those provisions are highlighted below.

## SCOPE OF EMPLOYMENT

The actor is generally employed to portray a particular role in a television series, with each program usually thirty or sixty minutes in length. The actor attends rehearsals, tests, lead-ins and lead-outs, added scenes, retakes, and other services required and specified in the agreement. The actor is usually hired for a cycle and will be notified of the start date in accordance with Screen Actors Guild requirements.

### Guaranteed Play Dates

An actor gains recognition by developing a following among viewers. It is to the actor's benefit to maintain and sustain visibility in front of the audience. The actor usually negotiates a firm commitment to be used in an agreed number of shows for the first cycle. In the event the series is signed for additional cycles, the actor generally negotiates an agreement to be used for an additional number of shows for the current and subsequent cycles. With the actor's popularity potentially explosive, the producer may attempt to lock the novice performer into an agreement with built-in options renewable at the producer's request.[5]

### Mid-Cycle Cancellation

Often, there are contingencies written into the contract. In the event a cycle is canceled midseason by a network, the producer generally maintains the right to cancel, upon demand, the employment agreement between the production company and the actor. Such termination would also nullify the producer's obligation to continue to pay the actor beyond the point of cancellation.

### Extension of the Show

Alternatively, if the cycle is extended beyond the intended initial period, the producer could insist on the assurance that the actor perform services for the extended period, with additional compensation for such work.

### The Down Period

There is generally a hiatus from the grueling schedule of taping episodic television. Production of new shows is suspended for a designated period of time every year. During that down period, the actor is, in most cases, free to accept roles in motion pictures, live theater, and certain televised programs and movies as long as those parts are not detrimental to the actor's role on the television series. The producer often requests the right of approval over the actor's selection of roles outside the series.

### Exclusivity

The producer generally expects the actor's services to be exclusive, within the broadcast medium, to the contracted show. The producer may also wish to regulate the amount of times the actor can make guest appearances during each cycle. Furthermore, the producer generally requires that the actor not portray a character similar to the series character on any guest appearances or motion pictures during the term of the agreement without first getting the producer's approval.

# THE YOUNG STAR

## CONTRACTS WITH MINORS

In the entertainment industry, it is not uncommon to see youngsters under the age of eighteen, the age of legal adulthood, working. Since the birth of the popular media, minors have been a consistent segment of the profession. Mickey Rooney and Shirley Temple were assured special protection while under contract with the major studios during Hollywood's golden years. Today, minors performing in television and in motion pictures continue to be protected by a more stringently controlled contract than that governing adults.[6]

## Minor's Uniqueness Under the Law

It is because minors hold a unique place in contract law that special care must be taken in drafting any agreement entered into by youngsters. The courts believe that minors require a higher degree of protection since they are considered susceptible to abuse based on their youth, inexperience, and innocence. A minor generally does not have the power to bind him- or herself by signing a contract. Usually, a minor can disaffirm any agreement without incurring liability. Even if a parent or guardian approves and guarantees the contract, it is not completely or unequivocally binding on the minor.[7]

## Legislation

Most states have legislation protecting the minor's right to disaffirm contracts on grounds of infancy and have established different criteria for judging minors in most legal situations.

## Judicial Approval

To secure a minor's compliance with the terms and conditions of an agreement, it is possible to obtain judicial approval for contracts entered into by minors that would, under most circumstances, establish a binding contract, even under a claim for disaffirmance on grounds of infancy. The theory behind such binding court approval is that since the court has taken a close look at the provisions of the contract, considered the reasonableness of the agreement, and reviewed the minor's working conditions and approved them, it is assured that the minor's rights will be adequately protected.

## Parental/Guardian Approval

Generally, agreements with minors contain a separate rider requiring the signature of the parent or guardian. The rider states that the person signing the agreement is the parent or legal guardian of the minor, and that they have read the agreement, consider it to be fair and reasonable, and consent to the performance by the minor under the conditions of the agreement.

## GUARANTOR OF MINOR'S PERFORMANCE

The parent or legal guardian will generally be asked to guarantee and become surety for the minor's performance. In essence, if the minor disaffirms the agreement, the party hiring the services of the minor – the producer – may be indemnified against all expenses resulting from the youth's disaffirmance, such as canceled production. The parent or guardian is generally asked to agree to cooperate fully in the event court approval is requested.

## PROTECTION OF THE MINOR'S INTERESTS

In many states, before the contract is approved by the courts, a designated portion of the minor's net earnings must be agreed to be set aside in a secure savings and investment account. This portion of the minor's earnings are beyond the scope of the family or guardian's reach until the minor reaches majority or until the court orders its release. The courts consider what percentage of the child's income (in many cases, a majority) is to be set aside, basing their findings on the financial conditions of the parents, the needs of the other children in the family, and, if the minor is married, the needs of the minor's immediate family.

Freeing the money from a minor's blocked account is usually not an easy matter. The courts protect the minor's income and typically require an application to the court before any funds are released. Compelling reasons must be shown to convince the courts to allow a guardian or parent the right to open the minor's vaults. Those reasons are often based on the welfare, educational requirements, or changed economic condition of the child and child's family.

### Working Conditions and Education

The court generally insists that the minor's working conditions meet the state's laws governing working children. It will also see to it that the child receives an education comparable to other youngsters of the same age and grade, with the producer providing private tutors, if necessary. The court has the responsibility to assure that the working child has as normal a life as possible, taking into consideration the unorthodox condition of the film location.

## REVOCATION OF CONTRACT

The court also has the right, in its desire to represent the best interests of the minor, to revoke its approval of the contract in the event there is a finding that the minor's health, education, and general well-being are being unnecessarily damaged by adhering to the contract.

## FAILURE TO PERFORM

The producer generally requires the right to terminate the agreement, without liability or damages, in the event the minor becomes incapacitated, drastically changes in appearance, undergoes a voice change, or suffers mental or physical incapacity, following written notice by the producer. The minor generally receives an agreed portion of compensation in such cases.

If the producer is hampered or prevented from filming the motion picture because of a *force majeure*, including war, floods, earthquakes, strikes, and so forth, the producer is usually free of obligations under the agreement, without incurring any liabilities or damages, and is generally not required to pay the minor the previously agreed compensation.

## UNENFORCEABILITY

In the event a condition in the agreement is ruled to be unenforceable by a change in the law, or by an interpretation of the courts, the parties can agree that the rest of the contract will remain in full force and effect. This will insure consistency in the performance of the terms of the contracts, without the fear that one error could void the whole agreement and the fruits of labor.

# 5

---

# THE SCREEN WRITER AGREEMENT

The role of the writer is unique and easily identifiable. The writer creates the blueprint for the final motion picture, which is the story used as a basis for the action. The employment contract entered by the screen writer is typically a personal service contract, considered an "above the line" budgeted item as opposed to a "below the line" production cost.

There are two types of motion picture writer agreements commonly employed in the entertainment business: the standard employee for hire agreement, which covers the majority of the writers, and the loan-out agreement, which is used by the remaining group. The loan-out agreement is often used as a vehicle or model when the writer is also the producer and/or director.

Under the latter arrangement, the producer typically enters an agreement with the company employing the writer's loan-out company instead of directly with the writer.

This chapter concentrates primarily on the conventional employee for hire agreement, a preferred contractual arrangement entered into between the writer and producer.

The writer's contract is basically an employment agreement that details the points negotiated by and between the producer and writer. The writer would agree and understand that he or she is employed to write a screenplay. The writer may be employed to provide other additional specified services with a particular project (e.g., to write the treatment or suggested story outlines for the motion picture or, if a multipicture deal, to provide services for a series of upcoming projects).

In general, the screen writer as well as the producer are aware of the various union agreements concerning compensation for the writer. The theatrical and television basic agreement of the Writers Guild of America

(WGA) is the standard union agreement used as a basis of comparison by both the producers and writers.[1]

The issue of the writer's credit on the screen is usually of great importance. For the writer, proper credit can mean the difference between professional stagnation and the successful progression up the hierarchy so important in the writer's career. The writer's earning power and credibility are often reflected by the placement, dimension, and position of a writer's credit on a particular motion picture.

While a director may make the script come alive, it is the writer who creates the screenplay. The writer is generally considered to be a prime creative contributor to the motion picture and, as such, may be likened to a central and main driving force of the project. To quell any doubts about the writer's contribution on any future projects or sequels, the writer's contract will generally include clauses on the use of sequels and ancillary projects based on the writer's work.

## EMPLOYEE FOR HIRE

The writer is employed, as an employee for hire by the producer, to author a complete and finished screenplay, based on a original idea by the writer, the producer or by a third party. The contract should specifically name the motion picture, though all parties understand and agree that the name presently being used in the agreement is tentative and subject to change.

Under the employee for hire structure, the Copyright Act dictates that the employer and not the employee, is typically considered the copyright owner.[2]

## UNION OR GUILD REQUIREMENT

As part of the writer's agreement, and generally under the writer's status as an employee for hire, the writer may be required to be a full member, in good standing, of the WGA prior to commencement of duties.[3] If the writer is, at the time of the signing of the contract, not a member of the guild, and if the producer is a signatory of the WGA, the producer will insist that the writer join the WGA in order to maintain good relations with the WGA. Furthermore, the producer will promise to abide by all the rules, regulations, and by-laws of the guild.

The writer and producer usually acknowledge that, as part of the limitations imposed on them, if a conflict arises between any provision of the agreement and the WGA basic agreement, the latter generally prevails.

The producer generally agrees to comply with all the union requirements, including making the necessary contributions to the pension, health, and welfare fund.

## DUTIES

The writer's employment duties generally include the writing of the first draft as well as the scripting of all future drafts. In addition to pre-production screenplay writing obligations, the writer's services may be required during the editing and postproduction phases of the motion picture.

The producer often retains the right to employ the services of additional writers if required to rewrite or doctor the screenplay by the original writer. This right is usually at the sole discretion of the producer. Generally, as more writers are employed to work on the screenplay, the original writer's chances of having full and solo screen credit may wane. The WGA has established guidelines regarding the placement and inclusion of screen credits to follow in the event multiple writers are attached to a particular screenplay.

### Limitation of the Writer's Duties

Since the role of the writer is considered unique, the producer generally maintains strict control over the work product, including all research, notes, treatments, and drafts. The writer may be prohibited from employing any personnel, contracting for the purchase or rental of any research materials, or making any agreement that would bind or commit the producer to pay any sum of money for any reason whatsoever in connection with the picture without first obtaining the written approval of the producer. The producer generally maintains strict control over the disbursement of funds relegated to the budget for the motion picture.

## EXPENSES ON LOCATION

A sizeable number of motion pictures are produced on location. The writer's contract should reflect the additional expenses imposed on the writer in the event he or she is required to travel to the production location. Typically, in the event the producer requires the writer to render services at more than an agreed upon distance from the writer's residence of record, the producer will provide the writer with round trip air transportation to the location.[4]

In addition to air transportation, the producer may furnish and pay for, or reimburse the writer for, reasonable living and traveling expenses incurred while on location, with an agreed weekly ceiling. The agreement may also provide for any savings below such a ceiling to revert to the production company. The amount the producer relegates to the writer for living and traveling expenses often relates to the stature of the writer, taking into consideration the motion picture budget and shooting location.

## RIGHTS

In most cases, the producer insists on retaining all rights, including copyrights, patents, and trademarks accruing from the creative output of the writer during the term of employment.[5] The producer may also insist on retaining other rights, including all rights stemming from, and relating to, incidents, plots, dialogue, characters, action, and titles used in the motion picture. The writer may be required to sign a separate agreement conveying such ownership to the producer.[6]

### Moral Rights

The writer's agreement may refer to what many European countries label *droit moral,* or moral rights. In the United States, the producer generally requests that the writer waive the moral rights of authors.[7]

When the writer waives moral rights, he or she grants the producer the unlimited right to cut, edit, rewrite, or revise the screenplay in any manner, to make variations on the writer's work and themes, and to change the sequence of events as originally drafted by the writer without liability or fear of legal recrimination. The producer generally also acquires the right to change the characters, alter their personalities, and modify their histories. The producer may also demand the right to change the title of the screenplay and to translate the title into other languages. In much of Europe, *droit moral* is a right inherent in any artistic or creative work. It is not as yet a recognized right in the United States, unless specifically agreed upon in a written agreement, usually the writer's contract.

Congress has not, as of the publication of this book, amended the U.S. copyright laws to reflect such a moral right by the writer.

### Additional Rights

The producer normally secures all the rights in the screenplay scripted by the writer and will list those rights in a manner that clearly elucidates the producer's intent and puts to rest all present or future confusion regarding ownership of those rights.

The rights secured by the producer from the writer under the employee for hire agreement usually includes, but may not be limited to, motion pictures, sequels, television, video cassettes, music, publishing, radio, merchandising, and advertising, and to all other rights that are attached, or will attach themselves, to the motion picture in any and all media that are known at the time of the agreement or which may be devised in the future.

The contemporary producer should realize that the entertainment industry is a rapidly changing business. Forms of media not even dreamed about at the time of this writing may be in full operational use in the future. The producers would not want to be omitted from a future revenue source stemming from a new technology. Historically, the failure to include such a broad sweeping clause into contracts during the earlier days of the entertainment industry resulted in the failure of many rights owners to receive revenue from newly discovered means of distribution, such as the highly profitable video cassette industry, a form of media not known several decades ago.

## FORCE MAJEURE

The writer's contract is an agreement entered into by and between the parties for the performance of a specific task for which time is generally considered to be of the essence. Generally, a clause is included to detail provisions in case events external to the control of the producer or writer make the performance of the writer's duties impossible or impractical. A *force majeure* clause generally covers such unforeseen events that require tolling or suspending the performance obligation.[8]

The *force majeure* clause usually serves to avoid a breach of contract by either party and may further provide for a cure. Typically, the contract provides for the resumption of the obligation as soon as the *force majeure* is declared over.

In order to clarify what exactly triggers the *force majeure* clause under the agreement, it is generally prudent to enumerate possible events. Aside from the standard events – fire, earthquake, labor dispute or strike, act of God or public enemy, municipal ordinance, state or federal law, governmental order or regulation – there should be wording that covers incidents unique to the entertainment industry, including the suspension of the production company's business, or the illness or incapacity of a principal member of the cast, director, or producer.

The *force majeure* clause should include a termination provision that is mutually beneficial and that will have the effect of avoiding an indefinite suspension of the agreement.

## TERMINATION

The writer may demand the right to terminate the agreement if the production company's unforeseen disability results in a suspension of compensation for a specified period of time. The amount of time required before the suspension takes effect is generally negotiated between the parties.

The contract may grant the producer the right to cure the disability in the event the writer executes his or her right to terminate the agreement by granting the producer an agreed upon period of time to cure the disability. Typically, the producer notifies the writer, in a signed writing, of its ability and desire to cure the disability within the stipulated time period.

## TIME PERIOD WITHIN WHICH TO PERFORM

The writer's agreement generally includes the date when the writer would be obligated to commence agreed upon services for the producer. The agreement may go on to indicate, in a flow chart or by a schedule, the time table within which the writer is obligated to present various stages of work to the producer.

A screenplay is usually developed through the following phases:

1. general outline
2. detailed treatment of the story in narrative or short story form
3. first draft
4. second draft
5. all additional drafts of the screenplay until the final draft is agreed upon
6. shooting script, with the scenes broken down by shot, location, exterior or interior location, time of day, and cast member

The agreement usually stipulates that the writer will follow the agreed upon schedule and present the completed work, on or before the due date, to the producer for review. Story conferences with the producer, writer, and cast often help the writer draft the screenplay, since location, story development, and dialogue are often discussed at those conferences. Typically, the story conferences are considered part of the writer's service obligation, without any additional sums due him or her. This aspect of the contract, as well as the time frame allotted the writer, may often be deemed material.

The final output of the writer's work generally determines the budget of the film. Even a minor modification in a location shoot or the addition or deletion of a character may heavily affect the cost of the film.

## COMPENSATION: FLAT DEAL VERSUS PROGRESSIVE
## OPTIONS

### The Progressive Option

Depending on the bargaining strength and reputation of both the producer and the writer, the compensation due the writer for services under the agreement may be paid by a flat fee or made according to an agreed schedule, broken down by the various stages of the screenplay.[9] Often, a writer with a weaker bargaining position may agree to perform services according to a schedule of progressive options. Using the progressive option, the producer may not be responsible for any payments to the writer beyond those contracted for under the executed option requirements, unless the producer exercises the option and chooses to proceed to the following option period.

The option periods are usually tied to the various stages of story development and may follow the following schedule:

1. treatment or outline
2. revisions and/or drafts of treatment
3. first draft screenplay
4. option for initial screenplay following draft
5. revisions/drafts of submitted screenplay
6. option for revision and/or draft of screenplay
7. rewrite of screenplay
8. polish of screenplay
9. other media rewrite options (e.g., movie of the week)

Using the progressive option approach, the producer may benefit by maintaining a steadier rein on the budget and more control over the development of the screenplay. The advantage of the progressive option approach for the screenwriter may be the producer's willingness to take a chance with the writer, knowing in advance of the option to search out other individuals in the event the writer's work product is not totally satisfactory.

### The Flat Deal

Unlike the option deal, the flat deal usually obligates the producer to use the full services of the screen writer from inception of the story idea through revisions made on location. The flat deal, under most circumstances, still obligates the writer to perform services according to a designated schedule. In order to provide continuity for the producer and distributor, who may have agreed to distribute the completed motion picture based on its delivery date, the delivery period and review period for each aspect of the story development scripted by the writer is generally specified in order to provide the time for total performance of the writer's output under the agreement.

The writer's agreement typically establishes a schedule for payment. Often, the beginning writer will receive a portion of his or her compensation upon the signing of the agreement, a portion on the delivery of the first draft screenplay, and the remaining portion on the first day of principal photography.

If the motion picture is scheduled to be filmed as a low-budget production, and if the writer is being paid the minimum amount allowable by union requirements, or, in the case of a higher budgeted production, if the producer intends to sweeten the deal offered the writer, the producer may offer the writer additional compensation in the form of a percentage of the producer's net profits (or, on rare occasions, a portion of producer's gross profits).

The writer's agreement usually refers to additional writers if required as collaborators, script doctors, or writers of added drafts. If the new writer is hired after the original writer has been hired on a one-time flat payment deal, the additional writer is generally paid a fee in addition to that paid the original writer. Unless agreed otherwise, the original writer does not generally suffer loss of compensation, though he or she may relinquish a portion, or all, of the credit. The WGA has established guidelines regarding the placement and inclusion of screen credits in the event multiple writers are attached to a particular screenplay.

## PRODUCER'S NET

Producer's net, a term used in the entertainment industry, should be clearly defined in the contract. Producer's net is usually defined as the difference between gross income and expenses, or as all revenues received by the producer after all production costs are paid, including overhead, taxes, deferred payments, expenses, distribution costs, attorney's and professional fees, insurance, salaries, and other costs. The definition can be as broad, or limited, as the parties choose.

Producer's net may exclude from its definition of gross income such items as receipts of any television network or stations, theaters, or any other exhibitor or user of the motion picture. Only the actual license fee or rental paid by such user to the producer or distributor is included under that definition.

In addition, any subsequent revenues generated by a distribution company that has purchased the rights to the motion picture by an outright sale or by bulk license may also, if agreed, be excluded from the calculations used to determine producer's net. Also often excluded from the definition are any unearned or outstanding advances, deposits, refunds, or rebates, and any portion of the receipts contributed to charitable organizations.

The producer generally insists on not factoring into the definition of net or gross such ancillary incomes generated by the movie, such as spin-off rights, radio rights, legitimate stage rights, remake rights, or sequel rights.

Other income usually excluded from the definition includes any salvage value or receipts derived from print stocks, stock footage, stills, props, sets, wardrobe, or other items included in the actual cost of the production of the motion picture.

## CONDITIONS AFFECTING OR RELATING TO COMPENSATION

Administrative elements of compensation are often discussed in the writer's agreement. The contract generally provides for such basic clerical and administrative functions such as where and to whom payments should be delivered, should the payments be delivered by mail or messenger, and the often standard provision that payments will be due upon the writer's performance of services, as agreed.

In the event the producer is forced or required by court order to withhold or to pay all or any portion of the compensation due the writer to any other person, firm, or corporation pursuant to the requirements of an attachment, garnishment, writ of execution, lien, contract, or assignment, the producer is generally obligated to follow such order without claims of default or breach of contract.

The producer may require that a clause be inserted in the agreement entitling the producer to offset any overpayment or indebtedness of the writer to the producer.

### Pay or Play

The producer usually negotiates to include a provision relieving the producer of the obligation to use the writer's services in any form, including producing, releasing, distributing, advertising, exploiting, or otherwise making use of the results and proceeds of the writer's work product.

The producer may also negotiate for the right to terminate the screen writer's obligations and responsibilities under the writer's agreement at all, without cause, legal justification, or excuse within the confines of any locally applicable labor relations laws. Under the guidelines of such a termination, the producer may insist that all other rights of the writer under the agreement are to be voided and deemed ineffective, except such rights that may have accrued to the writer, such as credits and payment, in accordance with the terms of the WGA or other applicable guilds and unions.[10]

### Accountability

When the writer is involved in an equity participation agreement with the producer, an accounting period should be included in the agreement.[11] The producer may agree to furnish the writer with semiannual audits and a general accounting of the receipts generated from the exploitation of the motion picture in the media and agreed upon territories, accompanied by a detailed statement clearly demonstrating the net profits generated from the exploitation of the motion picture, underlining the amount due to the writer under the terms of the equity agreement.

In order to protect the producer from unexpected expenses and payments, the writer's agreement may grant the producer the right to establish, from one or more accounting periods, a reserve for reasonable anticipated future distribution expenses, production expenses, and anticipated losses during subsequent accounting periods.

## CONFIDENTIALITY AGREEMENT

The writer may be required to sign a confidentiality agreement, wherein he or she agrees not to divulge the name or subject matter of the screenplay.

## WARRANTIES AND INDEMNITIES

The importance of averring the originality of the screen writer is a crucial aspect of the writer's agreement.[12] The writer is generally required to warrant that the work will be original, will not be plagiarized or copied from another work, and that the characters will not infringe on the rights of privacy of any person, alive or dead.

Moreover, the writer usually states that the screenplay does not constitute a libel or slander against, or violate any common law or any other rights of, any person, firm, or corporation. The warranty made by the writer is generally subject to limitations contained in the WGA agreement.

The writer generally agrees to make his or her best efforts to complete the picture. The writer also claims that he or she is free to enter this writer's agreement. Once entered into the agreement, the writer will warrant that his or her services under the agreement will not infringe on the rights or obligations of any other party.

The agreement may further provide that both the writer and producer agree, upon reasonable notice, to convey all documents necessary to effectuate the intent of the contract. Those documents may include statements from the writer underscoring unequivocally that the story is an original idea belonging to the producer, if applicable, and that the producer retains all rights, including the copyright, to the finished screenplay. If required, if negotiated, or if the idea is original to the writer, the producer may demand that the writer assign the copyright to the producer for a predetermined consideration.

## CREDITS

Credits are highly important in the entertainment industry. A hierarchy exists, signified by the placement of credits above or before the title, or by having full or shared screen credit. Credits establish the order of success and near success in the motion picture industry. The writer and the producer abiding by the requirements of the WGA, generally agree as to the wording and placement of the credit.[13] For example, the writer may demand, and the producer may agree, that the screen credit be included on all copies of the film, video cassettes, and promotional trailers. It may be a solo, full screen credit, the size of the director's credit, it may remain on screen for an agreed time period, or it may be a shared credit with the originator of the story idea. The credit may read, "Screenplay by (name of screenwriter)."

In the event an additional writer is granted screen credit, the original writer may request first credit.

## INJUNCTIVE RELIEF

Getting a finished motion picture into the stream of commerce by a particular play date is of major importance to the marketing scheme of the production and distribution companies. In order to prevent the writer from obtaining an injunction that may have the sole objective of preventing the film from entering active distribution, the contract usually stipulates that the writer shall be entitled only to money damages for an inadvertent noncompliance by the production company with its credit obligations.[14]

The writer, on the other hand, should be able to secure a statement from the producer that requires the producer to rectify or correct any inadvertent error on prints and materials prepared subsequent to notice of that error.

## NAME AND LIKENESS

The producer usually accords credit to the screen writer in certain promotional material, such as posters, marquee displays, and newspaper advertisements. Generally, the producer must secure in the writer's agreement the right to use the writer's name and likeness for such purposes.

To protect the exploitative value of the writer's reputation, the name and likeness clause typically imposes a limitation on the producer regarding the use of the writer's name. The agreement may state that such advertising may not include the direct endorsement of any product other than the motion picture without the prior consent of the screen writer.

The producer may insist the agreement stipulate that exhibiting, advertising, publicizing, or exploiting the motion picture by any media, even though a part of or in connection with a product or a commercially sponsored program, not be deemed an endorsement of any nature, and thereby relieving the producer of even the inference of the improper use of the writer's name and likeness.

## SEQUELS AND SPIN-OFFS

Ordinarily, the producer will not be obligated to use the services of the writer for any sequels, serializations, or novelizations of the screenplay. The producer may be better served by keeping free of the contractual obligation to use the writer's services in the future. If not granted the right to write any future screenplays based on the original motion picture or develop the picture's characters and story, the writer may request the right to submit ideas for such a sequel or spin-off.

## NO OBLIGATION TO USE SCREENPLAY

The producer is generally not obligated to use materials submitted by the writer. The screenplay may be rejected completely, and the producer typically insists on retaining the capacity to rewrite the product without any encumbrances or obligations to the writer. The ownership of the screenplay will, under most circumstances, remain with the copyright owner of record, usually the producer.[15]

## INSURANCE BENEFITS

As a key member of the production team, the writer is generally covered by adequate health and life insurance for the duration of the making of the motion picture. The agreement generally provides that the writer fully cooperate with the production firm and underwriter in obtaining such insurance.

Depending on the negotiating strength of the writer, he or she may stipulate that if the producer is unable to provide the writer preproduction or cast insurance at prevailing standard rates and without any exclusions, restrictions, conditions, or exceptions of any kind, the writer would have the right to pay any premium in excess of prevailing standard rates in order for the producer to obtain such insurance.

The agreement may also stipulate that, should the writer fail to observe all the conditions required for continuing the insurance plans, the producer may terminate the services of the writer by giving adequate written notice of pending dismissal, unless a cure can be effected within a certain period of time.

# 6

---

# The Producer Agreement

The motion picture producer is the packager, the promoter, the business executive, the member of the production team who combines all the creative elements in the effort to bring the audience an entertaining motion picture. Generally, the producer acquires the underlying literary property through acquiring the rights to a story, and then attempts to raise the finances necessary to make the motion picture independently. Alternatively, the producer could attempt to interest a production company or distributor to finance the production of the motion picture. The producer's agreement outlined in the following pages will be a producer's employment agreement between the producer and a production company/distributor. In this agreement, the producer will generally agree to perform certain prenegotiated and predetermined services for the distribution company, in consideration for both financial compensation and promotional credit.

## DUTIES

The distributor usually agrees to employ the producer to perform services customarily performed by a producer in the motion picture industry. Those services generally require the producer to develop the basic story line based upon a designated property. The producer then guides the production through the motion picture's preproduction phase, production phase, and postproduction phase. The producer is, in many cases, obligated to provide the literary work, the outline of the motion picture, and the final draft screenplay upon which the motion picture will be based.

The producer, furthermore, is contractually obligated to perform all services required to develop and successfully produce the motion picture. The distributor, and major financial backers, are typically granted the right to maintain a representative, supervisor, auditor, or executive producer on the production team. The distributor's representative may be allowed access to all production facilities at all times, including the often secretive preproduction, production, and postproduction phases. If agreed upon, the producer may be obligated to follow the instructions of the distributor's representative in accordance with the standards of reasonableness.

The producer is generally obliged to perform to his or her best ability, with the intention to comply with the budgetary, time, and artistic constraints agreed to by the production company.

In general, the producer acknowledges that his or her services are unique and extraordinary and are not replaceable. Since there is no adequate legal remedy for the producer's breach of the producer's employment agreement, the distributor is, if the situation arises, generally entitled to equitable relief by way of injunction.[1]

Furthermore, the distributor is generally entitled to own, exclusively, all contributions made by the producer relating to the motion picture, whether they be to the motion picture's themes, ideas, or compositions, or any other creative literary, dramatic, musical, or mechanical contributions. The producer usually relinquishes all rights of *droit moral* in the motion picture. In addition, the distributor may also be entitled to the proceeds due the producer from efforts in the exploitation of the motion picture, including merchandising or licensing products based on characters or events in the motion picture.

## ACQUISITION

Generally, the producer acquires the property, which the distributor perceives to be a viable and commercial product. The producer is usually required to demonstrate, through a signed agreement, proof that he or she has obtained those underlying rights.

Unless the producer is the writer, the producer will generally retain, in most instances, only an option to a literary work. In this way, should the producer be unsuccessful in obtaining the financial or creative support necessary to produce the motion picture, the most at stake is the option payment, which often represents only a small percentage of the total purchase price.

The agreement may also stipulate that if the distributor agrees to hire the producer based on the proposed basic property, the producer will transfer the option to the literary work, and all inherent rights in that option, to the distributor. This can take the form of a letter from the producer to the distributor stating that the producer relinquishes all rights in the basic property to the distributor.

## ASSIGNMENT

The producer generally assigns the rights to the underlying property to the distributor, agreeing to execute all documents necessary to perfect the chain of title to the distributor. The distributor may reimburse the producer the cost of securing the rights to the underlying literary property. If the producer is unable to obtain all the necessary elements to insure proper title to the property, the agreement typically stipulates that the agreement may automatically be terminated.

## DEVELOPMENT AND PREPRODUCTION PHASE

This general clause, covering the producer's obligations during the preproduction stage, typically states that the producer is obligated to work in consultation with the director and distributor's representative in performing other duties required during the preproduction phase.

The producer, usually in consultation and with the consent of the distributor, engages a writer to create a screenplay based on the underlying property. The producer may supervise the development and writing of the screenplay and, if he or she exerts creative control, often supervises all revisions to that screenplay, if agreed to by the distributor.

The agreement may also require, on occasion, that the producer take an active role in selecting proposed casting for the filming of the motion picture, as well as selecting applicable locations. The producer is also asked to assist in the preparation of the proposed motion picture budget. The producer's activities usually require the distributor's approval.

The producer, who may have other projects in development, will generally insist that the agreement for his or her services be nonexclusive. The producer may consent to the distributor's request that this production be granted a priority position on the production slate and may further require the assurance that the rendition of his or her services to any third parties will not interfere with obligations to the distributor with regard to the production of the motion picture. As a result of such nonexclusivity, the producer may agree that any and all reimbursable expenses are to be specifically approved by the distributor prior to the incurring of such charge or expense, for reasonable expenses incurred by the producer in connection with scouting trips, location surveys, and general entertainment expenses.

On the other hand, the producer, if possessing sufficient clout in the entertainment business, may negotiate for a multipicture contract, insuring an active production slate for over a contracted time period.

## Development Fee

The distributor generally pays the producer a fee to develop the screenplay from the underlying property and, if agreed, will not be required to reimburse the producer for any overhead, such as legal, living, travel, or business expenses expended by producer during the development phase of production except if stipulated elsewhere in the agreement. The actual dollar amount negotiated for expenses usually depends on the status and stature of the producer and the overall budget of the project.

In what could be analogous to a pay or play agreement, the producer's agreement may further state that the producer will receive a development fee irrespective of whether the movie is produced or not.[2] However, if the services of the producer are ultimately used in the making of the motion picture, the producer may agree to have the development fee offset against the total compensation package. Under those circumstances, if the distributor proceeds with the movie, the development fee would be deemed an advance against total compensation due the producer, as agreed to in the contract.

## Election to Proceed

The distributor generally has a specific period after delivery of the final draft of the screenplay, proposed budget, and approved cast and director to elect to proceed or abandon the production. Generally this election provision is not self-executing. Written notice of such election to the producer is usually required. Failure to give notice during the election period may void the opportunity.

The cost of development is usually minimal when compared to the overall cost of production. The distributor generally retains the right to abandon the production at this phase, in case the distributor loses faith in the economic viability of the motion picture. Under the agreement, the distributor is often able to abandon production without incurring liability or damages.

## Turnaround

In the event the distributor elects not to continue with the development and production of the motion picture, the producer may be granted the exclusive right, for a specified period of time, to acquire the distributor's rights, titles, and interests in the underlying property.

The producer may acquire the rights to the motion picture by reimbursing the distributor for all its costs, plus an administrative overhead charge. If the producer chooses not to exercise his or her rights within the turnaround period, all rights in the underlying property usually remain with the distributor.

The distributor, upon receiving funds from the producer, generally agrees to warrant that it has not, in any manner, transferred or otherwise disposed of any of its right, title, and interest in the motion picture.

In addition, the distributor generally insists that the producer furnish an indemnity agreement covering all obligations and liabilities in connection with the motion picture, relieving the distributor from any legal problems and liabilities relating to the basic property or the making of the motion picture.

### New Elements During Turnaround Time

Often, the distributor's final decision as to whether it will accept or reject the option or election of producing the motion picture rests on the total package offered them by the producer. The distributor generally evaluates the financial risk inherent in the production of the picture, the creative staff, the talent, and the likelihood for success in all manner of distribution, including domestic and international theatrical, pay, and free television, home video and pay-per-view.

If a new set of circumstances develops that could materially affect the likelihood of success, then the distributor usually insists on factoring in those new elements.

The agreement may stipulate that, if the producer, during the period of time in which the turnaround period remains valid, yet prior to the producer actually buying back the project, obtains any new or material changes in the project, thereby making the production more valuable in the distributor's eyes, the producer is required to bring such modifications to the attention of the distributor for review. The distributor would then be granted a specific time period within which to affect a cure of the original denial of the election and decide whether to go ahead with the project predicated on the new elements.

Generally, the agreement states that during this period of turnaround, should any new elements become available, the distributor reserves the right to accept it on a first refusal basis. The producer is therefore under an obligation to keep the distributor apprised of whatever changes the producer may have created, or may have arisen, with regard to the motion picture.

### DISTRIBUTOR'S DEMANDS

If the distributor elects to proceed with the production of the motion picture, it often demands approval of the final shooting script, the principal cast, the director, the director of photography, the negative cost budget, and the schedule for the production and postproduction phases. The distributor's intent is to protect its investment by maintaining overall supervision of the production.

### Right to Loan-Out Service

On occasion, the distributor will turn over the actual production of a film to a third party. Since the contract with the producer is typically a personal services contract, a loan-out provision may be inserted to prevent the possibility of a misunderstanding to the effect that the distributor and producer had entered into an exclusive employment arrangement and therefore would be precluded from entering the loan-out agreement.

The loan-out provision typically states that the distributor has the right to lend the producer's services to any of the distributor's subsidiary or affiliated companies, or any other distributor of motion pictures.

Depending on the bargaining strength of the producer, the producer may request the right to consent to any loan-out agreement entered into by the distributor and a third party, agreeing that consent will not be unreasonably withheld. This clause may also contain a time limit in which the producer must notify the distributor of objections to the proposed loan-out, together with a written explanation to justify such a withholding of consent. Typically, the lending out of the producer does not relieve the distributor of its obligations to the producer.

## APPROVAL OF KEY PERSONNEL AND ELEMENTS

The producer's right to approve key personnel generally depends on several factors, such as the bargaining strength of the producer. The right of approval addresses the issue of who is able to hire key creative and production personnel without an impending veto hanging overhead.

Generally, the distributor insists that after consultation with the producer, it retains the final approval of the budget, production schedule, postproduction schedule, release title, and all other artistic and production elements in connection with the production of the motion picture. Those elements will account for both the above-the-line and below-the-line personnel and elements, including all production commitments and contracts.

### Creative Control

The creative control element of the contract generally relates to two independent, but often complimentary, areas: approvals and selections of key creative and production personnel, and the final cutting and editing of the motion picture. These two points are often negotiated when the producer has gained a certain status in the industry. If the producer is inexperienced or does not have a meaningful track record, the producer naturally carries less of a bargaining position and may not be able to insist on retaining maximum creative freedom for the entire picture.

Creative control of key personnel generally relates to what is referred to as above-the-line matters as compared to below-the-line matters. The term *above-the-line* relates to that part of the budget enumerating the key production personnel, such as the actors, director, and producer, typically deemed to be variable costing items. *Below-the-line* items are those that for the most part, are more fixed in nature, including costs of wardrobes, sets, locations, wranglers, living expenses, sound and camera elements, editing, and so forth.

Creative control over the final cut, which shapes the final look of the film, is usually the responsibility of the distributor. If the producer has a successful string of box office hits to his or her credit, the producer may be able to wield some negotiating clout and capture creative control over the final cut.

In most situations, the producer and distributor fully consult with each other in the production of the film. The producer, if experienced enough, may be able to get mutual approval on the overall making of the picture, including its casting and cost distribution.

If the less experienced producer is granted certain consulting rights, that term should be defined clearly in the agreement. If not so defined, the degree of control granted to the producer depends on the definitions and needs of the distributor. One distributor may define consultation as nothing more than the right to express a judgment or opinion usually unheeded, on a production decision. The contract should, therefore, be as specific about the consultation procedure as possible.

The agreement may include the following areas of mutual consulting:

- the principal members of the cast
- budgeted negative costs
- preproduction schedule
- production schedule
- postproduction schedule
- final approved screenplay
- locations for shooting sites, including exterior and interior locales
- the laboratory used to process the film
- the main and end titles of the motion picture
- the final cut of the movie

If not granted to the producer, or if not subject to mutual consent, the distributor usually retains final approval of all production elements, both above- and below-the-line, and all production commitments and production-related contracts. In addition, the distributor generally demands the right, in its sole discretion, to select and designate the location auditor.

The agreement often addresses the question of conflict regarding approval or consultation. A typical example is the conflicting decisions between a powerful producer and a powerful director. The contract may state that, in the case of such a deadlock, the producer will be the sole arbiter. Likewise, if the producer is absent from the set or cannot be accessed for consultation over a key decision, the agreement may state that the producer's right of approval and consultation under such a situation would under the agreement be waived.

## Employment of Others

Although the producer appears to have authority over the production, in reality, the producer is often limited with respect to hiring and firing employees. The agreement may establish that the producer does not have the right to hire or commit the distributor to hire anybody without the express prior approval of the distributor.

Depending on the stature of the producer, he or she may be able to insert a clause giving the producer the discretionary right to hire specific individuals or job functions. The implication of such a right generally means that the producer has the right to fire that person as well.

Since it is the responsibility of the producer to keep the production of the movie on schedule, the producer normally has the right, as stated in this provision, to remove any individuals deemed an interference from the set. Such a ban, however, does not necessarily grant the producer the right to fire that person if the producer did not hire him. The distributor generally wants to retain the right to fire personnel hired by the distributor, unless that discretionary right was granted the producer in the agreement.

The producer with enough of a bargaining position may be able to insert a clause into the agreement stating that the producer has the right, subject to applicable guild and union requirements, and in addition to employing key above-the-line elements, to select and designate the following key personnel for the picture:

- Director of Photography
- First Assistant Director
- Production Manager
- Unit Manager
- Costume Designer
- Sound Engineer
- Sound Editors
- Lighting Director
- Casting Director
- Special Effects Director

- Music Composer/Director
- Film Editors

Naturally, the discretion granted the producer may be constrained by certain preconditions, such as that the costs involved for engaging a particular person for a key job should not exceed the accepted rate within the motion picture industry. Furthermore, the accepted rate should not exceed what is allocated for such a person in the operating budget. In addition, the track record of the person to be employed should be acceptable to the distributor, with special emphasis on whether that employee had done satisfactory work with the distributor in the past. Finally, the particular person should be ready and able to perform when required by the distributor.

The contract may grant the distributor the right to approve and select any key person that the producer fails to hire in a timely manner or with which the distributor cannot fully agree.

### Dailies

Editing the hundreds of thousands of feet of film shot during principal photography helps shape the final look and feel of the picture. Each day's filming, which together constitute the dailies, is typically viewed by the producer, the director and upper management production staff. The dailies are then passed to the editor, whose job is to string those dailies together into a workable print.

The distributor may demand that it be given the right to inspect the dailies and view and approve each version or cut of the picture as it goes through the editing process.

### OVERHEAD

The distributor may elect to furnish the producer with an office, secretary, and general office facilities. Furthermore, if the services of the producer require travel to an out-of-town location, the producer is generally furnished with round trip transportation tickets and living expenses.

### SERVICES

The producer generally performs services under the terms of the producer's employment agreement, which is subject to the distributor's rights of approval. Depending on whether the deal with the producer is a single movie project or multititle package arrangement, the agreement generally states whether the producer's services are exclusive or nonexclusive.

Generally, the contract states that the producer's services commence at an agreed date prior to the actual first day of principal photography of the motion picture and continue until completion of the postproduction period.

The producer usually agrees to refrain from undertaking any new assignments conflicting with his or her duties on this motion picture.

Usually, the producer agrees to conform to the final shooting script as approved by the distributor, as well as maintain within budget the costs of production, such as the approved negative cost. Furthermore, the producer generally agrees to complete the filming within the approved production schedule, taking into account postponements caused by weather conditions, location unavailability, scheduling problems, *force majeure*, director's unavailability, or cast unavailability.

The producer usually understands that the final motion picture must have a running time of between ninety and 120 minutes. Furthermore, the date of commencement of principal photography should be stated in the contract and agreed to by both producer and distributor. The producer also understands that the final version of the motion picture should carry a rating of no less than the one approved by the distributor. Depending on the marketing target of the movie, the motion picture can be produced with a Motion Picture Association of America (MPAA) rating of G, PG-13, PG, R, or NC-17.

The MPAA uses a ratings formula that blends societal and cinematic requirements. The least restrictive rating is a G, for general audience. The G rating means that the content of the motion picture is suited for all age groups, including preschoolers. There is no profane language or scenes of partial or full nudity. The motion picture also has a theme that would be understood and enjoyed by all attendees.

The PG rating is intended for films considered general but that contain a slightly more mature content. PG means parental guidance suggested, and that parents should try to view the film before deciding if their children are mature enough to watch it.

The next level of rating indicates a film of a general nature, but with a special warning to parents that preteenagers may not be specifically well suited for the movie. Thus, the MPAA issues a rating of PG–13, or parental guidance 13, which means that people under the age of thirteen, or their parents, would most probably have difficulty with the film's subject matter, which may be too strong, offensive, or inappropriate for pre-teenagers.

The MPAA also issues a restricted, or R, rating. The R rating means that the contents of the motion picture are geared for adults, not for teenagers below the age of 18. The movie may contain scenes of partial nudity, profane language, and adult themes. The most restrictive rating is the NC-17 rating, issued to motion pictures that exhibit excessive violence, nudity, and patently adult themes. Children under 17 are not admitted to movie theaters exhibiting NC-17-rated motion pictures.

In addition, the producer generally insures that the motion picture will qualify for the union seal of the International Alliance of Theatrical and Stage Employees (IATSE). By being a signatory to the IATSE, the producer assures the motion picture industry that union labor will be used as set builders, lighting crew, and sound/audio technicians.

## FINAL EDIT

The distributor generally demands the right to control the final edit, or last cut, and all final credits of the motion picture, giving the motion picture its look, feel, and sound. This final cut usually includes the right, at the distributor's sole discretion, to film additional scenes; add or delete scenes or musical compositions; and mix, remix, or change the sequence of the musical compositions. The right of the final edit is usually the final word in the appearance of any motion picture.[3]

## TELEVISION COVER SHOTS

The producer generally agrees to film back-up television cover scenes that would be considered appropriate for airing over the public airwaves, television, based on the network continuity standards in existence at the time of principal photography.

## EXCLUSIVITY

Generally, for the period of production and postproduction, the producer agrees to perform services exclusively for the distributor in connection with the production of the designated motion picture. During the postproduction phase, or even during the preproduction phase, the producer may elect to commence development of another motion picture property, yet may not perform any services that would impede the producer's services to the distributor.

## TERMINATION

The distributor may wish to maintain the right to terminate the producer's services and substitute another producer in order to complete the production and postproduction of the motion picture. To do so, the distributor generally has to demonstrate that the producer had materially breached the agreement, either in creative or budgetary matters. If, for example, the producer had failed to maintain the production costs within the approved budget, the distributor may have ample grounds to demonstrate that the production is delinquently over budget and behind the shooting schedule upon which the budgeted negative costs are based. The distributor may also demonstrate that the producer is materially defaulting in the performance of his or her duties. Those grounds are generally the basis for termination.

The distributor is generally required to submit to the producer written notice of its desire to terminate its agreement. Upon the producer's receipt of the distributor's request, the producer will usually be obliged to assign to the distributor all contracts and agreements to which the producer is a party.

Following such termination and subsequent substitution of a replacement producer, the distributor has the right to proceed with the production of the motion picture. In the event the distributor terminates the producer based upon the producer's nonperformance, or if the producer materially defaults in the performance of services, the distributor may no longer be obligated to pay the producer the total compensation due. The remainder of the compensation is generally paid according to a previously agreed schedule.

## COMPENSATION

The producer may receive compensation as a fixed fee, payable at an agreed schedule. Usually, the producer receives a portion upon the signing of the producer's employment agreement, a portion in weekly installments over the scheduled period of principal photography, and the final portion upon completion of the final corrected answer print of the motion picture.

The producer may also have agreed to receive as compensation a percentage of the net or gross profits, as defined in the agreement, earned from exploiting the motion picture in the agreed upon territories and in the agreed upon media. The agreement may call for the producer to receive participatory compensation after the break-even point is surpassed.

## COPYRIGHT

It is generally agreed that the distributor is the copyright owner of the motion picture and basic property. The motion picture will bear the inscription "copyright ©, year, by distributor" on the credits. Furthermore, the distributor may acquire sole copyright ownership in all music publishing rights, and receive proceeds from the original music in the motion picture and from all sound track albums, and other commercial recording rights of the music in the motion picture.

## MERCHANDISING

Merchandising rights to all goods, items, and objects are based upon the characters appearing on, or incidents occurring in, the motion picture. The distributor may retain full ownership of all merchandising rights emanating from all characters and themes in the motion picture, or it may grant the producer a percentage of its merchandising revenues. The rights granted the producer should be clearly spelled out, since revenues earned from the exploitation of the merchandising rights inherent in the motion picture can result in substantial earnings, depending on the success of the motion picture at the box office.

## REMAKES AND SEQUELS

Generally, the producer grants the distributor the rights to all remakes and sequels, subject to the rights, if any, reserved by the original rights owner. With the popularity of the initial motion picture, a sequel may generate a substantial income, since the characters and incidents are already familiar to the public. A remake of a popular picture may also generate income from the sale or license of those sequel rights.

## NAME AND LIKENESS

The distributor is usually granted by the producer the right to use and display the producer's name and likeness for advertising, publicizing, and generally exploiting the motion picture.[4]

## INSURANCE

The production of a motion picture is a costly venture that often relies on the health and well-being of a few key individuals. A key producer's sudden illness can be costly to the distributor. Likewise, a producer's presence and creative vision are, at times, pivotal to the success of a picture.

The distributor, in order to insure its investment and interests, often requires that the producer submit to the examinations and obligations required by an insurer. The beneficiary of such insurance is usually the production company/distributor, who may consider this clause to be essential and usually requires the termination of the producer's agreement if the producer is unable to obtain insurance. The producer's refusal to cooperate with the underwriter may make him or her liable for termination with notice by the distributor.

## DISTRIBUTOR'S GROSS

Since the producer's agreement may call for the producer to receive, as compensation, a percentage of the royalties earned from the exploitation of the motion picture, it is important to define net proceeds and distributor's gross.

The terms are nebulous concepts that can be interpreted to mean all monies and receipts earned from the exploitation of the motion picture, without any deductions whatsoever, or all monies and receipts earned less specified deductions.

Those deductions must be clearly established and stated in the agreement in order to lessen the possibility of protracted litigation or arbitration at a later date. Clearly, the definition of gross as used in a particular agreement can be the difference between a sizeable earning and a minimal earning for the producer.

The stronger the distributor's bargaining position, the more it can dictate the definition of distributor's gross. In the case of a distributor of the stature of Paramount Pictures, Twentieth Century Fox, or Warner Brothers, for example, distributor's gross may be interpreted to mean receipts generated from all parties exhibiting the motion picture in theater and on television, all receipts received by the distributor from licensing or granting distribution rights, including video cassettes, pay-per-view, pay television and satellite, and all earnings of the distributor from the sale and license of advertising accessories and merchandising.

Often deducted from the distributor's gross receipts are certain expenses, including all taxes; duties; customs; imports; costs of acquiring permits; costs necessary to secure entry, license, exhibition, performance, use, and television play within any country; costs of transmitting any funds accruing to the distributor from any country to the United States and any discounts taken to convert such funds into U.S. currency; the cost of litigation or arbitration to contest any of the matters in the agreement; all payments due to actors, writers, directors, unions, guilds, pension funds, or other participants based on contractual agreements entitling them to gross or net profit participation in the earnings generated from the exploitation of the motion picture.

Usually, the following are not included in the definition of gross receipts: receipts of any theatrical, or other, user of the motion picture; receipts contributed to charitable organizations; and receipts received by a subdistributor, if any, from the gross earnings of such subdistributor.

## STATEMENTS AND RECORDS

The producer should insist that the distributor agree to furnish the producer with an accounting, at regular intervals, of the gross receipts earned from the exploitation of the motion picture. The distributor normally agrees to keep complete records and send statements to the producer, or to grant the producer or the producer's representatives, usually CPAs, the right to inspect the books, upon reasonable notice, at the places where the books and records are normally held.

## MONIES HELD IN TRUST

Funds held in trust by the distributor for the benefit of the producer represent a fiduciary obligation of the highest degree, comparable to the fiduciary obligation a bank has to its depositors. The distributor generally prefers limiting its liability by specifying clearly that funds it holds in its bank accounts are not held in trust for the producer.

## NO GUARANTEE OF SUCCESS

The distributor usually warrants to the producer that it has not made any representations regarding the gross receipts the motion picture will generate. The entertainment industry is a speculative business with a high degree of risk, and no such guarantees can be made with certainty.

## RIGHTS

The producer usually agrees to forfeit all rights, titles, and interest in the screenplay and finished motion picture, as well as in the gross receipts earned from the exploitation of the motion picture (unless the producer receives a percentage of the distributors gross receipts as a portion of compensation). The distributor, by this clause, is usually granted the unencumbered right to sell, transfer, assign, pledge, or encumber the motion picture and the gross receipts, and to produce, distribute, license, or exploit the motion picture in any manner throughout the world without requiring the producer's consent.

Moreover, the producer generally warrants and agrees that all material, works, writings, ideas, jokes, or gags written, composed, prepared, submitted by the producer in connection with the picture or its production are completely original and not copied in whole or in part from any other work.

In addition, the agreement may warrant that any original material used in the motion picture will not violate the rights of privacy or constitute a libel or slander against any person, firm, or corporation, and that the material will not infringe upon the copyright, literary, dramatic, or photoplay rights of any person or entity.

The distributor usually owns outright, solely and exclusively, the results and proceeds of the producer's services, including production, reproduction, and manufacture. The distributor generally owns copyrights, trademarks, and patents emanating from the motion picture. In addition, the distributor's ownership generally extends to include all forms of creation, idea, theme, composition, or product.

## TRAVEL AND EXPENSES

Filming a scene in the motion picture may require that the producer travel a distance away from home. In the event the filming occurs more than an agreed upon distance from the producer's home, the producer generally receives round trip transportation and reasonable living expenses.

The producer is generally entitled to a reasonable per diem expense draw, in addition to living accommodations. An escalation clause providing for a greater weekly payment may be negotiated and stated in the contract if the producer can establish that the actual cost of living for reasonable and necessary expenses exceeds the allowance.

The agreement may stipulate that any expense monies saved by the producer revert back to the distributor.

## CREDITS

The wording, size, and placement of screen credits are significant to the producer, who often negotiates forcefully for full screen credit on a separate card (alone on the screen) above or below the title of the motion picture. In addition, the producer generally requires credit on all advertisements, publicity, billboards, television and motion picture theater trailers, as well as on all promotional campaigns on the screen, radio, television, and in print.

Credits, for the producer, are a reflection of his or her professional stature and experience. They are the producer's calling card. Credits serve a valuable economic purpose too, since an established and popular producer can generate audience attendance and increase revenues for the distributor.

The producer prefers a credit above the title reading "Produced by _____" or "A _____ production," or "A _____ film." The size, wording, and placement of the credit is generally indicated in the agreement.

An additional point to be negotiated covers the size of the credit in relation to the main title of the picture, and whether the credit is to be placed on a separate frame, or card. The name of a top-drawing producer may often be equal to, or even larger than, the film title or star.

Also depending on the bargaining strength of the producer, the producer may insist on a provision limiting the size and placement of other credits. This covenant may stipulate that only star billings may have a credit as large as the producer's. All other cases – the performers and production staff cited on the credit roll, the crawl – must have credits smaller than the producer's. In some rare instances, the clause may stipulate that the producer's name must be the largest on the screen.

Also to be negotiated at this point is the size of the producer's name in advertising, both for the consumer and the trade. The producer may require that his or her name be placed in an appropriate location within the advertisement.

## REMEDIES AND BREACHES

Generally, this clause indicates that no casual or inadvertent failure to comply with the provisions of the agreement will be deemed a breach of this agreement by distributor.

The agreement further stipulates that the producer recognizes and confirms that, in the event of a failure or omission by the distributor constituting a breach of the distributor's obligations, the damages to the producer are considered insufficient to entitle the producer to injunctive or other equitable relief.

This clause may prevent the producer from obtaining a court injunction demanding that the distributor relinquish its rights and title to the motion picture in the event of a mistake or omission, even a mistake in the size, placement, or wording of the producer's credits. The producer may be entitled to legal remedies, usually money damages, which may be quite difficult to measure.

The agreement may specify that the distributor will, if an error or mistake is realized, correct any credit error as additional prints are made. In addition, the distributor may agree to include an explanation and clarification of such an error within print advertising of the movie.

The services rendered by the producer are generally considered to be unique, irreplaceable, and extraordinary. The distributor may claim that the loss of the producer's services will cause the distributor injury and loss that cannot be adequately compensated in legal action. The distributor typically requires a clause permitting it an injunction or other equitable relief against the producer in an effort to prevent a breach. Such injunctive relief for the distributor ordinarily prevents the producer from working elsewhere during the term of the agreement.

## NEGATIVE COVENANTS

The distributor may wish to control the dissemination of news items to the press. The company may intend to coordinate the release of the motion picture with a planned press release. The producer is usually restricted from issuing news stories or publicity relating to the motion picture, unless directed to do so by the distributor, until such time as the distributor shall decide to commence with the release of publicity.

## FORCE MAJEURE

*Force majeure* may be defined as any force or action, beyond the distributor's control, that results in postponing or suspending production.[5] In such a situation, the distributor may postpone the commencement of, or suspend the rendition of, services by the producer as long as the disability continues. The distributor may not be required to pay the producer during the period of suspension.

The agreement generally grants the distributor the right to terminate the contract with the producer in the event the event lasts beyond an agreed upon time and upon providing written notice of termination to the producer. Likewise, the producer may terminate his or her commitment to the distributor if the disability lasts for a prenegotiated amount of time and the prerequisite written notice is provided.

Upon the expiration of the *force majeure* event, the provisions and time limits originally stipulated in the contract revert back to its original contracted conditions, and the distributor must resume its obligations under the contract.

## BREACH OF CONTRACT

In general, if the producer fails or refuses to comply with any of the material terms or conditions of the contract as a whole, the distributor reserves the right to terminate the agreement and replace the producer, providing that advance written notice is provided to the producer. A producer with ample bargaining strength may insist on including a subclause requiring the distributor to allow the producer to cure the breach within a reasonable amount of time.

The term material breach may be used to soften the potential harshness of the contract. What may be characterized as a harmless breach of some technical aspect of the contract could not be used as a pretense for firing a producer.

The contract may provide, as an alternative to termination, for the temporary suspension without pay of the producer's services. The contract typically states that any incapacity or default of the producer would be deemed to continue until the distributor receives a written notice stating that the producer is ready, willing, and able to perform the services required under the agreement.

Since this provision prevents the producer from carrying out commitments to the distributor, the agreement may also stipulate that the producer will not render production services for any person, firm, or corporation other than the distributor, unless agreed to by the distributor.

# 7

## The Director Agreement

The director is the captain of the set. He or she charts the course, working to create a final product that is a masterful blend of creative artistry and keen business sense. The director must answer both to the public and to the producer. The public is interested in being entertained. The producer is interested in the bottom line.

The director is hired to tell the story spelled out in the screenplay in visual language. The director moves the story from scene to scene, blends action with dialogue, and instructs the talent and crew in the performance of their duties.

Because the director is the key person responsible for the entire filming, he or she bears the responsibility of keeping the production on budget. Mistakes are expensive, especially when one considers that the cost of daily expenditures for principal photography can easily run into tens of thousands of dollars.

On most occasions, the producer judges the various attributes of a director, screening the director's past work and looking for indications that the director's vision is in line with the theme of the film to be produced. A director's ability to handle action scenes, to direct tender love scenes, to get the most out of two male pals in a buddy film, to direct car chase scenes, or to use lighting to its maximum effect are considered in relationship to the motion picture being produced. The director's temperament and manner on the set, track record of past successes, and ability to complete the principal photography within the allocated budget is reviewed. The revenues generated from the exploitation of the director's films are tallied. The director's history is open for all to see and evaluate.

Successful directors can negotiate from a position of strength, while less experienced directors deal from a more vulnerable position. Creative freedom, as well as compensatory rewards, hang on the definitions of the clauses included, or excluded, from a director's contract.

## RIGHT TO LOAN OUT SERVICE

From time to time, a producer may want to turn over the actual production of a film to a third party. Since the contract the producer enters with the director is generally considered a personal services contract, a loan-out clause may be inserted in the employment agreement to clarify any ambiguities which may arise.[1] The loan-out agreement typically states that, in the event of any future disputes affecting the director that may arise between the producer and a third party production company, the director was in the employ of the third party production firm rather than the producer who initially entered into a contract with the director and had bargained for the right to loan out the director's services.

The agreement typically stipulates that the producer has the right to lend the director's services to any of producer's subsidiary or affiliated companies, or to any other producer of motion pictures, provided certain obligations are fulfilled. These obligations usually include the assurance that the third party producer has granted to the original producer the right to distribute the motion picture, if the original producer is a production company/distributor with the capacity to distribute the motion picture domestically and internationally.

Depending on the bargaining strength of the director, an added provision requiring the consent of the director to the loan-out agreement may be included. Usually, the consent clause is couched with the added caveat that the consent of the director will not be unreasonably withheld. This consent clause may also contain a time limit within which the director must notify the producer of his or her objections, if any, in a written explanation.

The consent clause generally provides that the lending out of the directors services does not relieve the producer or the third party producer of the contractually negotiated and agreed upon obligations to the director.

## EDITING

The editing of hundreds of thousands of feet of film shot over the months of filming shapes the final look and feel of the motion picture. Rough film footage of each day's shooting, called dailies, is viewed by the director, the production staff and the editor. It is the editor's job to string those dailies together into a workable print.

It is usually agreed that the director is entitled to the first cut, commonly known as the director's cut, whereby the editor complies with the director's vision of the film. The director is generally required to present to the producer the director's cut on an agreed schedule.

## The Final Cut

A point of contention and repeated negotiations is the final cut, the final and decisive edit of the film that will be presented to the public, theatrically, on television and in all other media. The comparative strength of the producer and director's prestige and box office histories are usually the deciding factors in this battle for creative control.

Since the final cut is typically limited to a rare handful of prestigious and successful directors, in most instances it is the producer or distributor who demands and receives the final say in the ultimately released version of the motion picture.

## Running Time

The producer generally requires that the director keep the running time of the film within limits considered peak for audiences' attention. The typical modern film runs between ninety and one hundred and twenty minutes.

## CREATIVE CONTROL

The creative control element of the contract typically relates to two independent but often complementary areas: approvals and selections of key creative and production personnel, and cutting and editing of the final cut of the picture.

The sensitive subject of creative control is generally negotiated with the director only after he or she has gained a certain status in the industry. If the director is inexperienced or does not have a meaningful box office track record, with a string of successful hits, often the director will have less of a bargaining position to insist on the right of final cut. The final cut is the last haven for creative control, the ultimate assurance of maximum creative freedom for the entire picture, the final opportunity to place a personal identifiable mark on the motion picture. In addition, the ability to exert creative control generally concerns the employment of above-the-line as well as key below-the-line personnel.

Above-the-line elements classically relate to that segment of the motion picture budget encompassing the key production personnel, including the actors, director, producer, and writer. The costs of hiring and maintaining above-the-line personnel and items is typically deemed to be the variable costing items. In contrast, those items that are for the most part fixed in nature are the below-the-line personnel and items and typically include wardrobe, sets, locations, sound and camera elements, living expenses, musical elements, and so forth.

## Consultation

The creative control provision may grant the director the right to consult with the producer regarding the motion picture's final cut. It is important that the term consult be defined clearly in the agreement in order to lessen the chance of any ambiguity. While on the surface granting the director the right to consult with the producer on every aspect of making the motion picture may appear to give some semblance of creative control to the director, it may in reality be a worthless phrase. In many instances, the degree of control granted to the director depends on the definition accorded that phrase by the producer. Producer A, for example, may define the director's right to consult on the production of a motion picture as the right to express a judgment or opinion. Often, the director's right to be consulted on a scene may be little more than the producer paying lip service to the director.

The agreement may include the following areas, which would require mutual consultation between the director and producer:

- the principal members of the cast
- budgeted negative costs
- preproduction schedule
- production schedule
- postproduction schedule
- final approved screenplay
- locations for shooting sites, including both exterior and interior locales
- the laboratory used to process the film
- the main and end titles of the motion picture
- the final mix or release of the movie

If the director is in a weaker bargaining position than the producer, the contract generally states in clear and unambiguous language that the producer retains final approval of all other production elements in connection with the production of the motion picture, including above-the-line and below-the-line elements, commitments, and contracts. In addition, the producer may retain the right, in his or her sole discretion, to designate the location auditor.

## EMPLOYMENT OF OTHERS

Regarding the employment of personnel, the agreement generally stipulates that the director may not hire or commit the production company to hire anybody without the express prior approval of the producer.

If the director has enough bargaining clout, though, the director may be able to insert into the agreement a provision granting him or her the right to select and designate the following key personnel for the picture:

- Director of Photography
- First Assistant Director
- Production Manager
- Unit Manager
- Costume Designer
- Sound Engineer
- Sound Editors
- Lighting Director
- Casting Director
- Special Effects Director
- Music Composer/Director
- Film Editors
- Cameraman
- Principal Cast Members

The discretion granted the director to hire and fire may be constrained by certain preconditions, which can include the costs involved for engaging a particular person for a key job (the cost of replacement may exceed the price generally allotted for such a person in the operating budget), the assurance that the track record of the person to be employed is acceptable to the production company, with special consideration given to whether that selected employee had done satisfactory work with the production company in the past, and finally the insistence that a particular person be prepared to perform the services required by producer within the production schedule.

Generally, the contract provides that, notwithstanding the right of the director to select personnel, the producer is granted the right to approve and hire any key person the director fails to select within the agreed time period, or upon whom the producer cannot agree.

In the event the director fails to hire appropriate personnel in a timely manner, the agreement may state that such action will be deemed a material default of the basic agreement and may subject the director to liability under the agreement or, in extreme cases, may result in voiding the contract as a whole.

Since it is the responsibility of the director to keep the production of the movie flowing, the director may have the right to remove any individuals he or she deems an interference, encumbrance, or detriment to the filming. However, such a ban from the set may not necessarily require the firing of such a person.

## DUTIES AND TERMS

The director typically agrees to perform services as director of the motion picture under the conditions outlined in the agreement, to the best of his or her ability. Furthermore, the director usually agrees to comply with reasonable directions and requests from the producer.

In addition, the director usually agrees to be available for story conferences with the writer and for meeting with financiers and studio executives.

## TERM OF EMPLOYMENT

The director's period of employment is generally divided into three phases: the preproduction period, the production period, and the postproduction period. The director's term of employment may include additional periods for reshoots or television cover shots. With television, cable, pay-per-view, and other broadcast rights in mind, the producer may prepare, during the actual filming of the motion picture, two versions of the movie: the PG version designated for television broadcast, and the original version designated for theatrical release. The difference between the versions may be scenes featuring violence or sexual activity. Generally, the broadcast version of the motion picture is more subdued and could require alternate scenes and dialogue in order for the final version to comply with network standards.

It is usually the director's task to film such less controversial scenes — cover shots — and to complete the director's cut of the television version within an agreed upon date, typically within several weeks following the delivery of the final answer print of the theatrical version of the motion picture.

The preproduction period is generally considered the period from the date the director is first employed to the first day of principal photography. During this period, the director's duties usually include guiding the screenplay into its final, shooting version, casting the principal roles, deciding upon the locations, and the creation of the props and sets for the filming.

When preparing a contract in advance of the commencement of the director's duties, potential conflicts may arise regarding the director's work schedule on other projects.

Depending on the stature of the director, the producer generally demands that the director's services be exclusive to the production for a period of time prior to principal photography. Prior to that period of exclusivity, the director may be granted the right to complete other previously committed obligations while guaranteeing availability to the production company of the new project.

The production period is when the motion picture is actually filmed. Often this period is well defined, since actors, directors, and below-the-line personnel may be contractually obligated to perform their services for another film with an established start date. Defining the production period locks in the cast, crew, and full production team.

The postproduction period commences at the completion of principal photography and usually ceases when the director presents to the producer the final version of the film, which is often described as the final corrected answer print.

The duties of the director during the postproduction phase is generally stipulated in the contract. When defining the terms for postproduction, the producer is typically concerned with the possibility that a scene or an element of a scene may have been inadvertently overlooked, filmed inappropriately, or should be added. These events may require that the director be available to shoot or reshoot those supplemental shots. To be prepared for such postproduction shoots, the producer usually tries to get the director's exclusive services during the postproduction phase. If such exclusivity is unacceptable to the director, the producer may settle for a nonexclusive, but a right of first call, agreement. The director may have another picture being planned during this phase of production and may not be prepared to become tied contractually to the producer. In the first call arrangement, the director is on call to complete the producer's motion picture.

The director may require that the agreement outline a specific postproduction schedule to insure that the director can fulfill other motion picture assignments without fear of creating a conflict.

Additions to the filming, or modifications to previously shot scenes required by the producer, may also include dubbing, trailers, sound track, process shots, or the taping of additional language versions. Since the director may already be committed to other projects during this postproduction period, the agreement generally takes into consideration future shooting schedules. The contract may contain the caveat the director, if involved in another picture, shall cooperate to make his or her unique directorial services available to the producer at the earliest possible date.

## RIGHT OF FIRST NEGOTIATION

The director's contract may also stipulate that the director will have the right of first negotiation for theatrical or television remakes or sequels, within a certain period of time, based upon the motion picture.

Some directors argue vehemently for this right, as the trend towards sequels in certain genres continues in the marketing strategy of many production companies. In such a situation, the producer is able to produce a sequel or remake with a certain degree of continuity, while the director will not only be able to secure additional compensation following the filming of a successful motion picture, but will be able to create a creative flow from one picture to the next. In addition, if sequels are produced, and they are directed under the helm of the original director, they may enhance the stature of the director in the motion picture industry.

The clause may require that both the producer and director show good faith when negotiating for the rights to direct the sequels. The term good faith is not necessarily a word of art, since many courts will define the term in various ways. Some jurisdictions will imply a good faith clause into the contract while other courts may require that some negotiations take place in order to have fulfilled the obligation to negotiate in good faith. The contract may state, for example, that the director has a designated period of time within which to negotiate in good faith to the terms offered by the producer before the production company has the right to offer the position to another director.

## EXCLUSIVITY

A director usually agrees to render services exclusively and solely for the producer until the director's cut is complete and accepted as satisfactory by the producer. While this will preclude the director from performing services as director of any other project during the agreed upon term, nothing prevents the director from developing other projects as long as such development does not interfere with the timely performance of the director's obligations under the agreement. After the director's cut is accepted by the producer, the director is free to commence preproduction work on another motion picture.

## PLACE OF PERFORMANCE

The filming of the motion picture may require that the director travel to several locations. Those locations, including interior and exterior locations, as well as sound stages and editing facilities, are usually spelled out in the agreement.

## UNION MEMBERSHIP

The Directors Guild of America (DGA), with principal offices in Los Angeles and New York, is the primary union representing directors. It is generally agreed in the agreement that the director, at his or her sole expense, be a member in good standing of the DGA, as required by the by-laws of the union.

As a result of being a member of the DGA, the contract includes the stipulation that nothing contained in the director's agreement will be construed to require the violation of the DGA basic agreement. Moreover, the contract generally states that wherever there is any conflict between any provision of the agreement and the DGA basic agreement, the rules regulating the DGA would prevail, but only to the extent necessary to permit compliance.

## INSURANCE

The production of a motion picture is a costly venture that often relies on the health and well-being of a few key individuals. A director's sudden illness can cost the producer millions of dollars in unfinished footage. The director's presence and vision are often pivotal to the success of a picture.

The producer, in order to insure investments and interests, often requires that the director submit to the exams and obligations required by an insurer. The beneficiary of such insurance is usually the production company, which may consider this clause to be material and require the termination of the director's agreement if the director is unable to obtain insurance.

However, the contract may mitigate that problem by the insertion of a clause stipulating that, in the event the director is able to secure proper insurance, the producer reimburses the director the amount of the premium that the producer would ordinarily pay, provided the director pays the balance and adheres to policy conditions. If the director refuses to cooperate with the underwriter, then the director may be liable for termination with notice by the producer.

## COMPENSATION

The director's fee can be paid in several ways: as an agreed salary of a fixed sum, as a percentage of the revenues earned from exploiting the motion picture, at times referred to as contingent compensation agreement, or as a combination of both.

The fixed sum is often paid according to a defined schedule. One such schedule may be as follows:

1. an agreed sum upon the signing of the agreement
2. a sum upon the approval of a budgeted negative cost (negative costs being defined as the amount expended on the motion picture up to the point of positive prints being made)
3. an additional sum upon commencement of principal photography
4. a sum upon delivery of the director's cut
5. the remaining sum upon completion of the final cut and delivery to the laboratory of the composite print

When negotiating with an experienced director, the producer may agree to pay the director a nonrefundable deposit, payable at the time of the signing of the director's agreement. For the majority of lesser established directors, such an up front payment is generally not a conventional source of compensation for the director.

The producer may argue that the director not be entitled to extra pay for work performed at night or on holidays.

In addition to a salary, the director may be entitled to deferred compensation, which may include contingency payments and bonus payments. The contingent compensation, a percentage of the revenues earned from the distributor's gross or net receipts and earnings from exploitation of the motion picture, generally depends on the director's stature, past track record, and experience. A bonus payment may be earned if the director completes production on, or below, the contracted budget. In addition, a director may be entitled to a bonus if the motion picture earns, at the box office, in excess of an agreed sum, or if the picture is nominated for, and wins, an academy award.

In negotiating the agreement, it is imperative that the director know the producer's history regarding such methods of compensation. Specifically, if a producer has a policy of refusing to offer percentages of gross or net profits, the director may try to negotiate for a larger fixed compensation package. Conversely, if the director is confident in the script and his or her ability to turn out a successful production, the director may be better off financially by arguing and holding out for a smaller salary but an increased percentage of the profits. Of course, by accepting a portion of profits as compensation, the director accepts a greater proportion of risk. The motion picture may be unsuccessful at the box office, and the director's net or gross returns could be relatively small.

In entertainment contracts, definitions used when drafting what constitutes net profits and gross profits are critical, since the percentage of the amount negotiated by the director is related directly to the definition of net profits and gross profits.

## Pay or Play

In order to limit liability, the producer may state that he or she is not required to produce or release the motion picture, and that the producer alone is entitled to decide whether, for commercial or creative reasons, the production is to be aborted and the distribution agreement nullified.[2] Furthermore, the contract often states, in clear language, that the producer is not in general obligated to produce, release, distribute, advertise, or exploit the motion picture.

The agreement may go on to stipulate the exact amount of fixed compensation that will be paid to the director in the event the producer, without legal justification or excuse, elects not to use the director's services. This provision often provides for installment payments to the director, rather than the director receiving the entire fixed compensation agreement in one flat fee payment.

As a further negotiated point, the pay or play requirement may be considered fully vested if, not withstanding the termination of director's services to direct or the director's incapacity or default under the terms of the director's agreement, the director receives "directed by" credit pursuant to the DGA basic agreement. On the other hand, if the director is not entitled to receive director's screen credit, as determined in the DGA basic agreement, then the director may receive a proportion of his or her fixed compensation based on the same ratio of completed footage in the completed picture as released, which was directed by the director but which may have been completed by other directors. Should the director's contribution to the completed motion picture be roughly 30 percent of the released movie, for example, the director's fixed compensation and deferred compensation would equal that ratio.

Inclusion of the pay or play clause may require the producer to pay the director for the full compensation due, irregardless of whether the director's services are utilized in the production of the motion picture. While contract law in general provides that the person claiming a breach by the other party should mitigate damages to the utmost, the pay-or-play provision has been interpreted to mean that the director need not have to mitigate damages. The director, therefore, would not be obligated to find a new project in the least amount of time reasonably expected in a similar situation in the entertainment business unless the producer demands a mitigation subclause be inserted into the agreement.

## NO OBLIGATION TO PRODUCE

The producer generally stipulates that he or she will not be obliged to complete production of the motion picture. In addition, if the final version of the motion picture does not meet the producer's standards, or if the motion picture is considered to be noncommercial and therefore not a prime candidate for general distribution, the producer is under no obligation to distribute the final, completed motion picture.

This could be considered an economic saving for the producer since, by avoiding the obligation to complete the production or to commence distribution of the finished product, the producer may generate substantial savings by ceasing involvement with the production of the motion picture and halting production.

## GROSS PROFITS

Since the director's agreement may grant the director the right to earn a percentage of the royalties or profits earned as a result of the exploitation of the motion picture, it is important to define the exact definition of gross profits clearly and unequivocally.

Gross profits are a nebulous concept whose meaning can include all monies and receipts earned from the exploitation of the motion picture, without any deductions whatsoever, or it may restrict the director's potential income by being defined as all monies and receipts earned, less specified deductions.

Those deductions must be clarified in order to lessen the possibility of protracted litigation or arbitration at a later date as the courts, or arbiters, wrangle with the definition of gross profits. Clearly, the definition of gross as used in a particular agreement can be the difference between a sizeable earning and a minimal earning for the director.

The stronger the director's bargaining position, the more the director can dictate the definition of gross profits. In the case of a major director of wide repute and noted stature, for example, gross profits may be defined as receipts generated from the production and subsequent distribution and general exploitation of the motion picture from all parties exhibiting the motion picture in theaters and on television; all receipts received by the distributor from licensing or granting distribution rights, including video cassettes, pay-per-view, pay television, and satellite; all earnings of distributor from the sale and license of advertising accessories and merchandising; all revenues generated from the novelizations of the motion picture, the motion picture sound track, the license and sale of the motion picture outside of the United States, and exploitation of the motion picture in all media, whether presently in existence or devised in the future.

Certain expenses may be deducted from the gross profits, including the following:

- all taxes, duties, customs, imports, costs of acquiring permits, and any other costs necessary to secure the entry, licensing, exhibition, performance, use, and television play within any country

- expenses to transmit any funds accruing to the distributor from any country to the United States and any discounts taken to convert such funds into U.S. currency

- the cost of litigation or arbitration to contest any of the matters agreed to in the agreement

- all payments due to actors, writers, directors, unions, guilds, pension funds, or other participants based on contractual agreements entitling those persons or entities to gross or net profit participation in the earnings generated from exploiting the motion picture.

Usually, the following are not included in the definition of gross profits receipts:

- receipts of any theatrical, or other, user of the motion picture
- receipts contributed to charitable organizations

- receipts received by a subdistributor, if any, from the gross earnings of such subdistributor.

## STATEMENTS AND RECORDS

The director typically requires that the producer furnish the director with an accounting, at regular intervals, of the gross receipts earned from the exploitation of the motion picture. The producer normally agrees to keep complete records and should send the director statements at agreed intervals.

## MONIES HELD IN TRUST

Funds held in trust by the producer for the benefit of the director represents a fiduciary obligation of the highest degree, comparable to the fiduciary obligation a bank has to its depositors. The producer generally prefers limiting liability by specifying clearly that such funds are not held in trust for the director. The director generally argues otherwise, negotiating for the establishment of a trust account, in his or her name.

## NO GUARANTEE OF SUCCESS

The producer usually warrants that he or she has not made any guarantees or representations regarding the gross receipts the motion picture will generate. This clause generally protects the producer from liability in the event the director claims that he or she was induced to direct this motion picture, in lieu of another, based on claims made by the producer guaranteeing the motion picture's success.

## RIGHTS

The director typically agrees to forfeit all rights, titles, or interest whatsoever in the screenplay or finished motion picture, or, if so agreed in the compensation clause, in the gross receipts earned from the exploitation of the motion picture. The producer, by this clause, is usually granted the unencumbered right to sell, transfer, assign, pledge, or encumber the motion picture and the gross receipts, and to produce, distribute, license or exploit the motion picture in any manner throughout the world without the director's consent.

## WARRANTY RELATED TO CREATED MATERIALS

The director usually affirms that any material he or she created is original, created or conceptualized by the director alone, without infringing on the protected rights, including copyrights, of any other person or entity. The director usually warrants that all material, works, writings, ideas, jokes, or gags written, composed, prepared, or submitted by the director in connection with the picture or its preparation or production are wholly original and were not copied, in whole or in part, from any other work, except if material was submitted by the producer as a basis for such material.

Typically, the clause further ensures that the director's original material does not violate the rights of privacy of or constitute a libel or slander against any person, firm, or corporation, and that the material will not infringe upon the copyright, literary, or dramatic rights of any another person or entity.

## OWNERSHIP OF MATERIAL

The director, in most cases, agrees that the producer owns outright, solely and exclusively, the results and proceeds of the director's services, including production, reproduction, manufacture, copyright, trademark, and patent, and any form of creation, idea, theme, composition, creation, or product. The director is generally asked to waive all rights of *droit moral* in the motion picture, in any country and in any capacity connected with the motion picture. The director generally also grants to the producer all rights to the characters, themes, acts, and scenes as used in the motion picture. The characters popularized in the motion picture may be the basis for favorable merchandising or licensing agreements entered into by the producer to exploiting his or her rights in the motion picture.

## DIRECTOR'S NAME, VOICE, AND LIKENESS

The producer generally requires the right to use the director's name, voice, and likeness for the purpose of licensing, selling, promoting, advertising, and exploiting the motion picture.

## RIGHT TO ENTER AGREEMENT

The director is often required to affirm his or her right to enter the agreement without infringing on the rights, contractual or otherwise, of any other person or entity.

## TRAVEL AND EXPENSES

The filming of a scene in a motion picture may require that the director travel a distance away from home. In the event the filming occurs at more than an agreed distance from the director's home, the director generally requires round trip transportation (first class travel, if he or she has the bargaining strength) and reasonable living and per diem expenses.

This provision may stipulate a weekly dollar expense account. The reasonableness of the amount usually depends on the bargaining strength, track record, and stature of the director.

Where the anticipated living expenses may exceed the permitted ceiling, an escalation of the director's weekly payment may be negotiated and stated in the contract if the director can establish that the actual cost of living for reasonable and necessary expenses exceeds the agreed upon allowance.

## CREDITS

The director's credits are an integral and important provision in the agreement. Credits are a reflection of a motion picture professional's stature and experience within the industry. It is a director's calling card, history, and curriculum vitae. The credit often adds to the economic success of the movie, increasing earned revenues for the producer.

It must also be remembered that credits and their wording and placement are also significant in the established hierarchy of the motion picture industry. The director, if he or she fully and completely fulfills the obligations required by the agreement, is entitled to screen credits.

The director typically prefers a credit above the title reading, "A (name of director) Film" and a credit below the title reading, "Directed by (name of director)." The size, wording and placement of the credit is generally also agreed upon in the agreement.

A negotiated point may involve the size of the credit in relation to the main title of the picture, and whether the credit is on a separate frame or card. In the case of a highly successful director, the director's name is often equal to or even larger than the star actor.

Also, depending on the bargaining strength of the director, the director may insist at this point to include a credit limitation clause, which stipulates that only a recognizable star may be entitled to billing and credit as large as that accorded the director. In all other cases, credits of all the performers and production staff cited on the credit roll must be smaller than the credit accorded the director. In some instances, the clause may simply stipulate that the director's name be the largest on the screen.

Another point to be negotiated under this clause and finalized in the contract is the size of the director's name in advertising, both for the consumer and the trade. The agreement may require that the director's name be on a separate frame or card and placed in a central location, along with his or her name and likeness, in all promotions and advertisement.

## Remedies and Breaches

In the event the producer inadvertently fails to comply with the credit requirements, the producer may argue that the inadvertent failure should not be deemed a breach of the agreement. In the event of such a failure or omission by the producer, which would be considered to constitute a breach of the producer's obligations under the contract, the directory may be contractually required to agree that the damages, if any, that the producer feels resulted from this breach will not be considered irreparable or sufficient to warrant injunctive or other equitable relief.

This clause may be of prime importance to the producer, since it may prevent the director from obtaining a court injunction demanding that the producer refrain from the continued distribution of the picture in the event of a mistake in the credits.

The agreement may also state that the director is entitled to legal remedies, which translate into damages in money. However, determining what money damages are to be received may be quite difficult.

The producer may add that, if an error or mistake is realized, the producer will be granted a reasonable amount of time to cure such an error on all additional prints. Furthermore, the producer may agree to an acknowledgment of such an error in print in advertising.

## UNIQUE SERVICES

The services rendered by the director are generally considered to be unique and extraordinary.[3] The producer may claim that the loss of the director's services will cause the producer irreparable injury and damage, a loss that could not be adequately compensated in a legal action. The producer typically requires that a clause be added to permit the producer to demand an injunction or other equitable relief against the director in order to prevent a breach of the agreement. Such injunctive relief ordinarily prevents the director from working elsewhere.

## NEGATIVE COVENANTS

The producer may wish to control the dissemination of news items to the press to coincide with a planned press release. The director is usually restricted from issuing news stories or publicity relating to the motion picture, unless directed to do so by the producer or until such time as the producer decides to commence the release of publicity.

## FORCE MAJEURE

*Force majeure* may be defined as any force or action, beyond the producer's control, that results in a tolling or suspension of production.[4] During the occurrence of the *force majeure*, the production company receives the benefit of suspending time limits together with relief from its obligations.

Conditions that execute *force majeure* generally include fire, earthquake, labor dispute or strike, act of God or public enemy, municipal ordinance, state or federal law, or governmental order or regulation. Other conditions that might trigger the *force majeure* clause include the death, illness, or incapacity of any principal member of the cast. In such a situation, the producer may postpone the commencement or suspend the rendition of services by the director for as long as the disability continues. The producer is generally not required to pay the director during the period of suspension. Generally, the producer retains the right to terminate the contract with the director in the event that the disability generated by the *force majeure* lasts a certain reasonable period of time. In that event, the producer may terminate the services of the director by providing written notice of termination. Likewise, the contract may also provide the director with the option to terminate the commitment if the disability lasts for a prenegotiated amount of time and if the prerequisite written notice is provided.

If the agreements have not been nullified upon the expiration of the event of *force majeure*, the time limits stipulated in the contract revert back to normal, and the producer must resume fulfilling its obligations.

## DIRECTOR'S INCAPACITY

As a key member of the production team, the director must be available at all times. A protracted illness or accident may put the entire film project in jeopardy. Consequently, the employment contract between the director and the producer should provide for such a contingency.

This clause generally states that, if by reason of mental or physical disability, the director is incapacitated from performing his or her duties stipulated in the contract as a whole for more than an agreed upon number of days in a row or an agreed upon number of days over an aggregate period of time, the producer has the right to terminate the services of the director pending written notice to the director of such termination.

The provision may contain a provision granting the director the opportunity to cure this disability, rather than be terminated.

## BREACH OF CONTRACT

In the event the director fails or refuses to comply with any of the material terms or conditions of the contract as a whole, the producer generally reserves the right to terminate the contract and to replace the director, providing that advance written notice is provided to the director. A director with enough bargaining strength may insist on including a subclause allowing the director to cure the breach within a reasonable amount of time.

The term material breach is often used to soften the potential harshness of the contract. By defining what may be characterized as a harmless breach of some technical aspect of the contract as a harmless breach rather than a material breach prevents its use as a pretext for getting rid of a director.

The contract may provide, as an alternative to termination, the temporary suspension of the director's services without pay. The contract typically states that any incapacity or default of the director would be deemed to continue until the producer receives written notice that director is ready, willing, and able to perform the services required under the contract. Since this provision suspends the obligation of the director to carry out his or her commitment to the producer, this clause may also contain the provision that the director will not render services for any person, firm, or corporation other than the producer during the suspension.

The contract may also state that, in the event the director is suspended without pay and subsequently reinstated, the term of the entire contract would be extended the same time period as the suspension. If, for example, the contract was to run eighteen months from the inception to the completed release of the movie, and if the director is suspended for six months, then the contract would be extended for that period, that is, six months.

A director of sufficient caliber and stature may insist on inserting a clause that gives the director the right to render directorial services to third parties during any period of suspension, based upon a producer's disability, but subject to the producer's right to require that the director resume services upon notice.

# 8

---

# MASTER RECORDING USE
# FOR A MOTION PICTURE AND
# SYNCHRONIZATION RIGHTS

The music soundtrack is an integral aspect of a motion picture. Ownership of a musical composition—lyrics and music—must be clearly defined.

## COPYRIGHT OWNERSHIP

Normally, the writer of a composition is the original copyright owner of that work and is afforded the protection provided by the copyright act.[1] The writer may assign that copyright to a music publisher, who will often pay the writer an advance payment for the right to represent the composition. Under those conditions, the publisher often continues to pay the writer royalties derived from the exploitation of that composition, for the term of their agreement.

Publishers, producers, or other employers may hire musical composition writers as employees for hire.[2] The compositions then are, in most cases, the property of the employer, who owns them for the duration of the copyright. A work made for hire is usually prepared by an employee within the scope of his or her employment responsibilities.

### Length of Copyright Protection

Original compositions created after January 1, 1978, will usually be protected by the copyright laws of the United States from the moment of their creation, extending for the life of the writer, plus an additional fifty years following the writer's death. In the event the work was created by two or more authors, the term of the copyright protection lasts for fifty years following the death of the last surviving author.

Works that are made for hire, on the other hand, have the benefit of copyright protection for seventy-five years from publication or a hundred years from the creation of the work, whichever is shorter. For compositions written prior to January 1, 1978, the copyright protection will last for seventy-five years from the year the copyright was originally secured, as long as renewal of the copyright is timely.

### Notice of Copyright

A notice of copyright is generally placed on all publicly distributed phonograph records of sound recordings and on all publicly distributed copies of visually perceptible material. The symbol ℗, is followed by the year the recording was first published and the name of the owner of the copyright, for example, ℗ 1990 XYZ Inc. The notice on copies of literary, dramatic, and other visually perceptible work is ©, followed by the year the work was first published and the name of the owner of copyright, for example: © 1990 XYZ Inc.

### Transfer of Copyright

Generally, all, or a portion of, the exclusive rights of the copyright may be transferred. The transfer of copyright must be effected by a signed writing. The exclusive rights may be bequeathed by will and pass as personal property, subject to the laws and regulations of the various states.

A publisher generally has the authority to transfer some of the rights of a composition to subpublishers for the purpose of exploiting that work in the various territories of the world for a determined period of time. It must be noted that foreign copyright laws differ from those of the United States. Each country's laws, regulations, and terms should be reviewed individually.

### Fair Use of Copyrighted Material

The copyright owner of a composition typically has the capacity to restrict the use of that composition under particular circumstances. However, protected works may be used in certain situations without the owner's consent. The fair use of copyrighted material usually applies where there exists significant public interest in the dissemination of ideas and information. The fair use doctrine justifies limits of the copyright owner's rights. When copyrighted material is used for news reports, commentaries, scholarship, and educational purposes, the fair use doctrine usually applies, granting the user the right to limited use of the copyrighted material.

## CLEARANCE OF RIGHTS

In most situations, it is the producer's responsibility to clear music material used in a television, film, or video production. The producer must locate the copyright owners of the composition for the territory and media to be used to secure the copyright owner's permission to use the composition in those limited circumstances in exchange for a license fee or royalty.

The use of such copyrighted material without properly obtaining such rights by the copyright owner may result in a copyright infringement suit, an injunction that would block the exhibition of the production and possibly incur costly re-editing of the motion picture or movie. Under the copyright laws of the United States, the unauthorized exploitation of such copyrighted material may result in paying statutory damages as well as compensating the copyright owner for lost profits.

Music rights for compositions in motion pictures are often granted for a worldwide territory for a term of years equal to the length of the copyright. At other times, the grant of copyright may be limited to a contracted term of years. The rights granted are usually broad, awarding the producer the license to exploit the picture, along with the musical compositions, in as wide a range of media possible, including recordings; music publishing; laser or electronic recordings; theatrical motion pictures; free, pay, and cable television; radio; live theater; advertising; and in all other media, including those forms of media now known or devised at any time in the future.

## SYNCHRONIZATION RIGHTS

The reproduction rights for using a composition on television, film, and other forms of visual production are protected by what is commonly known as synchronization, or "synch" rights. These rights are most often obtained by the producer when the musical composition is recorded in synchronization with visual images. The synch rights are generally obtained by negotiating with the copyright owners or their representatives.

*The compositions.* The synchronization agreement generally lists the compositions covered by the granting of the synchronization license from the owner of the composition to the producer of the motion picture. The list often includes the name of the composition, its writer, performer, and publisher.

*The motion picture.* The license generally names the motion picture that will use the composition. In addition, the license typically includes the sequels, remakes, video cassettes, television productions, and all other visual renditions based on the story or characters of the motion picture.

*Territory.* The synchronization license granted by the composition owner to the producer is generally granted in a broad territory. In most instances the producer insists upon worldwide rights, since the distribution of the motion picture is typically not limited to a certain region.

*Parties.* The license to use a particular musical composition or series of compositions in a motion picture is generally granted by the copyright owner of the composition – to the producer of the motion picture.

*The term.* Under most circumstances, the length of the synchronization license extends for the full term of the copyright (or grant of copyright) of the composition and/or of the motion picture, in the United States and in the territory granted by the synchronization license. The term is generally extended to all modifications and extensions of the original agreement.

*Consideration.* The producer generally pays the copyright owner a flat fee for the synchronization license – the right to synchronize the musical composition to the motion picture.

## RIGHTS GRANTED

All rights are typically granted directly by the copyright owner, often the publisher, to the film producers for theatrical performances within the United States. The contract typically states that the publisher grants to the producer the nonexclusive right and license to perform publicly in the United States and its possessions, either for profit or nonprofit. The license may be limited only to synchronization or timed relationships to the motion picture.

The issue may be more complex when dealing with licensing for overseas markets. Depending on the bargaining strength of the producer and the songwriter/publisher, the latter may insist upon a clause that requires the producer, in the event the movie is exhibited outside the United States and its possessions, be subject to clearance by performing rights societies in accordance with their customary fees. Consequently, the publisher may stipulate that, to the extent it controls the performing rights, it will license an appropriate performing rights society in the respective countries to grant such performance right.

The granting of synchronization rights to the producer from the composition owner generally include the right to record, in any manner, medium, or form, one or more uses of the composition in synchronization with the motion picture. Those rights typically include the right to use the composition during the main and end titles of the film as a theme composition, or at any time and place during the motion picture. The grant of rights usually includes the right to synchronize the composition to the motion picture on all copies of the motion picture. The producer generally acquires the right to edit, change, or alter the musical composition in its sole discretion.

The owner of the composition usually grants to the producer the unreserved right to publicly perform and to authorize others to publicly perform the composition in the motion picture in all media.

*Theater* rights include motion picture theaters and other places of public entertainment where motion pictures are generally exhibited and where admission fees are charged, including but not limited to the right to perform the composition by transmission of the movie to audiences in theaters and such other public places for the duration of the U.S. copyright of the composition.

*Television* rights include the public performance and exhibition of the composition of the motion picture by means of free, pay, subscription, or cable television; networks; local stations; satellite transmissions; and any other form of television use presently existing or to be devised in the future.

*Audio-visual* rights include using the composition on any audio-visual device, including video cassettes and discs for noncommercial home use. This clause generally gives the producer the right to market the movie and the musical compositions for the home video market, irrespective of the medium used. Depending on the track record and popularity of the composer, this clause may require a royalty agreement based on the number of video tapes sold. In some instances, the copyright owner may enter into a buy-out or modified buy-out arrangement, where the producer pays the rights holder a flat sum for unlimited copies of the home video.

In this connection, the royalties arrangement is virtually identical to that of phonograph records and compact discs (CDs). It often includes precise terms on when royalties should be paid, the thresholds for such payments, as well as a stipulation that, in the event of a bona fide dispute, both parties will submit their grievance to arbitration.

*Trailer* rights include radio, screen, television, and all other uses of trailers intended to advertise or promote the motion picture using the compositions.

*Nontheatrical media* rights, as the term is commonly known in the entertainment industry, include the exploitation of motion picture and musical compositions on military bases, ships at sea, educational outlets, airplanes, and all other nontheatrical means of distribution.

## REPRESENTATIONS

The owner of the musical composition generally warrants and represents that he or she has the right to grant to the producer the synchronization rights granted in the synchronization agreement, and that by granting these rights, the owner does not infringe on any rights, including copyrights, of any other party. The owner generally continues to warrant that he or she owns the composition or shares ownership with another party who consents, in a signed agreement, to granting the synchronization rights.

## INDEMNIFICATION

For added protection, the producer generally requires that the owner of the composition indemnify the producer in the event the owner has made any representation that causes the producer loss, damages, or liability. The producer generally bases his or her actions and production activity on the composition owner's warranties and representation regarding ownership of the compositions. The use of copyrighted material owned by another party can cause the producer economic harm and loss of esteem in the industry. The producer would be forced to bargain with the actual owner for the use of the composition and would be at a disadvantage, since the motion picture is already in distribution and all production costs have been expended.

## RESTRICTIONS

The agreement generally stipulates that the producer does not have any license, permission, or authority to make changes in the original lyrics or in the fundamental character of the music of the composition. The producer may also be restricted from using the title, subtitle, or any portion of the lyrics of the composition as the title or subtitle of the motion picture, or to dramatize or use the plot or any dramatic contents of the lyrics of the composition without the owner's grant of rights.

## FREE TELEVISION SYNCHRONIZATION LICENSE

The synch rights for television are actually grants of permission to record the music on film or tape. The rights granted typically do not include public performance rights, which are licensed by the American Society of Composers, Authors, and Publishers (ASCAP), Broadcast Music Inc. (BMI), and the Society of European Stage Authors and Composers (SESAC). Although increasingly difficult to find, some contracts limit the music synch rights to free television only and not for subscription (STV) television or pay or free cable television. Such limitations put a severe damper on the marketability of the television movie and would most likely be unacceptable to producers and production companies, especially since they are actively involved in all media.

Synch rights are typically licensed for a specific time unless a buy-out arrangement is made. Generally, buy-outs are found in television movies rather than television specials (e.g., musical variety shows).

Because of the underlying synch license, a portion of movies that may have gone into public domain for a variety of reasons still have a viable copyright with respect to airing and presenting the music over the film medium.

# 9

## THE MOTION PICTURE DISTRIBUTION AGREEMENT: THE WORLDWIDE PICK-UP DEAL

The motion picture distributor is the marketing link between the film producer and the general public. The distributor takes the finished product and licenses it to various media, such as theaters, broadcasters, home video companies, and cable/television systems. In general, the distributor wishes to obtain all media rights and then license those specific rights it will not use through its own infrastructure.[1] In most instances, the distributor negotiates to acquire worldwide rights.

With the proliferation of international business combinations, mergers, and acquisitions, the major motion picture studios have remained increasingly involved in both production and distribution, although there are some legal restrictions relating to theatrical distribution and the right to own theaters.[2] If the majors are not the actual producers, they may assist in financing a project in return for the right to be the exclusive distributor. Under that arrangement, the independent producers are often assured a greater possibility for national or international distribution in the major theater chains and territories.

There are basically two types of distribution deals: the acquiring of a completed project and the financing or cofinancing of a production as consideration for the acquisition of all or some of the distribution rights. Under the latter, the distributor, protecting its distribution interest in the motion picture, often assumes an active part in the actual production of the project.

### DISTRIBUTOR VERSUS PRODUCER

As financier or cofinancier, the distributor generally insists that the producer be obligated to certain requirements. For example, the producer is typically required to produce the motion picture based upon the screenplay, starring designated actors, written by the designated writer, and directed by the appointed director under the guidance of an executive producer assigned by the studio. In the event any of those principal or key members of the production team and cast are unable to render their services, the producer is generally required to consult the distributor in selecting replacements.

Prior to funding a film, the distributor generally insists upon the general approval of the look, contents, and length of the final version of the motion picture. The distributor typically insists on including those ingredients that are proven box office winners, thereby increasing the probability of distributing a commercially successful movie. The distributor, for example, usually demands that the motion picture be filmed in color, with a running time between 90 and 120 minutes. Another demand may be that the finished film be delivered to the distributor within a specified period of time following the conclusion of principal photography.

The distributor generally requests the right to view all dailies (the raw, unedited film shot on any particular day) and usually requires that the final version of the film be rated by the MPAA. In addition, the distributor usually requires that the final version of the motion picture not vary from the approved screenplay.

In this manner, the distributor attempts to protect its investment, which is based on information it was given, such as the original screenplay, key actors, and a noted director. If the motion picture is changed dramatically, the distributor does not receive what it had bargained for and may have the right to rescind the distribution agreement.

The producer is generally required to grant and assign to the distributor the sole and exclusive right, license, and privilege to distribute, license, market, reissue, and exploit the motion picture in all media, including theaters, nontheaters, television, and cassettes, and in all other forms of media now known or to be devised in the future.

Defining the rights provision in such broad terms takes into account the new forms of presentation, distribution, and exploitation that become available to the entertainment market. The distributors learned their lesson by failing to include any future form of media in agreements consummated prior to the 1970s. Cassettes, pay-per-view, and cable are some of the markets excluded as revenue sources by contractual oversights in the early days of the entertainment industry.

The rights the distributor acquires often include other, ancillary forms of distribution, including the distribution rights to the armed forces, ships at sea, and in-flight motion pictures, to mention only a few.

### Final Cut

The distributor usually demands the right to make the final cut of the motion picture to be presented to the public in theaters, on television, and in the other acquired markets.[3] Moreover, depending on the arrangement with the producer, the distributor may insist on the right to rescore the film.

### Synchronization License

The distributor tries to protect its investment by ensuring that all licenses to all the inherent rights pertaining to a motion picture, including the copyright, were obtained by the producer. One such copyright – the right of synchronization – relates to the music or underlying score in the movie.

The synchronization license is the granting of permission by the owner of the music rights to the user of the musical composition. Because, under strict legal definitions, the music is not part of the movie but a separate element, specific permission must be obtained prior to the release of the movie. (The sound track is not integrated, but is, rather, physically and legally a separate property right.) In addition, the composer is usually required to warrant that he or she has the right, power, and authority to enter the synchronization agreement.

## RIGHTS ACQUIRED

In order to be confident that it has secured all synchronization and musical composition rights, the distributor generally demands that the license it has acquired contain all the necessary elements specific to the contracted motion picture and musical compositions, including:

- The name of the motion picture,
- The title of the compositions,
- The territory covered by the license,
- The term of the license (usually granted for the full term of the copyright of the compositions, film, and any derivative copyrights),
- The right to the composition in synchronization with the film; the right to publicly perform the musical composition; the right to edit, change and alter the composition; the right to publicly perform the composition in theaters, on free or pay television, in the nontheatrical media, and in all media, now known or hereafter devised.

## OWNERSHIP

The distributor generally requires that the producer grant and assign all rights in the motion picture, including copyright, to the distributor.[4]

Typically included in these rights are: the screenplay, musical compositions, all subsidiary rights, remakes, and sequels. The latter is somewhat of an insurance policy in the event the original project is a huge success and the public wishes to view a sequel. Without the right to remakes and sequels, the distributor may not be able to secure those rights at a later date without paying a substantial premium to the producer.

To be prepared for any potential changes in the U.S. copyright law, the distributor may insist that the producer provide documented evidence that the motion picture contains not only the proper copyright indication on each print released (e.g., © XX Corporation, 19XX), but that it is also registered with the Copyright Office, Library of Congress in Washington, D.C. Failure to register may result in the distributor losing the opportunity to obtain any damages relating to copyright infringements.[5]

## COMPENSATION

Upon the signing of the distribution agreement, the distributor usually agrees to pay the producer a percentage of the agreed sum required to acquire all the rights granted in this agreement. A portion of the total amount is generally paid to the producer during the actual production, or principal photography phase, and the remainder is usually payable upon the satisfactory completion of the motion picture and upon its acceptable delivery to the distributor.

The distributor may have agreed to pay, as part of the producer's compensation, a percentage of the gross receipts received by the distributor. Generally, the distributor makes payments to the producer after the distributor breaks even from the worldwide exploitation of the motion picture. Often, the distributor retains 100 percent of all gross receipts earned, until an agreed threshold is reached. That sum typically reflects the break-even sum.

A distributor is generally considered to break even when it has recouped all the monies it has expended in the production and exploitation of the motion picture. The definition of break-even may fluctuate from contract to contract; therefore, it should be defined clearly and concisely in each contract. Upon attaining the break-even level, the receipts are apportioned at an agreed percentage.

In order to induce certain third parties to participate in the motion picture, the producer, with the approval and agreement of the distributor, may have agreed to pay to those third parties (actors, writers, director, etc.) a certain percentage of the motion picture's profits, either net or gross profits. The standard used should be clearly defined in the agreement, as there exists no standard definition of either net or gross in the motion picture lexicon.

## NET PROFITS

The term net profits has a definition specific to the entertainment industry. Definitions are as different as the various persons who wield the term during negotiations. It is imperative, in order to clarify any future disputes, that the meaning of the term as used in the agreement be defined.

Generally, net profits are the gross receipts remaining after deducting from gross receipts certain payments agreed upon by the parties to the agreement. Those payments often include:

- The distribution fees owing and due distributors as compensation for its services as distributor.

- All expenses and disbursements due and owing the distributor incurred in the performance of its services as distributor.

- All deferments, gross participants, and other amounts due to any party for rights, services, materials, or other facilities used in connection with the motion picture prior to the initial break-even point and after the initial break-even point.

- The negative costs incurred by the distributor. The "negative costs" of a motion picture generally include all costs incurred by the distributor in connection with the acquisition of literary and musical rights, in connection with the pre-production, production, and postproduction of the motion picture, all above-the-line and below-the-line costs, all costs covering fringe benefits and insurance. In addition, the distributor generally includes administration overhead charges, regardless of where the motion picture is filmed.

- The interest incurred, on a continuing basis, with respect to all sums chargeable to negative costs.

- In the event the negative cost exceeds the previously agreed and budgeted negative costs, the amount expended to complete the production of the picture – the excessive budget – including all additional negative costs, union and guild costs, and overruns.

## RATINGS

The MPAA is an independent organization that, through a series of screenings to film professionals and selected members of the community, rates motion pictures released for public viewing as G (general public), PG (parental guidance), PG-13 (parental guidance geared to children above the age of thirteen), R (restricted), and NC-17 (patently adult).

In deciding what rating the picture will be awarded, the MPAA is required to evaluate the amount of violence, nudity, and descriptive language found in the motion picture and, based upon a formula, designates the movie with a certain voluntary rating. When the distributor enters a distribution agreement with a producer, it usually requires that the producer obtain a specific rating, an R or a PG rating, for example, upon the completion of the production. In this manner, the distributor insures that it will receive the product it bargained for and be able to present it to the focused audience it originally intended.

In the event the producer does not comply with the rating committee requirements, the distributor normally insists that it have the right to take whatever steps necessary, including re-editing the motion picture, in order to acquire the rating it bargained for. The contract typically adds that, in the event the producer cannot or will not edit the movie to the extent necessary to achieve a certain rating, that any work by the distributor to ensure such a rating will be paid for by the producer.

## PRODUCER'S WARRANTIES

A motion picture is a collection of rights, including property rights, copyrights, and rights of privacy. It is usually the producer's obligation to secure the rights of the screenplay, the rights of privacy of individuals represented in the motion picture, the copyrights, and all other applicable rights.

The producer generally warrants that he or she is the sole and exclusive owner of all the motion picture rights, including the rights upon which the motion picture is based.

In the event the story is based on the personal history of an individual, a portion of which is not in the public domain, it is generally the responsibility and obligation of the producer to secure those rights from that individual or, if deceased, from that individual's heirs, executors, or administrators.[6]

Those rights must be clearly demonstrated in writing, signed by the owner of the rights or the owner's representative. The producer normally acquires those rights following some form of payment to the right's holder, be it a one-time fee or an equity position in the finished motion picture.

In the event the story is based on a published novel or magazine article, it is generally the producer's obligation to secure the rights to dramatize that story in all media, including broadcasts, satellite, cable television, cassettes, and theatrical productions. Those rights, and the payment schedule, should be clearly demonstrated in a separate agreement signed by the rights holder or a representative and the producer.

## WORKS FOR HIRE

The distributor generally requires a document from the producer stipulating that the producer has obtained clearances from any employees who worked for the producer in the capacity of work for hire. Unlike the case of the self-employed composer or writer who usually retains a property right in his or her work product, when the creative artist is employed to perform work for hire, and if the terms for such employment are in writing, the copyright is generally retained by the employer.

A work for hire is typically defined as a work in which the creator acknowledges that all rights in the work, including copyright, for all uses and purposes, are the sole and unencumbered property of the producer, and that the producer may assign, license, sell, and generally exploit those rights in any manner at the producer's sole discretion.

## RIGHTS TO ENTER THE AGREEMENT

The distributor usually requires that the producer warrant that he or she has the right to enter this agreement without infringing on any rights, including copyrights and rights of privacy, of any individual or entity. The producer is generally required, upon demand, to demonstrate ownership in writing of all rights in the motion picture.

## UNIONS

Typically, the producer enters into collective bargaining agreements with all the unions and guilds representing the members of the motion picture community. Those unions and guilds include the Screen Actors Guild (actors), DGA (directors and assistant directors), Writers Guild Association (screen writers), American Federation of Musicians (composers), and the International Alliance of Theatrical and Stage Employees and Teamsters Union (working crew).

## ADVERTISING

The manner in which the motion picture is presented and marketed to the viewing public may help determine if the film is a box office success or a failure. Consequently, the agreement between the exclusive distributor and the producer generally contains a clause stating that the distributor has the absolute, sole, and exclusive right to advertise and publicize the motion picture in the territories it has acquired by the distribution agreement.

## MERCHANDISING

The right to merchandise objects—clothing, furniture, accessories, games, toys, dolls, and so forth—based on the characters and incidents in the motion picture is a valuable right that can result in a substantial portion of the gross revenues derived from the general exploitation of the motion picture. The merchandising of established characters, such as Rambo, Mickey Mouse or Darth Vader represents a business in itself and is usually a bargaining chip in the distribution agreement. The distributor generally retains a substantial percentage of all revenues earned from merchandising the elements in the motion picture. Motion picture studios generally have strong merchandising divisions equipped to license the characters and incidents derived from the motion pictures it releases.

## OWNERSHIP OF MUSIC COMPOSITIONS

The distributor generally requires that it be consulted regarding the selection of musical compositions performed in the motion picture. Generally, the producer demands the right to issue or license the issuance of a sound track album containing part or all of the compositions and background music composed for, and used in, the motion picture. The distributor usually specifies the royalty payments due it from the exploitation of the sound track album.

## CREDITS

It is typically the producer's obligation to deliver to the distributor the names and credits of those persons whom the producer is contractually obligated to accord credit on the screen.[7] It is also the producer's obligation to present the distributor with the proper wording and placement of such credit.

Credits that generally appear on motion pictures include: "Produced by _____," "A _____ film," "Written by _____," "Based on an original story by _____," and "Sound track album available on _____ Records."

## ACCOUNTING

The producer usually demands the right to inspect the books and records of the distributor, in the location where those books and records are generally kept, upon reasonable written notice to the distributor. The distributor generally agrees to furnish the producer with regular statements, accompanied by a remittance of the amount reflected in such statement as being due and owing the producer.

## DISTRIBUTOR/EXHIBITOR

There are several ways in which the distributor can distribute and exploit the motion picture theatrically. The most common is the percentage deal. The percentage arrangements typically range from the straightforward 50/50 arrangement, wherein 50 percent of the box offices gross receipts are committed by contract to the distributor, to 80/20 or 90/10 arrangements, where the distributor receives 80 percent or 90 percent of the box office gross receipts while the exhibitor receives the remaining percentage. Generally, the exhibitor must earn an agreed minimum weekly amount, the "house nut," before the percentage break down takes effect.

Another, less popular, manner of distribution is to "four wall" a motion picture. In this method, the distributor rents the theater for an agreed upon price and retains 100 percent of all box office gross receipts. Although this manner of distribution is not popular, there has been some success in its use.

# 10

---

# The Pay-Per-View Agreement

As the penetration of cable television expands not only in the United States but also in much of the developed world, an increased desire to maximize profits and compete with home video is materializing. One such ancillary service is the offering of motion pictures and other programs on a pay-per-view basis. Capitalizing on pay-per-view technology, a cable system that uses state-of-the-art technology can address its signals to each household. Unlike the traditional pay channels that present movies already released in theaters and home videos, pay-per-view often presents movie fare that competes for the theatrical and video audience.

## PARTIES CONCERNED

Typically, the pay-per-view film license agreement is entered into by the owner of the right to distribute the motion picture using pay-per-view technology over the cable television or broadcast television systems and the pay-per-view distributor. In some instances the producer retains the pay-per-view right and is thereby the owner, while at other times the motion picture distributor licenses all media rights from the producer. The owner of the pay-per-view rights is generally a negotiated point agreed on during the initial negotiations among the owner of the rights to the work, the producer, and the distributor. The name of the party the distributor must pay in exchange for the pay-per-view rights is therefore generally the one stipulated in the agreement as the owner.

## TERRITORY

The agreement generally establishes the territory or market areas licensed by the distributor. In some instances the territory may be described as a named cable television system, while at other times the contract names a specific city or county. Usually, if the cable television system has acquired the exclusive franchise for a particular market, the agreement stipulates such a market. However, in those areas or territories where a franchise may be split, it only causes possible legal uncertainties to state a city as a territory of license. It is therefore important to state clearly which territories will be used in the agreement.

## TITLE OF PROGRAM

The agreement should state the title of the motion picture included in the contract. The listing usually includes the MPAA rating, the year the motion picture was released, its running time, and the list of talent involved.

The MPAA and its sister organization, the Motion Picture Export Association of America (MPEAA), are the entertainment industry organizations representing major industry-related subjects, including ratings, copyright infringement and anti-piracy programs. The rating system is available subject to their inspection pursuant to the payment of appropriate fees. The rating system is also available to non-MPAA members. The MPAA, therefore, not only represents the major studios in the motion picture industry, but also acts as the guardian of what is considered to be appropriate viewing material for various age groups. While such ratings are voluntarily accepted by independent producers, economic reality often dictates that most, if not all, domestic movies be submitted to the MPAA for their rating.

It is generally necessary to be as specific as possible when listing the motion pictures included in the agreement, since titles of films have traditionally not been able to be registered as a copyright, trademark or service mark. Producers may generally use any name they please as a title for a motion picture. By stipulating the year, running length, actors, directors, and writers involved in the production of the motion picture, the owner and distributor give more specificity to the licensing process.

## LICENSE FEE AND TERMS

When preparing a pay-per-view agreement, the license term or fee may be structured on a royalty or per subscriber basis, rather than on the more traditional method of a flat fee based on a limited number of runs found in commercial television and possibly cable. In the case of pay-per-view, the distributor may agree to pay an agreed dollar amount per subscriber or an agreed percentage of accountable receipts, whichever is greater.

The term accountable receipts as used in pay-per-view entertainment agreements may be interpreted to designate not the sum of money collected or received by the cable firm but rather what is owed to the system. Accountable receipts in pay-per-view agreements may be interpreted to mean all monies actually received by the distributor from exploiting the rights granted in the agreement, less all taxes actually payable with respect to the exploitation of the motion picture by the distributor. All such monies and taxes are usually calculated upon the close of the applicable accounting period, as defined in the agreement. Generally, the contract is concerned with the total number of television sets tuned into the pay-per-view presentation. This method of payment usually provides the distributor with an equitable amount of profit sharing while still allowing the system to retain a sizeable portion of the earned revenue.

Since the distributor has certain fixed costs (e.g., the distributor may have contractually agreed to pay the owner a minimum fee), the agreement may contain a provision that designates the distributor to pay the owner a minimum flat fee per viewing set. The flat fee per television set is generally based on the strength of the motion picture.

The license fee is generally established clearly within the agreement and typically states that, in full consideration of all rights granted within the agreement and in exchange for all services performed under the agreement, the distributor will, in exchange for the right to present the motion picture using the pay-per-view technology, pay fees, collectively referred to as license fees, equal to the percentage of accountable receipts specified in the agreement, or the agreed upon flat fee per television set. All fees are generally computed, determined, and paid in accordance with an attached schedule.

## ACCOUNTING

The contract may also define how statements and payments will be calculated. The agreement generally defines the accounting period as each calendar or fiscal month in which accountable receipts are received by the distributor. Within a designated number of days following the end of each accounting period, the owner is sent a statement showing the computation of accountable receipts for that period, and the owner shall be paid the license fees, if any, based on such accounting. The agreement may further state that any withholding or deduction required by law may be made by the distributor.

In addition, the owner may request, at his or her sole expense and upon reasonable notice, to have a CPA inspect and make copies of any books and records directly relating to the distributor's exploitation of the motion picture. Such inspections are usually done at the distributor's offices at times agreed to among the parties.

The agreement may add that such inspection be completed within a designated number of days. In the event a discrepancy of more than an agreed percentage is determined by such audit and examination, the owner and distributor may agree that the costs of the audit shall fall solely on the distributor. The rationale behind this may be to distance the owner from the responsibility of paying for an audit, and to fine the distributor when owed revenues are not paid.

## RELATIONSHIP OF THE PARTIES

The agreement may state that neither party shall be deemed a fiduciary, partner, or joint venturer of the other party. Moreover, the agreement may go on to declare that, as between the distributor and the owner, the distributor has sole discretion in the scheduling and number of exhibitions of the motion picture. The distributor generally makes no representations or warranties as to any minimum amount of accountable receipts or license fees that may be due to the owner. This provision may protect the distributor in the event the revenues expected by the owner fall short of projections.

### License Period

The agreement generally provides that the owner licenses to the distributor the right to exhibit the motion picture for an agreed number — perhaps an unlimited number — of presentations using pay-per-view technology in its cable systems. The term cable systems may be defined as both the geographic territory as well as the name of the system. The agreement may further add that the right to exhibit the motion picture over the pay-per-view systems is granted during the applicable license period only.

### Incidental Rights

Since the pay-per-view agreement is often based on a royalty-per-airing system, it may be in the best interest of both parties to adequately exploit the motion picture as widely as possible. Subject to prior consultation with the owner, the distributor is often granted the right to advertise, promote, and publicize the motion picture in any media, including the distribution of synopses or excerpts of the motion picture. The distributor may request the authority to authorize others to do so as well.

Subject to possible restrictions of which the owner may be obligated to notify the distributor in writing upon the execution of this contract, the distributor may use and authorize others to use the name, likeness, and voice of anyone who rendered services in connection with the motion picture for the purpose of advertising, promoting, or publicizing the distributor's exhibition of the motion picture to be aired over the pay-per-view form of media. Generally, endorsements of any product or service are prohibited. Moreover, the distributor may request the right to exhibit commercial, promotional, or other announcements before, during, or after the exhibition of the picture.

### Retail Prices

In order to assure that all parties to the agreement are in agreement, the contract may include the price charged to the end user – the viewer – for a pay-per-view showing. In some instances the pricing may be multi-tier, depending on how local distributors promote their pay-per-view operations. A distributor may have created, for example, a viewer's club whereby viewers agree to purchase a fixed amount of pay-per-view screenings a year at a discount over a one-time only showing. Such a break down is outlined within the body of the agreement.

### Warranties

As in most contracts of this nature, the warranty clause primarily protects the pay-per-view distributor. The right's owner is typically required to warrant and represent that he or she has the right to enter into the pay-per-view agreement with respect to the named motion picture. The owner generally warrants and represents that the motion picture is not libelous, does not infringe on any copyrights or trademarks, does not invade the privacy or otherwise interfere with the property or personal rights of third parties and that the motion picture is free and clear of any liens and claims.

The owner typically warrants that he or she will not license the motion picture to another competing pay-per-view system in the same franchise area or during the term of the agreement, and that the motion picture has not been licensed in the agreed territory prior to the agreement. In addition, the owner is generally required to warrant that he or she has proper title to the motion picture and owns or controls all the rights licensed under the agreement.

The owner generally warrants that he or she has obtained proper and effective licenses for the use of the sound recording system employed in producing the film, any copyrighted music or other material within the movie, and any patented processes, methods, and inventions employed in the production of the movie.

Not only does the owner warrant that he or she has obtained all the necessary licenses, but that all license fees, royalties, and payments previously required in connection with the production of the film have been paid in full.

To insure the compliance by the talent to the terms of the agreement, it may also state that the owner warrants to the distributor that the former has obtained or will obtain, prior to the execution of the agreement, all the proper and effective licenses or grants of authority to guarantee the use and results of the services of the talents, performers, director, writers, and all other persons connected with the production of the motion picture. The statement may go on to stipulate that the talent has agreed to the exercise of all the rights granted under the terms of this agreement, including the consent of the licensee to use their names, likenesses, and biographies for the purpose of advertising and exploiting the picture.

With the proliferation of video and signal piracy in much of the third world, as well as within the developed world, the warranty clause may state that the owner will, at his or her own expense, take whatever steps necessary to secure and maintain copyright protection for the motion picture in the licensed territory, and that the owner has affixed a legally sufficient copyright notice to the motion picture, thereby granting the pay-per-view distributor a license to the motion picture not subject to claims of copyright infringement.

The owner generally continues to warrant that all permits required by any union or guild are in place; that he or she has made, or will make, any payments required by such unions or guilds; and that all required payments will be paid for by the owner to cover such provisions as residuals, reuses, reruns, and any other third party payments presently due or that may become due in the future to any performer, actor, musician, or other person employed in the production of the picture.

In the event no proceeds were sent in the form of royalty payments, the distributor may agree to advance the owner the amount of any residual payments due with respect to the pay-per-view broadcast of the motion picture providing they do not exceed the overall minimum guarantee stipulated in this contract.

The agreement may also state that should the residuals exceed the guaranteed minimums agreed to by the owner, the owner may be responsible for any excess residual payments required. Moreover, the owner may have the right in the succeeding accounting periods to deduct the amount of such advances from the amounts due.

The owner may also warrant that all musical compositions contained within the film or its sound track are either in the public domain, in the legal control of the owner in the form of an employee for hire arrangement, or that all proper synchronization licenses controlling the performance of musical compositions in motion pictures have been secured.

The owner usually warrants that the motion picture is free from technical defects and is of broadcast quality. In addition, the owner also warrants that the motion picture has been rated by the MPAA.

## Indemnity

Despite the inclusion of the warranties clause, the contract should nonetheless contain an indemnification clause, wherein each party to the agreement stipulates that it shall at all times indemnify and hold harmless the other, its assignees and affiliated companies; and the officers, directors, employees, and agents of all the foregoing, against and from any and all claims, damages, liabilities, costs, and expenses, including reasonable counsel fees, arising from the exercise of any rights granted within the body of this pay-per-view agreement. Moreover, such indemnification is usually broad enough to include any breach by either party of any representation, warranty, or other provision. The contract may also stipulate that each party notify the other in writing of any claim within an agreed period of time after such claim is brought up or received.

## Entire Agreement

To protect the parties from any deletions or misunderstandings based on oral agreements, the pay-per-view agreement generally stipulates that the written contract entered into by the owner and distributor contains the parties' entire understanding and supersedes all prior understandings of the parties relating to the contract. Moreover, both could agree that this agreement cannot be changed or terminated orally but only in writing.

## VENUE AND STATE OF JURISDICTION

The agreement generally provides for the venue and jurisdiction of law of the contract in the event of disputes between the parties.

## CREATIVE EDITING RIGHTS

Subject to any prior agreement with the director (or any other creative member) of the motion picture, the pay-per-view agreement typically grants the distributor the right to edit the final product to comply with market requirements.[1]

The agreement may grant the distributor near absolute discretion of what may be edited out or retained. This discretion usually covers the right to make final cuts, alterations, translations, and variations of the title and subtitles. Depending on whether this deal is primarily international or domestic, the agreement may also provide for the distributor's right to edit the motion picture in order to comply with government regulations, including censorship requirements.

### Dubbing

The market place typically requires the presentation and transmission of the motion picture in the various languages of distinct nationalities acquiring the product. The Spanish market in the United States, for instance, represents a burgeoning portion of the viewership. In consideration of that market, the agreement may require a motion picture to be transmitted in the Spanish language. The distributor may require the right to freely dub the motion picture in order to effectively distribute the product in the territory acquired. The agreement may establish that the actual dubbing costs are subject to recoupment by the distributor. Dubbing costs would be subtracted from the payment or royalty rate due the owner.

The practice of subtitling generally falls under this category since it in effect offers the movie in a different language than the original.

### SATELLITE DELIVERED PROGRAMS

Importing distant terrestrial stations is accomplished by Master Antenna Television (MATV), where one antenna may serve an entire apartment building or complex usually receiving local on-air television stations; Satellite Master Antenna Television (SMATV), which is basically similar to MATV except the antenna used is known as TVRO, or Television Receive Only, which can bring down television shows originating directly from the satellite; and Community Antenna Television (CATV), the forerunner of modern cable, where a common antenna may be used to serve an entire community in a geographic location, such as a deep valley, that distant television signals cannot reach with clear reception. Absent a clear intent in the agreement, litigation to settle the issue of who has the right to transmit the motion picture may result in the pay-per-view market utilizing the various means of satellite delivery systems.

### OPTIONS

Depending on the size and general financial wealth of the pay-per-view network operator, the owner may offer the distributor an option to obtain additional territorial or media rights in the motion picture, or the owner may provide for an option to extend the exclusive deal for a further amount of time.[2]

The option may be in the form of a guaranteed option or, alternatively, the clause may be drafted providing the owner with the right of first negotiations or first refusal. The right of first negotiations is generally interpreted to mean that the owner agrees, prior to discussing with any third party or distributor the granting of pay-per-view distribution rights to the motion picture for a term subsequent to the original term, to negotiate in good faith with the distributor as to the granting of such rights. The contract may also state that the pay-per-view distributor has a stipulated amount of time within which to notify the owner in writing if it is interested in obtaining any additional rights.

Should the distributor decide to negotiate for those additional rights, it will, within a reasonable time period, be required to submit a bona fide offer for those rights. If the owner fails to accept that offer as a good faith submission or rejects it as not being a bona fide offer, then the owner is generally free to negotiate elsewhere for a more favorable agreement.

If the clause includes a right of first refusal, the owner is typically free to negotiate with bona fide companies for the most advantageous licensing agreement. However, any offer that the owner receives may be matched by the original licensee within an agreed period of time. Usually the contract stipulates that the third party offer be submitted within a reasonable amount of time so that the original distributor can adequately evaluate it and make counter proposals.

## MATERIALS TO BE DELIVERED TO THE LICENSEE BY THE OWNER

The licensor usually authorizes the release of, and makes available to the distributor at the distributor's sole cost and expense, a master videotape.[3] The master tape is typically held for the distributor at a designated film laboratory. In addition to paying the costs of transferring the motion picture onto the master tape, the distributor is usually responsible for all laboratory charges, together with all the costs of shipment and freight. The owner usually furnishes to the distributor, if available and upon request, trailers, stills, advertising mats, and other publicity material that may be used by the distributor for any and all exploitation purposes.

In general, the owner agrees to make available to the distributor the following:

- Laboratory access letter, directing the laboratory to process all orders placed by the distributor to duplicate positive prints, trailers and master video tapes.

- A 35mm or 16mm positive print, or answer print, of the motion picture, which is cut, main and end titled, edited, scored, and assembled with sound in perfect synchronization.

- A 35mm or 16mm three-stripe magnetic master of the complete sound track of the motion picture.
- A 35mm or 16mm trailer and trailer negative.
- Master video tape of the motion picture.
- Promotion of publicity materials.
- Copy of the music list setting forth the name of the composers, titles of the compositions, and names and addresses of the publishers.

## MARKETING RIGHTS

Given the intensely competitive environment in the domestic and international television sales arenas, it is important that the pay-per-view agreement define, clearly and concisely, the rights and obligations of the distributor.

The distributor generally attempts to retain complete control and discretion regarding all matters of distribution within the context of the pay-per-view agreement. A point of contention or negotiation usually arises when the motion picture licensed to the distributor is licensed as part of a package, that is, as part of a collection of motion pictures.

When the distributor acquires the right to distribute a package of films to the pay-per-view market, it generally demands the right to determine the price of each individual film within the package offered. On the other hand, the owner, in an attempt to ensure that the motion picture is not offered at a price that could affect its license in other markets, may insist that the distributor's contract guarantee that the owner be granted the right of approval or consultation regarding the number of airings, time of airings, and price charged to the user to view the airing. A compromise may be reached assuring the owner the right of consultation prior to a sale, while granting the distributor the final decision. Another compromise between the owner and distributor may be reached by granting the owner the right of final approval in smaller markets while allowing the distributor all final rights of approval in all substantial markets. The markets under this compromise should be clearly spelled out.

### Marketing The Motion Picture

The distributor may agree to use its best efforts to promote and market the film in all the territories for which it has received a license. The agreement may add that the distributor, at its sole discretion, has the authority to remove a film from any territory to which it has the syndication rights. Such a strategy may be related to issues such as piracy, or it may be part of a marketing ploy to increase the value of the picture. In either instance, the distributor generally requires that flexibility be reflected in the contract.

## CREDITS

The pay-per-view agreement may reiterate the credit obligations[4] the owner made with the talent and production staff, ensuring that the distributor follows the contractual requirements on the motion picture trailers, printed advertising material, or promotional flyers, as well as on the motion picture itself. The distributor may include a disclaimer in the event proper and timely notice was not received.

### Logo

The distributor will often require that it be granted the right to affix its logo or credit at the beginning and end of the motion picture, irrespective of credit arrangements made by the owner with the distributor, key talent, and production staff.

## PROTECTION OF THE MASTER

The distributor generally warrants that it will protect the film negatives or prints against illicit use and will further protect the copyright of the motion picture by prohibiting any sublicensee from removing or deleting the copyright notice from the movie.

## LICENSING TO A SUBDISTRIBUTOR

The owner is rightly concerned that his or her product receive the maximum revenues possible. As such, the agreement may state that, in the event the owner licenses the motion picture to a distributor who, in turn, licenses that motion picture to any of its pay-per-view subsidiaries, the distributor will deal at arms length with such pay-per-view systems regarding the terms and conditions of any license or sublicense granted in the motion picture. This attempts to ensure that the owner receives fees equal in price and terms if the motion picture is licensed to nonaffiliated independent companies.

## BREACH OF CONTRACT

The general default clause states that, should either of the parties breach the aforementioned warranties or misrepresent itself, then the agreement is considered null and void. The clause may go on to state that, should either of the parties become financially insecure and file for bankruptcy protection, the other party has the opportunity to entirely vacate the contract. In such a situation there is typically a built-in cure element that enables the breaching party to solve or mitigate the breach within a certain amount of time.

A breach is usually defined as a failure or refusal to comply with any of the contract's material obligations. In case a breach of contract cannot be cured, the agreement generally provides the owner with the option of voiding the agreement, obtaining equitable relief, and personally servicing the existing contracts together with 100 percent of all revenues generated by the distributor, minus unrecouped portions of the costs and charges the distributor is entitled to under the terms of the agreement as a whole.

## FORCE MAJEURE

Since the pay-per-view contract is created to ensure the fulfillment of a specific performance, where time is of the essence, it is important to provide a clause that details what will occur if events external to the control of the owner makes the performance impossible or impractical. The *force majeure* clause[5] covers such unforeseen events that require the tolling of the performance obligation.

The practical effect of the *force majeure* clause is to avoid a breach of contract and to provide a cure. This typically provides for the resumption of the obligation as soon as the event triggering the clause is declared gone.

The pay-per-view network or local cable television system may have the right to terminate the agreement if the production company's disability results in an unacceptable programming delay. Naturally, the exact length of the delay and a stipulation on how such written notice is to be delivered is to be negotiated between the parties prior to the signing of the agreement.

# 11

---

# Licensing Feature Films for Television Syndication

Television, traditionally a steady market for feature film distribution, represents a substantial portion of the revenues received from the exploitation of the motion picture in the established ancillary markets. In today's multimedia society, the three major networks, NBC, CBS and ABC, along with the Fox Television Network and other independent stations, are constantly acquiring products to fill their program schedules.

While first-run independently produced syndicated series, network reruns, news shows, and sports events comprise much of what is offered on independent television stations, movies are, to a large degree, still a key ingredient in the overall program programming mix. Usually, if the motion picture distributor does not acquire all the rights in a motion picture, those nontheatrical rights can be offered to distributors specializing in licensing motion pictures to free television and other nontheatrical markets.

The television syndication agreement typically stipulates that the producer grants to the television distributor a license to distribute the completed motion picture, as well as the various rights to properties normally associated with that motion picture, including the screenplay, music, and sequels, as well as literary, publishing, and merchandising rights.

A television syndication/distribution agreement may involve finalizing an agreement with the major American networks or entering a contract with those television stations considered to be nonnetwork, independently owned and operated (O&O) stations. The contract for both are somewhat similar, yet material differences exist which should not be overlooked. The contract discussed in this chapter covers points of primary interest in a non-network distribution agreement.

## THE GRANTING OF RIGHTS

The producer generally grants to the television distributor the sole and exclusive right and license required in order for the latter to distribute, license, and exploit the motion picture over free television in the designated territory.[1]

In the case of a domestic agreement, the territories usually consist of the United States and its possessions and territories. Since much of the population of Canada is within reach of an American television station, either directly or through use of a powerful television antenna or cable services, the distributor may require that Canada be considered within the territorial boundaries of a domestic agreement. The distributor may negotiate to include the condition that the Canadian broadcaster's television release of the motion picture be coordinated with the U.S. broadcaster's airing schedule.

If the television syndication agreement is an international contract, it usually details the specific territories or regions authorized to be licensed under the agreement. Depending on the location of the contracted territories, the agreement may cite a specific country, group of countries, or a boundary constructed by a common language. In the case of South America, for example, the territory may include all of Spanish-speaking South America. Generally, the agreement specifies any exclusions in order to avoid the possibility of ambiguities. For example, the territories of Argentina and Peru are Spanish speaking, but if they are excluded from the agreement they should be specifically listed.

The agreement may state that the distributor has the right to sublicense the motion picture on a regional or local basis, and that the distributor has the sole right to select the sublicensee.

## WARRANTIES

The warranties represented by the distributor are generally considered to be the primary legal basis upon which the entire contract is constructed. The producer usually warrants that he or she has proper title to the motion picture and owns or controls all the rights licensed under the agreement. The producer may also warrant that he or she has the right to enter the agreement and that the motion picture is free and clear of any liens, claims and copyrights.

The producer also usually warrants that he or she will not license this motion picture to another distributor for the territory granted during the term of the agreement.

Moreover, the warranty clause generally warrants that the producer has obtained proper and effective licenses for the use of the sound recordings employed in the production of the motion picture, any copyrighted music or any other material within the movie, as well as any patented processes, methods, and inventions employed in the production of the movie.[2]

Furthermore, the producer typically warrants that he or she has obtained all the necessary licenses and that all license fees, royalties, and payments previously required in connection with the production of the film have been paid in full. The warranty clause may additionally state that the producer has not infringed upon the property or personal rights of any third party, including the rights of individuals who may be affected by the story line.

Regarding the actors in the motion picture, the warranty clause generally states that the producer warrants to the distributor that the producer has obtained, or will obtain prior to the execution of the agreement, all the proper and effective licenses or grants of authority required in order to use the work products of actors, performers, and other persons connected with the production of the motion picture. The producer usually has the actor's release and may be required to issue a warranty to the effect that the producer, and by contract the distributor, have the right to use the names, likenesses, and biographies of the actors and other performers for advertising and exploiting the picture in any medium.

With the proliferation of video and signal piracy in a substantial part of the world, this clause may include a warranty that the producer will take whatever steps are necessary or required by existing law to secure and maintain copyright protection for the motion picture in the licensed territory. Generally, the producer is required to bear alone the burden of the costs of those protective steps. The producer may also warrant that he or she has affixed the required copyright notice at the appropriate and designated areas on the motion picture.[3] The distributor generally insists that there be clear and undeniable language in the agreement granting it clear rights to the motion picture without the possibility of copyright or other infringement claims from any party, whether it be on the part of the actors, writers, original rights owners (e.g., original novelist), or other possible rights holders.

The producer usually warrants that he or she has, or will have acquired by the time the contract is effective, all permits required by any trade union or guild and has made or will make any payments required by such trade unions or guilds, including residual, reuse, and rerun costs. If negotiated, the distributor may be required by the agreement to advance to the producer the amount of any residual payments due with respect to the broadcast of the movie.

In the event the residuals due exceed the guaranteed minimums agreed upon by the distributor, the distributor may insist that the producer be responsible for any excess residual payments that may be required. Moreover, the distributor generally negotiates for the right to deduct the

amount of such advances from the amount due the producer in the succeeding accounting periods.

The producer is generally required to warrant that all musical compositions contained within the film or its sound track are protected by the
proper synchronization licenses controlling the performance of musical
compositions in motion pictures, are in the public domain, or are under
the legal control of the producer by virtue of the producer having entered
an agreement, such as an employee for hire agreement, with the musical
composition creator. The producer may also warrant that the motion picture has not been licensed or aired in the territories covered by the agreement unless clearly and unambiguously agreed and stipulated elsewhere
in the agreement.

The distributor generally insists that the producer warrants that the
film is free from technical defects and is of broadcast quality. The producer may be required to represent that the contents of the motion picture has been rated by the MPAA and has been edited and judged
acceptable for general television audiences.

## LICENSED MEDIA

The contract generally states clearly whether the agreement covers the
right to broadcast the motion picture over nonsyndicated television only,
or whether the parties have entered an all-inclusive broadcast agreement
that may include subscription television, premium or pay cable, and pay-
per-view television.

It is important to clarify clearly and concisely the particular media over
which the distributor has the right and license to exploit the motion picture.[4] Without such clarification, in light of the proliferation of methods
of distribution, there is potential for confusion and ambiguity if the contract merely grants the distributor generally defined broadcast rights.

Often, the means of transmitting the motion picture over television and
pay cable is in the form of video tapes and cassettes. In the agreement the
distributor should be granted the right to supply video tapes and cassettes to television licensees who may require them for transmission. In
addition, it should be clarified that the use of such video tapes and cassettes is not to be construed as a general grant to the distributor of the
right and privilege to distribute the motion picture by video tape or cassette.[5]

## ADVERTISING

The distributor is usually granted the right to advertise and publicize
the motion picture by all reasonable means, including television, print,

radio, billboards, publicity stills, press booklets, fan magazines, and other means, in order to effectively execute its function.

Since the director and principal members of the cast of the motion picture are important assets in the distribution of the motion picture, the distributor is generally granted the right to advertise and publicize the names and likenesses of those individuals through the agreed methods of advertising and promotion.

## CREATIVE EDITING RIGHTS

Subject to any prior agreement with the director of a motion picture, the distributor's agreement for television syndication rights typically includes the right to edit the final product.[6] This provision generally gives the television distributor discretion over what may be edited. This discretion usually includes the right, in addition to the right to edit the motion picture itself, to complete control over cuts, alterations, translations, and variations of the title and subtitles. Depending on whether this agreement is primarily for international or domestic territories, it also provides for distributor control over all editing due to government regulations, including specific censorship requirements.[7]

Unlike theatrical releases, the syndication market is regulated. Broadcasters face license renewals from the Federal Communications Commission (FCC) and are extremely aware of the effect viewer opinions have on government watchdogs. With the many hundreds of television stations in the market, the distributor should be able to offer a product acceptable to a broad customer base.

Local stations are forced, on occasion, to cut the length of a motion picture, not only to alter content but also to accommodate scheduling time restraints. Typically, a two-hour motion picture on television represents approximately 100 minutes of the actual movie. The balance is generally allotted by the broadcaster to advertising spots. In order to prevent problems with the producer and director, who may insist on maintaining creative control over their product, the distributor may demand that the right to edit clause be a mandatory aspect of any contract, and that it be considered material under the law.

### Dubbing

The broad spectrum of the contemporary market place requires the presentation and transmission of motion pictures in the various languages of the distinct nationalities acquiring the product. In order to accommodate that growing foreign language segment of the market, the distributor often demands the right to freely dub the motion picture in order to effectively distribute it in the acquired territory. Typically, the actual dubbing costs are subject to recoupment by the distributor. In such a case, the cost of dubbing may be subtracted from the payment or royalty rate due to the producer.

Subtitling a motion picture may fall under this category. Subtitling would, like dubbing, offer the movie in a different language than the original.

If the contract stipulates that the distributor has acquired all television broadcast rights, without regard or mention of language, the distributor may be justified in dubbing or subtitling the movie in whatever language it may decide the market will bear in the agreed upon territory. Naturally, clarification in drafting tends to negate all such ambiguities.


## DURATION OF TERMS

The length of the syndication distribution agreement is generally spelled out.[8] The length of the term may depend on various factors, including whether the distributor had invested any funds in the production of the picture and therefore negotiated for a longer period as exclusive distributor. There is typically a set term allotted for distribution of the motion picture over the television syndication market. After the agreed allotted time period, or window, the motion picture may be presented over other media by the license holders of those additional modes of exploitation and distribution.


## OPTIONS

Depending on the size and general financial condition of the distributor, the producer may offer the distributor an option to obtain additional territorial or media rights in the motion picture. The agreement may also provide an option to extend the exclusive syndication agreement for a further amount of time.

The option may be in the form of a straight option or, alternatively, the clause may be drafted in such a manner as to provide the distributor with the right of first negotiations or first refusal with regard to acquiring the license to exploit the motion picture in any additional territory or medium. Generally, granting the distributor the right of first negotiations requires that the producer negotiate in good faith to grant such rights to the original distributor at comparable terms to the best offer the producer received from a bona fide third party distributor.

The agreement generally states that the distributor has a designated amount of time in which to notify the producer in writing if the distributor is interested in obtaining any additional rights. The requirement for a written statement negates the possibility of any confusion or misunderstanding.[9]

Should the distributor decide to negotiate for any additional rights, the agreement usually requires that it submit a bona fide offer for those rights within a reasonable amount of time in order to set in motion the right of first negotiations grant. If the producer fails to accept that offer as a good faith submission or rejects it as not being bona fide, then, subject to a decision on the validity of such an offer, the producer is generally free to solicit and accept a better deal.

If the agreement includes the granting of the right of first refusal to the distributor, and if the offer is deemed reasonable, the producer is generally free to submit the motion picture to competing distributors to acquire a better, more favorable proposal. However, under the right of first refusal, any offer the producer receives is usually granted an opportunity to be matched by the original distributor. Usually the contract stipulates that, if the offering distributor submits a proposal more favorable than the one submitted by the original distributor, the original distributor is granted a reasonable amount of time in which to adequately and thoroughly evaluate the additional proposal and prepare a counterproposal.

## DELIVERY

To facilitate the distributor in the performance of its services, the producer usually agrees to deliver to the distributor a final print of the motion picture, a letter granting the distributor access to the laboratory in order to make prints, and all press materials.

## COMPENSATION

As payment for granting the television distributor the right to distribute, broadcast, and exploit the motion picture in the agreed territories over the negotiated media, the distributor usually pays the producer an agreed flat fee. Partial payment may be made upon signing the agreement, with the remainder to be paid according to an agreed schedule.

## MATERIALS TO BE DELIVERED TO THE DISTRIBUTOR BY THE PRODUCER

In general, the producer agrees to make available to the distributor the following:

- Laboratory access letter, directing the laboratory to process all orders placed by the distributor to duplicate positive prints, trailers, and master video tapes.
- One 35mm or 16mm positive print of the motion picture that is cut, main and

end titled, edited, scored, and assembled with sound in perfect synchronization. This is usually referred to as the answer print.

- One 35mm or 16mm three-stripe magnetic master of the complete sound track of the motion picture.
- One 35mm or 16mm trailer and trailer negative.
- One master video tape of the motion picture.
- Promotion of publicity materials.
- One copy of the music list to include the names of the composers, the titles of the compositions, and the names and addresses of the publishers.

## MARKETING RIGHTS

Given the intensely competitive environment in both the domestic and international television sales arena, it is important that the television syndication agreement provide some flexibility for the distributor within the framework of both the producer and distributor's needs and requirements. It is within the parameters of the marketing rights clause that the rights and obligations of the distributor are stipulated, clearly and concisely.

The television distributor often negotiates for the right to retain complete and total control, in all matters of distribution, within the context of the agreement. The distributor's chance of successfully negotiating this point, as well as many others in the agreement, often depends on the strength of the distributor's prior successes in the television distribution arena. The distributor's track record aside, a general point of contention or negotiation in the television syndication agreement tends to be defining the exact role the producer will have concerning the right of consultation and approval regarding the distributor's business decisions affecting the distribution of the producer's motion picture in the defined marketplace.

### Packaging the Motion Picture

Licensing the broadcast rights of the motion picture to television distributors is often structured as a part of a package of several motion pictures. The package is usually licensed as one entity. If the producer's picture is part of an overall package licensed by the distributor, and if the producer, as is often the case, believes his or her product is worth proportionately more than other films licensed within that package, the producer may insist that the motion picture return a higher license fee than the other similarly packaged films. The stronger the producer's motion picture with regard to quality, box office appeal, and cast, the stronger tends to be the producer's hand in such negotiations.

## CREDITS

The credit arrangements the producer finalized with the talent, director, and writer are often reiterated in this syndication agreement, ensuring the distributor's obligation to fulfill the producer's commitment.[10] Usually included is a disclaimer freeing the distributor from any fault or liability resulting from failure to fulfill the obligation of credit placement, in the event that proper and timely notice was not given to the distributor by the producer.

In general, the distributor is granted the right to affix its particular logo or credit at the beginning and at the end of the motion picture print, irrespective of credit arrangements made by the producer with key talent and production staff.

## ILLICIT ACTIVITIES

The agreement usually stipulates that the distributor will protect the film negatives and prints against illicit use and will further protect the copyright of the film by prohibiting any sublicensee from removing or deleting the copyright notice from the movie.

## PROMOTING AND SUBLICENSING

The contract may further stipulate that the distributor will use its best efforts to promote and market the film in all the territories in which it has received a license. Generally, though, the distributor, at its own discretion, is able to withdraw the motion picture from any territory to which it has the right for syndication. Usually, the distributor is forced to remove from syndication or license a motion picture based on piracy of the print. The distributor may also decide to remove the print based on a marketing strategy aimed at increasing the value of the picture.

The agreement usually addresses the issue of the distributor licensing the motion picture to subsidiaries or subdistributors. In the event the distributor owns television broadcast facilities or if the distributor licenses the motion picture to a subsidiary company or subdistributor that it wholly owns or controls, the producer generally demands assurance that the product will receive the maximum exposure possible. The agreement may state that, where the distributor licenses its product to any of its subsidiaries, it shall deal at arms length with systems or television stations it owns or controls with regard to the terms and conditions of any license or sublicense granted in the motion picture. The producer attempts to insure that he or she will receive fees equal in price and terms as if the picture had been licensed to nonaffiliated independent companies.

## BREACH OF CONTRACT

The default clause is generally aimed at both parties. Typically, this clause states that, should either of the parties materially misrepresent any of the warranties, then the agreement may be considered null and void. The agreement typically has a built-in cure element that enables the breaching party to mitigate the breach within a certain amount of time. Usually, a breach is defined as material and a failure, refusal, or neglect to comply with any of the contract's material obligations and provisions.[11]

# 12

## INTERNATIONAL COPRODUCTIONS

As production costs and deficit financing continue to increase, and globalization of markets becomes the norm, there is a greater tendency by the original producer to consider coproductions and cofinancing ventures on an international level. An international coproduction might consist of a British-based producer, an Italian-based writer who created the idea and story, a German-based venture capitalist partnership, and an American-based television or cable television network. Each party has its own interest, be it television distribution rights, profit participation, or international distribution following a U.S. network presentation. A contract typically labels some of the parties producer, network producer, and executive producer. The latter often represents those involved primarily for the revenues, and not in distribution, such as the producer, distributor, or venture capitalist.

When negotiating and drafting such an agreement, key issues should be addressed, including financing, production, distribution, apportioning of gross and net revenues, accounting, producer's warranties, and television network warranties.

### FINANCING

When drafting the financing clause of the contract, it is important to stipulate not only the exact amount that each party will contribute towards the project, but also a time schedule indicating the projected infusion of cash from each source. Generally, the amount that each partner contributes is balanced in part by the nonmonetary contributions made by some partners to the project, including distribution guarantees, introduction of key financial and creative elements, production management, and administrative services.

The cash flow budget is typically broken down as follows:

1. Amount paid in advance
2. Amount payable on execution of contracts
3. Amount payable on commencement of principal photography
4. Amount payable on completion of 50 percent of principal photography
5. Amount payable on completion of principal photography
6. Amount payable on completion of the rough cut
7. Amount payable on completion of the fine cut
8. Amount payable on delivery of all materials

Generally, the amount paid in advance is a small portion of the total amount due. The amount usually paid during the course of actual principal photography constitutes the bulk of the budget. The submission of the rough cut, fine cut, and all materials generates much of the remainder of the total cash contribution.

Aside from the calculated budget, the contract may include a clause stipulating that each party will contribute a certain sum in the event the project goes over budget. In general, the television network is not responsible for the additional funds. The duty to supplement the budget typically lies with the producer and executive producers. Should the coproduction find itself with excess funds due to the producer's success in completing the project under the agreed budget, the agreement may provide for a bonus due the producer.

### Completion Bond

The coproduction company generally requires that the producer obtain, at a cost consistent with the budget, a completion bond—a virtual necessity in financing any independently produced project. This completion bond, which may be underwritten by an insurance firm or by a major distributor who has given a sizable advance to secure the rights to the project in certain markets, generally costs between 4 to 6 percent of the total budget.

This provision typically also contains a clause that states that the producer must get the written approval of all the partners before exceeding, or reallocating, the budget. This provision protects the partners from gambling in excess of their original budgetary projections. The contract states that, in the event the producer exceeds the proposed budget without prior approval of the participants, the producer is solely responsible for such funding and will not receive additional funds from the partners.

The contract may include a reference to each participant's approval of each phase of the production by requiring that each initial approval of the screenplay, budget, and choice of talent.

## CREATIVE CONTROL BY THE PRODUCER

An area that often spawns a heated debate between the creative and commercial factions of the production is the degree of creative flexibility the producer retains in the motion picture project. The producer often demands the full and unencumbered right and authorization to hire whatever staff the producer deems appropriate, including the writer, line producer, director, composer, director of principal photography, and principal cast members. Conversely, the coproduction and investing partnership may insist on retaining veto power over certain creative elements or decisions in order to protect financial investments or reputation.

The provision regarding control over the various elements comprising the completed motion picture may also include control over such important elements as the proposed length of a miniseries, date of actual production, date of final delivery, as well as provision of certain technical or format standards required for telecast. The format requirement is generally included as an amendment to the general agreement and consists of such requirements as having a "tease with voice over," a trailer of the coming episode of the miniseries, a network logo, and a space for local station breaks.

## CONSULTATION REQUIREMENTS

Since sizable investments are often required for productions, the participants may insist that the producer be obligated to consult with them on a regular basis as the project develops and grant them or their representatives access to the shooting set, editing rooms, and screenings.

## COPYRIGHT PROTECTION AND NOTICE

To insure copyright protection in the United States, the work must be registered in the U.S. copyright office, which then grants the owner certain benefits regarding rights of ownership and damages in the event such ownership is compromised. Consequently, this provision often requires that the producer place a valid copyright notice on all prints, tapes, and disks of the production according to the following model: Copyright © (producer's name) 19XX.

If the copyright is to be registered in all the participants' names, the contract stipulates that all the names be inserted within the copyright notice. If, for a variety of legal or accounting reasons, it is decided that only one of the partner's names will be listed, then the importance of the contract is greatly increased since, under copyright law, all rights in the film are usually presumed to belong to the copyright owner unless otherwise expressed in a written document signed by all the parties.

## ACCESS TO PROCESSING LABORATORY

Since there may arise subsequent disagreements or legal actions against one or several of the partners, either by interested parties outside of the partnership or by members of the production partnership itself, it is essential that the film negatives and assorted production materials be accessible to all the parties. This is generally accomplished by stipulating in the agreement that all bona fide representatives of the partners shall have access to the film processing laboratory. In addition, the contract should state that none of the material will be removed from that processing lab without prior written authorization from all the partners.

The agreement may also refer to an attached exhibit or laboratory access letter on file with the facility. The letter should contain essential ingredients, including the requirement that the laboratory will fill all orders upon request from the partners, producers, or licensees at the production partner's sole cost, and that the lab is not responsible for the costs incurred by the distributor or its agents, licensees, and so forth. An additional element which may be included is a clause stating that the lab will not assert any lien on the program or materials relating to the film by reason of the failure to pay any outstanding charges that may result from processing the order. The letter should also state that the lab will be prohibited from moving or releasing the preprint material from the labs without written authorization.

## PRODUCER'S PRODUCTION REPORTS

The contract should provide that the producer will submit weekly or bimonthly production status reports to the other partners in the coproduction. The report should include such important data as the costs incurred during the production week, status of the production, estimated completion date as calculated from the previous week, any significant current or potential problems that might delay completion past the previously agreed upon date.[1]

The producer may also be required to consult in good faith with the television network (if applicable) and distributor regarding potential distribution and broadcast problems as production continues. Moreover, the producer should agree to permit the other parties access to the daily rushes.

Since the investors in the project may, in turn, have their own investors who must be kept informed of the progress of the production, the producer may be asked to maintain a set of official books and records at a location to be mutually agreed upon during negotiations. For example, if most of the angels (financial backers) are located in Los Angeles, the agreement may require that the producer maintain an office in Los Angeles so that all the parties or their bona fide representatives will have complete access to financial records, contracts, licensing agreements, talent contracts, clearance forms, and the like. In addition, it is normally agreed that copies of all those documents will be made available to the representatives of the parties, providing that the parties pay for the cost of duplicating the documents.

## MANDATORY INSURANCE COVERAGE

The contract also requires that the producer maintain adequate insurance policies until delivery of the final production element – typically the completed motion picture. Insurance policies typically include general liability and negative, cast, and extra expense insurance in amounts necessary and appropriate to insure delivery of the picture.

The producer, in protecting the concerns of the television network, is generally required to carry, until the expiration of the network license period, standard errors and omissions insurance, in an amount to be negotiated by the parties. This type of insurance usually relates to copyright infringement, defamation, trademark infringement, and invasion of privacy. The premiums are typically incorporated into the budget.

In the event the coproduction deal is a licensed agreement rather than a joint venture in which title is jointly owned, the contract should clearly state to which partner the assets of the production belong. Often, the assets accrue to the producer. Such assets include, but are not limited to, all ancillary and subsidiary rights; the screenplay; all contracts and intangible rights relating to the production; all books, records, ledgers, schedules, shooting scripts, and checkbook receipts; all film materials and tapes; and so forth.

## DISTRIBUTION RIGHTS

Another important aspect of the agreement relates to rights of distribution. The parties of the coproduction may acknowledge that the producer will have, except as expressly agreed to otherwise, sole and exclusive rights regarding the distribution of the production.

The other participants may also agree that the producer will have no obligations other than to make a good faith effort to distribute or otherwise exploit the property in all territories, except those granted the other parties. In those instances, the burden of exploitation shifts to the partners who have obtained those territorial rights.

## NO GUARANTEES OF SUCCESS BY PRODUCER

The coproduction agreement should also state that the participants undertook the investment without relying on any representation by the producer that a guaranteed amount of revenue would be generated, unless certain presell agreements were signed and in place prior to the agreement. The contract also indicates that, in the event revenues so projected are not realized, the producer will not be held in breach of the agreement or liable for failing a lack of good faith.

## LICENSING ACCORD BETWEEN PARTIES AND NETWORK

The agreement should detail the licensing agreement between the parties and the U.S. network, if applicable. It may state, for example, that the network partner may broadcast the show an agreed number of times over a defined period through free television.

If the agreement calls for any exclusivity windows, such a provision should be included in this agreement. If the U.S. network partner did not obtain Canadian rights, for example, the network partner may insist that the producer or distributor provide the U.S. market with a predetermined threshold for initially airing the production during its first run. The rationale behind that provision could be that many Americans live close to the Canadian border, and Canadian channels are often relayed on cable systems in U.S. cities adjacent to the frontier. Naturally, the U.S. network prefers to maximize its audience and advertising revenue, and preventing the series from first airing in Canada would help.

## ANCILLARY RIGHTS

Aside from television rights, the license may include all rights to the nontheatrical distribution and exploitation of the production. That definition itself is subject to negotiations but generally includes a broad base of nontheatrical rights. Typically, those rights may include all formats, means, and technologies now in existence or to be hereafter invented or discovered. Those licenses typically include those related to film; video tape; video disc; closed circuit television; education; cable and off-air video taping for exhibition to nonpaying audiences in educational institutions (e.g., schools, public libraries, colleges, universities, dormitories, and residence halls); churches; synagogues; museums; hospitals; prisons; summer camps; business; transportation industry; hotels; clubs; organizations of an educational, cultural, religious, charitable, or social nature; and all other like entities and places.

### Producer's Obligation to Obtain All Ancillary Rights

The contract generally requires the producer to obtain, for all the elements of the production, broad rights sufficient to permit the network and distributors to exploit the production and all ancillary and subsidiary rights derived from the project in all media, in perpetuity, without in any way infringing upon or violating any third party rights. The rights in question usually include: copyright, trademark, privacy, and publicity.[2]

## ROYALTY AND PUBLIC PERFORMANCE PAYMENTS

In the event the producer will not function as distributor for the production, this agreement may provide that the third party distributor is liable for all residual and royalty payments to the appropriate unions, guilds, and musical royalty associations.

The agreement should state that the third party distributor, if it will pay these fees, may allocate those payments as advances against the participants' shares of income. These royalties are therefore generally 100 percent recoupable prior to the distribution of profits.

## EDITING

The network partner may insist on creative editing control in order to satisfy local requirements or standards of programming. The network may agree to assume the cost of such editing, and that such expenses are not recoupable against profit at the expense of the other parties.

Pending previous negotiations, the contract generally addresses the need for dubbing into predetermined foreign languages, in the event the project was not shot with multilanguage use in mind.

## GROSS REVENUES

Generally, revenues are apportioned according to the contributions and risks by each of the parties, or according to the relative bargaining strengths of the parties.

The terms gross revenues and net revenues must be carefully defined within the contract. Those terms, as used in the entertainment industry, are nebulous and leave themselves open for differing definitions by each party. The more concise the definition, the less the possibility of a hotly contested litigation battle over compensation. Generally, gross revenues are all sums actually received from all sources, both primary and ancillary, by the producer or distributor or any of their subdistributors or sublicensees connected with the production. Monies due but not received are often not deemed gross revenues. Moreover, any tax credits derived from doing business are generally not included as gross revenues.

On the surface, net revenues are gross revenues less all distribution expenses, incurred by the producer or distributor, that are required to be and are in fact paid out on account of such requirements. Several examples of such expenses include union fees; residual and royalty payments;

pension, health, and welfare payments; music license fees; the costs of manufacturing and processing prints; shipping, packaging, and delivery costs; promotion, advertising, publicity, and sales expenses; accounting and legal costs; the cost of copyright protection in each country where the miniseries is to be aired; insurance premiums; nonincome-related government taxes; bookkeeping; and so forth. Furthermore, the producer may require an administrative fee and the distributor may insist on a fee on top of commissions. After calculating all the percentages, the amount of net revenues may be a small percentage of the total income earned by the production.

## PRODUCER'S WARRANTIES

The producer's warranties are an important part of the coproduction agreement. This provision warrants that the producer is able to commit to the project at hand.

The producer is generally required to warrant and represent to the other parties the services of all persons performing services in connection with the proposed production; to provide all production, direction, and other picture elements; and to provide all recording, editing, and other production-related services.

The producer may further warrant and grant the television network, if applicable, the right to use and license others to use the voices and likenesses of all the talent appearing in the production; to promote and use the producer's name in advertising; and to use excerpts of the production for promotional purposes without it being deemed an airing.

The producer typically warrants that he or she is legally capable of undertaking this obligation and has secured, or will secure prior to the delivery of the production, all rights, releases, clearances, or licenses in connection with all materials and elements of the production. Furthermore, the production, upon delivery to the distributor or broadcaster, will be free and clear of any liens or claims by any third party.

In addition, the producer generally warrants that the production has complied with all appropriate collective bargaining arrangements, and that the copyright registration was properly completed and filed.

## INDEMNIFICATION

The producer generally indemnifies and holds harmless the distributor or broadcaster and all other parties to this coproduction from and against any and all costs, damages, claims, losses, liabilities, and expenses resulting from a breach or alleged breach with respect to any covenants, representations, or warranties.

Conversely, the distributor, broadcaster, and other parties to the coproduction may be required to warrant that they are authorized to make a production financing commitment, that all the parties are legally free to sign and execute the agreement, and that each will indemnify each other in breach of specific duties and responsibilities.

## FORCE MAJEURE

The agreement may also include a clause relating to *force majeure,* which will hold harmless the producer in the event of uncontrollable delays.[3] Depending on the complexity of the venture, the parties will negotiate a resolution period and deadline in the event the *force majeure* clause is applicable.

# 13

# The Home Video License Agreement

Home video rights are valuable assets. These rights are an integral part of the agreement between the owner of the rights and the distributor. If the owner, usually the producer, chooses to separate the home video rights from the theatrical rights, the owner may license them to different parties, licensing the motion picture rights to a motion picture distributor and the home cassette rights to a video distributor.

The license agreement between the owner of the home video rights and the distributor of those rights has developed as the industry matured over the years. The home video market did not substantially exist prior to the 1980s, and the license agreement grew into existence as the need warranted. The contract is now a sophisticated agreement that requires the knowledge and exactness of other entertainment contracts.

## DEFINITION

The video cassette is usually defined as a video disc record; cassette; magnetic tape record in cassette or cartridge form, or any form now or to be hereafter devised; or any other audio-visual system, now known or to be devised in the future, using a playback device for viewing on a television receiver or device.

## EXCLUSIVITY

The owner usually grants to the distributor the exclusive right and license to manufacture and distribute the video cassette for an agreed upon and determined period of years in a defined territory.

## TERRITORIES

The territories are a negotiated aspect of the agreement and may be limited to the United States and Canada, or to a particular area of the globe, such as the Benelux countries, Japan, or the Far East, or it may include the whole world. The agreement may clarify that the work could be exploited in all languages, in either the dubbed or subtitled format.

## SUBLICENSE RIGHT

The distributor generally retains the right to subdistribute the exploitation of the video cassette to a subdistributor, who shall be required to abide by the conditions of the license agreement.

## COPYRIGHT PROTECTION

The rights owner generally warrants that the work is fully protected by federal copyright laws, and that all required rights and licenses, including synchronization and performance, comply with the needs of the licensee. The owner usually further represents that he or she has the unencumbered authority to represent the work for the rights in question.

## PRICING

The home video distributor generally retains the right to determine the retail price of the video cassette, the number of cassettes to be manufactured, and the marketing and promotion strategies for the sale and exploitation of the video cassette in the market it controls.

## EDITING RIGHTS

Since the markets may be diversified, with varying needs and requirements, the distributor negotiates for the right to re-edit the work. If the owner retains the overriding creative rights, the editing rights may be highly contested.

## FUTURE WORKS BY OWNER/PRODUCER

The distributor may request the right of first negotiation during the term of the agreement, in order to license an additional number of the owner's works for the video cassette distribution market. This output deal insures the distributor a flow of goods to the market place and guarantees the owner an outlet for the goods.

## COMPENSATION

The owner may agree to an advance against future royalties, payable upon the signing of the contract, as an initial payment toward the licensing fee. The payment schedule for royalty percentage is mutually agreed and is generally required to comply with normal accounting procedures. The amount of the advance and the percentage of royalty usually depends on the success of the film at the box office, as well as the stars, the producer, and director attached to the project.

In addition, the parties usually agree on a royalty fee. The actual royalty paid by the distributor to the owner can be calculated based on the number of cassettes sold and the place of purchase. The royalty rate may be higher when the cassette is sold in established retail outlets than when sold by rack jobbers to mass market outlets.

The contract often details the formula upon which the royalty is calculated. Typically, such royalties are based either on wholesale prices or gross receipts. Generally, the wholesale formula is a fixed basis compensation. In some cases, it may be based on the number of units obtained by the distributor, the value established not on what is actually received but on what is deemed to be the wholesale price, irrespective of actual markups by the distributor.

The contract may refer to a published, prevailing, or otherwise established wholesale selling price. Gross receipts are generally defined, in a detailed definition, as monies actually received by the distributor, without any deductions whatsoever.

The distributor is often obliged to pay only the royalty rate and will usually not be obliged to make further payments to the talent, producers, or other participants in the original work, unless specifically agreed upon.

The contract typically discusses the calculation of distribution fees and the owner's share with regard to discounts, net billings, treatment of bad debts, retailer returns, spoilage, and the like. For example, the distributor may be liable solely for units actually sold and not returned by consumers or sublicensees. In addition, the contract usually addresses deductibility for bad or uncollected debts. Moreover, commerce-related taxes, such as excise, sales, use, VAT, foreign currency remittance, and other similar taxes should be addressed. Often, they are deducted from royalties due to the owner. However, taxes relating to the cost of doing business, such as income or franchise taxes, are generally the responsibility of the distributor as part of its overhead expense.

The contract should also consider the use of subdistributors and the calculation of income and royalties. Although subject to bargaining, royalties are typically based on the revenues remitted by the subdistributor to the distributor.

## THE WINDOW

Establishing a release window is essential in determining a motion picture's pattern of distribution. The window can be defined as the period of time between the theatrical release and the video release of the work. Usually, a movie is initially reserved for a theatrical showing, followed by home video, pay television, and free television showings.

The agreement generally includes both a domestic and international theatrical release window, during which period the home video rights may not be exploited. That window assures the owner that the video cassette will not interfere with the box office receipts generated from the theatrical release of the work.

A successful release could benefit from a longer window, since that lengthy period of time would insure that video cassette revenues will not detract from the theatrical box office receipts. On the other hand, a motion picture that is a disaster at the box office would be better off with a shorter window period. That would place the cassette into the retail outlets at an earlier date and bring in much needed revenues. The trend recently is a shorter window period.

The contract also generally states that the distributor will accelerate the window, or availability date, for home video release if the theatrical release date is delayed in a particular country or territory. This is usually tied in to the date of availability promised by the owner/producer of the motion picture.

## INCLUDED WORKS

If the contract applies to more than a single work, a list of the motion pictures to be licensed may be included in the contract. The agreement also generally establishes the time table for the fully edited, broadcast quality video tape master to be delivered to the licensee.

In addition, a compilation of the support materials the licensee requires should be detailed in the agreement. That list usually includes the 35mm internegative made from an interpositive of the original final cut negative, and a 35mm screening print to be used for time comparison; a 35mm color reversal intermediate; a magnetic sound track; a dubbed or subtitled version; a letter of access to the laboratory; full access to the reproduction master and sound track; and all other necessary materials, whether preprint or otherwise.

## CONVERSION

The distributor usually pays the cost of converting the work to master video recordings that will serve as the master for the duplication of all video cassettes of the work, as well as all other costs incurred in the exploitation of the video cassettes.

## INTERNATIONAL PROVISIONS

Since agreements for the exploitation of a motion picture's home video rights can include the exploitation of its worldwide rights, it is important to provide for that contingency. The contract should provide a clause clarifying who is responsible in the event government restrictions or barriers prevent the timely import of agreed home video titles. Such barriers could be the imposition of import duties, import quotas, or local work requirements in the actual manufacturing of the video cassettes, be they duplication or voice dubbing.

The issue of censorship must also be addressed when dealing on an international level. The agreement should provide the right to edit the home video to ensure its compliance with local authorities. It should also stipulate under whose creative control – the owner or the home video distributor – the editing takes place.

The contract should also note the financial costs inherent in the censorship process. In some countries there is a preclearance of products prior to the customs procedure, while in others the master tape must submit to customs and a censor. Also, in many countries it is necessary to get a postrelease approval from the local censorship authorities, so it is important to state in the agreement under what conditions the owner will bear the costs and which fees and expenses are left to the local distributor.

The agreement should also address the problem of the proper rating for the property, if that is a requirement in a particular market. In the United Kingdom, for example, the fact that a movie was given one rating does not automatically entitle that movie to a similar rating for its home video release. The costs associated with editing a movie to meet certain guidelines should if possible be established at the outset. The international home video agreement should contain a clause addressing the issue of foreign currency controls and the repatriation of royalties and fees to the U.S. licensor.

In some countries there are banking regulations designed to limit the outlay and export of hard or foreign, convertible currency. The contract should outline procedures for how a home video distributor fulfills its financial obligation when a portion of its earnings is blocked funds – revenues earned in a country that forbids the export of its currency. It is important to consider which party is in control of the blocked currencies.

In addition, the agreement should consider a rescheduling of payments in the event the distributor has to undergo additional expenses if required to apply for remittance approvals with that territory's central bank authorities.

The agreement should also take into account other registration and control requirements faced by the distributor, such as local copyright registration, video registration stickers, and other administrative requirements.

Likewise, the contract could provide for the mechanics of foreign currency payments and the audit of same, with particular attention to how records shall be kept in the event of local currency fluctuations.

## SECURITY INTEREST

The distributor may require a provision that it will receive a security interest in the picture in order to secure the performance of the producer's obligations.

## FLOW OF PRODUCT AND TITLES

Ideally, a distributor makes an output deal, thereby ensuring an adequate supply of titles. In that case, the contract addresses the minimum number of cassettes to be released, usually where the distributor has already paid front money or guaranteed certain sales levels.

Depending on the track record of the producer, the distributor generally insists on retaining the final prices and marketing policies for the home video titles it is exploiting. In addition, unless the producer has contracts to the contrary, the distributor generally argues for the right to maintain complete discretion on advertising policies and cover designs. The contract should also address the concerns of inventory requirements in light of who is responsible for such payments.

## CREATIVE AND BUSINESS APPROVAL

Depending on the strength and the investment of the distributor in the production of the motion picture, the distributor could request the right to co-approve the budget and casting of the motion picture. The contract may also stipulate that the distributor, prior to paying on delivery of the finished project, will receive a certified negative cost statement as well as a CPA-supervised audit of the records of the finished production.

Since the distributor is banking on a finished product for its own home video market, it may demand that the producer obtain a completion bond and insist on retaining personal approval over the terms of such a bond. Such a clause is easier for the distributor to get if the distributor advances monies prior to and during the actual course of production.

### Producer's Rights on Home Video

The producer often requests the right to control the creative and business decisions made during the production of the motion picture with the caveat that those decisions do not infringe on the rights granted the distributor. The producer may attempt to include a self-executing provision stating that any issues that would be liable for approval by the distributor must be in writing and submitted to the producer within a certain time frame. The failure to properly file a veto automatically constitutes approval.

The producer may also try to commit the distributor to act in a consensus with other financial investors and distributors so as to not frustrate the production of the motion picture.


## ESCAPE CLAUSE

This clause generally stipulates that the home video distributor may terminate the agreement if approval rights granted the distributor are breached or circumvented against its interests. Although a customary amount of time is permissible to allow the producer to cure the breach, the distributor may be entitled, under this stipulation, to a full refund of any monies already advanced or submitted, and to have no further obligation to pay any additional monies or distribute the movie for home video.


## QUALITY CONTROL

Because the success of a home video production is often tied in to its box office success during the motion picture's theatrical release, the distributor may insist that the producer guarantee that the finished work meet certain objective standards common to the theatrical film business. For example, the home video distributor may insist that the production company use the theatrical distribution services of a major or "mini-major" Hollywood studio. In addition, the contract may stipulate that the producer support the theatrical release by authorizing a minimum number of prints to be distributed to the major theaters domestically and/or internationally and apportioning a guaranteed amount for sufficient advertising and promotions. If the home video distributor has ample clout in the entertainment market place, it may require that the production team and theatrical distributor guarantee a minimum number of screens, theatrical venues, and play dates, prior to the home video release date in order to maximize the publicity of the movie.

In connection with these commitments, the contract may state that the home video distributor is entitled to a copy of all statements received by the producer from the theatrical distributor and that it will be entitled to do a complete accounting or audit of the books and records of the producer.

## FIRST-RUN HOME VIDEO PRODUCT

As the home video market continues to expand, home video companies are creating their own programming in addition to being involved in joint productions in which they license the home video works prior to or after actual production.

As in the case with theatrical filmmaking, the agreement with the home video distributor may initially be an option-based deal, whereby the decision to actually produce the movie can be revoked without penalty.

An important element in the contract is the ownership of the work upon which the home video production is based. The contract generally calls for the assurance that, in the event the material was not already published, the rights owner will register the work with the copyright office. The owner may also affirm that no other motion picture, video cassette, or dramatic version of the literary property has been manufactured, produced, presented, or authorized; that no radio or television development deal was made based on the optioned or fully acquired works; and that no oral or written agreement was made and executed with respect to the literary work, except those stipulated in print.

Establishing the proper copyright is of prime importance, so this clause may also state that the underlying property owner did not base the original literary work on any literary, dramatic, or other material of any kind, nature, or description, except that in the public domain. This clause generally includes the plot, scenes, sequences, or story line of the work.

In addition, the underlying property owner is generally required to warrant that the story does not violate the privacy of others, that the material is not libelous, and that the work itself is not in the public domain in any country in the world where copyright protection is available.

The owner of the literary rights is also required in most situations to warrant and guarantee that he or she is the exclusive proprietor throughout the world of the rights stipulated in the agreement. Moreover, the owner typically states that he or she has not encumbered, diminished, or impaired those rights, nor assigned them to a third party.

The contract generally provides that, in the event potential litigation does arise, the option terms shall be extended in direct proportion to the length of the controversy. Thereby, the option period will toll until there is no challenge or litigation regarding the ownership of the literary work.

The contract usually stipulates how notice of the acceptance of the option will work. The agreement typically provides for the home video licensor to notify the owner of the literary works in a documented writing, and that such a receipt constitutes the exercise of such an option. Moreover, if the option requires an additional payment to be credited against the original purchase price, the contract will stipulate how that amount of money is to be paid.

The contract may also grant power of attorney to the distributor in the event the agreement is exercised but there are failings in ownership. For example, if the work involved was never registered with the U.S. copyright office, this agreement could provide the distributor with the authority both to register it and to name the distributor as holder of the copyright.

Usually provided in the agreement is a clause stipulating that the rights owner may not take any action that will prejudice the rights granted the distributor. For example, the owner may be enjoined from negotiating with a third party in the event that the agreement fails, unless such negotiations do not conflict with the rights granted to the distributor.

In the event of a breach of any of these conditions by the owner of the work, and depending on the strength of the parties, the distributor may also have the choice of either permitting the owner to cure the defect and allow the agreement to continue, or completely canceling the agreement altogether, with funds advanced to the owner and returned to the distributor.

## MERCHANDISING: NAME AND LIKENESS

The home video distributor may request the right to merchandise the products derived from the production (clothing, furniture, accessories, toys, dolls, products, etc.).

The distributor generally retains the right to quote directly from the original property and use the name and likeness of the owner and producer, if such usage will help promote and market the home cassette. In the event of a successful response by the audience to the picture at the video rental or retail shop, the distributor may attempt to secure a percentage of the revenues earned from the republication of the work, if the original work appeared as a novel.

## CLARIFICATION OF RIGHTS

All the rights granted to the distributor should be clearly defined in the agreement, including the right to use, in other formats, the characters, plot, and setting incidental to the work. The right to take the characters and plot lines for a popular film or television character and use it as a basis for an animation series is a separate right that can represent a substantial amount of additional revenue.

The distributor may be permitted, if negotiated, to use a portion or portions of the property or the characters, plots, or theme in conjunction with any other literary, dramatic, or other material distributed by the distributor. The distributor may be permitted to add paid advertisement at the beginning, or end, of the tape, as long as it does not impede the creation of the work itself.

## Holdback

The owner may wish to retain several rights, including the rights to live stage presentations, publication, and, at times, production sequels that feature the same characters and setting as those in the rights acquired by the distributor. (e.g., When the owner or producer retains the right to use a character for additional works, written or filmed, such rights which fall outside the rights purchased by the distributor.) If the distributor fails to acquire those rights, it may request that the owner hold back the theatrical stage presentations for a period of time after the release of the production in the home entertainment market place. The home video distributor could rightfully argue that such a release at or around the time the distributor releases the original production on home cassette could critically damage the rights retained by the distributor, and could represent a substantial loss of revenue.

## *Droit Moral*

Since the acquisition of the work is for both domestic and international use, it is important that the contract contain a waiver of the *droit moral* clause. It should be noted that in some countries, such as France, the moral right of author may not be legally waived. In some other countries, the licensor may not have the right to permit such a modification without specific notice to the author or creator of the work.

## Waiver of Rights

If the producer and owner expressly agree that they have no right, title, or interest whatsoever in the screenplay or finished motion picture, or in the gross receipts earned from the exploitation of the motion picture in the home entertainment market, the distributor is usually granted the unencumbered right to sell, transfer, assign, pledge, or encumber the cassette, as well as to produce, distribute, license, or exploit the video cassette in any manner throughout the territory acquired, without the owner's consent. The owner and producer may also grant to the distributor all rights to use their names, voices, and likenesses for the purpose of advertising the motion picture.

## EXISTING CONTRACTS

The distributor may require contractual evidence that the actors have agreed to render their services to portray the agreed roles in the production, including rerecording their voices for sound effects in connection with the home video release. In addition, the actors may be obligated to promotional tours and advertising campaigns to aid in the sale, rental, and licensing of the home video. Furthermore, the actors may be contracted to make retakes, add scenes, shoot added close-ups, be available for dubbing (laying voices over the dramatic action) upon reasonable notice, and to be available for filming scenes for trailers and advertising and publicity shots required for the home entertainment market. The agreement could stipulate that the actors perform all the above additional services at no additional compensation, if rendered during the agreed term.

The distributor may request the right to substitute another voice for an actor's voice under agreed upon conditions, including the following:

- when necessary to meet the requirements of foreign exhibition
- when necessary to meet censorship requirements both foreign and domestic
- when the actor is not available despite advance notice
- when the actor is unable to meet certain requirements of the role, such as singing or other similar or comparable services requiring talents or abilities other than those possessed by the actor.

## THE FUTURE

The video cassette business shows no sign of letting up. VCRs will certainly become more technically advanced with time. Advances in the home entertainment business are progressing faster than originally thought. The majority of homes in the United States already has a VCR. Newly produced and advanced tape, laser disc, and high-definition equipment are already on the market, while engineers are busy developing the next generation of equipment.

The home entertainment market represents a substantial part of the entertainment business, with video sales and rentals accounting for a sizeable portion of a motion picture's earned revenue. All indications are that revenue earned from the home entertainment market has surpassed revenue earned from the theatrical release of motion pictures. The home market is considered so significant that the trade unions representing the various members of the entertainment and media industries (SAG, WGA, DGA) instigated strikes and work stoppages to ensure themselves a piece of the home video cassette market.

# 14

## ENDORSEMENTS

The use of endorsements, talents acting as spokespersons for products or services, has increased substantially as advertisers attempt to distinguish their products from the competition. The role of the talent may take various forms: as a voice over, as a performer talent in a mini drama or music video, as an on-camera spokesperson, and as a live performer making special appearances in conjunction with marketing promotions.

The talent may personally recommend the use of a product or service. In this form, the personal integrity and reputation of the endorser is often at stake.

In addition to personal endorsements, well-known public figures, be they in politics, drama, music, or sports, may be hired to participate in a promotional marketing strategy with the goal of generating sales by identifying the product with a known and respected personality. The retained talent may not view the assignment as a personal endorsement but only another film or television assignment.

The retained talent is often used to focus attention on the product logo or name as much as to sell the product or service. For the employer, the endorsement is typically part of a long-term marketing strategy. Irrespective of the type of campaign, there are certain basics common to all endorsement agreements that need to be explored and reviewed.

The talent who agrees to endorse a particular product usually grants to the manufacturing or licensing company the exclusive right to use his or her name and likeness in connection with the promotion, advertisement, and sale of the product for a designated period of time in the marketing area in which the company does its business.

## USE OF ENDORSEMENTS IN MEDIA

The endorsement contract generally provides a clause that states that the advertising agency or client (both hereinafter referred to as the client) permit the talent the full and exclusive use of the materials prepared for the endorsement. In conjunction with the other clauses of the contract, the agreement states in which territories the campaign is to be conducted (e.g., North America, Western Europe, the world).

The agreement usually states that the client, during the initial term of the contract and in addition to the extended options and modifications, will have the right to use the talent's name, likeness, photograph, or signature at the client's sole discretion on television, radio, and video cassettes, in print magazines, cooperative advertising campaigns, point-of-purchase campaigns, product packaging, and official business documents, such as annual reports to shareholders, and any other manner of advertising or promotion.

## USE OF MATERIAL FOLLOWING TERMINATION OF THE AGREEMENT

An area that should generally be fully negotiated is the use of the material following the termination of the basic agreement[1] or extended option agreements.[2] Because of long lead times and the nature of the advertised product, the client typically insists that the talent permit the client to continue distributing, for a predetermined period, any packaging materials bearing the likeness, name, or photograph of the talent. In addition, the client is usually not required to withdraw or remove from sales outlets, for a similar period of time, any of the packages or point-of-sale materials containing the client's name, photograph, or likeness.

## OVEREXPOSURE

Many leading talents are concerned about overexposure and the need to carefully regulate the public view of his or her performances. Depending on the strength of the performer's bargaining position, the endorsement contract may provide certain ground rules in terms of the number of exposures, the type of publications using the endorsement, and how the endorsement will be presented. The rationale for such a clause may be that the reputation of the performer is often attached to the endorsed product as well as the medium in which its advertising appears. A well-known actor may not want the commercial to appear in a certain genre of television program or publication. The client, conversely, may attempt to be as broad and vague as possible so as to maximize its own marketing discretion.

## CONTROL OF PERSONNEL

The talent, under this agreement, may insist that the commercials be produced by widely respected professionals in the field, be it specific photographers or directors. The talent may insist that the advertising campaign include a predetermined budget for first class postproduction services. Such clauses are generally negotiated on a case-by-case basis and may vary according to the strength of the performer.

## SERVICES

The services to be performed by the talent are generally spelled out in detail and usually include promotion of the talent's image in the print (magazine and newspaper) media, and the promotion of the talent's presence and recognizable voice on television and radio broadcast advertisements in connection with the product. The amount of actual days required for these functions should be clearly delineated in the agreement. The talent may require assurances that the binding contractual endorsement obligation will not interfere with prior commitments to a rigorous performance schedule.

The agreement generally stipulates the number and duration of television and radio commercials to be filmed or taped under the agreement, and the number of days for still photography shooting.

The endorsement agreement may include specifications for the noncommercial use of the material, such as for educational, the armed services, or charity. The rates for such noncommercial use might be different than for the commercial broadcast or print use of the talent's services.

Although clients may wish to use scenes of the actual video tape or film footage for print (magazine and newspaper) use, they may plan to use the services of a still photographer for customized still photography. The talent generally agrees in the contract to be available for such still photography for an additional fee.

The services portion of the endorsement agreement may also provide that the client will be granted the right to use the likeness, name, or statement of the talent for nonprint or broadcast areas, such as counter display cases and point-of-purchase advertising displays. Such material may be referred to as commercial materials in some agreements.

The agreement generally states that the talent will be ready and able to provide the services necessary to make the endorsement. In addition, the agreement could stipulate that the talent will be available for a minimum number of hours during each day of shooting.

Since the shooting schedule is contingent upon several variables, including the availability of the photographer, writer, director, and production company, the contract may not specifically stipulate a time or date.

In such a situation, the agreement may state that the scheduling of the agreed upon production days will be mutually determined by the client and the talent, subject to the talent's professional availability. In addition, the agreement may state that, should extra production time be needed as a result of factors beyond the control of the talent, the talent is entitled to receive additional compensation.

## RIGHTS OF APPROVAL

Depending on the stature of the performer, the talent may demand the right of prior approval before any of the talent's photographs, likenesses, and statements are released in an advertisement campaign. The contract may provide that the client must give the talent a predetermined amount of time in which to grant or deny such approval. In addition, it may be generally stipulated that the client will provide a broad selection of proposed commercial material and that the talent must select a percentage of the offerings. The percentage and the length of time required for approval is typically subject to intense private negotiations at the time the endorsement contract is entered.

Depending on the type and nature of endorsement contemplated, the talent may insist that the agreement provide more than just tacit approval rights. This concern may arise when direct testimonials are used by the client. In that case, the talent may demand that the script and layout material be reasonably compatible with the talent's personality or style. In addition, the talent may negotiate for the absolute right to approve the script and print copy, in order to insure that the script reflects the talent's personal experience with the client's products.

The client may require that the talent provide affidavits or assurances that the talent will not undertake any actions that will undermine the advertising campaign.

## MORALS CLAUSE

The client may insist on including a morals clause,[3] granting the client the unencumbered right to terminate the relationship if the talent becomes involved or associated with any public disrepute or scandal that offends the standards of the community in general. The talent may request a grace period to correct scandalous incidents and to erase wrong impressions from the public's mind prior to termination taking effect.

In addition, the talent may be asked to refrain from activities that, while they may not be restricted by the morals clause, may nonetheless cause embarrassment or problem. For example, if the talent is being paid to be a spokesperson for a leading car manufacturer, the talent should not be seen making public appearances using a competitor's brand of automobile. Naturally, such behavior could weaken the credibility of both the talent and the endorsement.

## EXCLUSIVITY

The agreement may contain a limited "noncompete" or exclusivity clause that restricts the talent from performing similar services for a similar product during and following (for an agreed upon period) the termination of the agreement. Working with a competing company may detract from the objective of the endorsement and derail the company's expensive sales campaign.

As a general rule, the more restrictive the agreement with respect to other outside employment, the higher the compensation is to offset the loss of that potential income. The type of exclusivity recommended may be as broad as an industry or as narrow as a type of product. For example, the spokesperson may work for a car manufacturer, but the restrictive covenant could prevent the talent from also working for trucking firms. As another example, if the talent endorses a certain food or drink product, he or she may be prevented from endorsing any other food or drink product, whether or not it competes with the initial product.

The issue may be further complicated when dealing with large multinational firms with overlapping interests. For example, if a talent is asked to endorse the photocopiers of a major electronics conglomerate that happens to also be a major camera, radio, and television manufacturer, the performer may or may not be able, depending on the precise drafting of this clause, to accept an assignment from a competing camera manufacturer because the corporate name of the photocopier is the same as that of the camera. If such a covenant prohibits even that type of association, compensation should reflect those lost opportunities.

The contract should be constructed in such a way as to insure that the talent will not be limited in future employment opportunities in similar fields unless the talent has given the client an exclusive on such services. At times, a commercial success might hamper a talent in future endeavors, particularly if the talent becomes linked with a particular brand or client.

## EXPENSES

The contract may also address the issue of per diem expenses due the talent in the event the client requires location shooting outside the performer's immediate environs. The exact amount of money often depends on the track record, status, and stature of the performer in the entertainment field. In addition, the definition of distant location shooting should be negotiated.

## TALENT'S REPUTATION

As the talent continues to remain a recognizable icon in this culture of mass communication and instant recognition,[4] the talent's endorsement of a commercial product can be an effective marketing tool if used correctly by advertising agencies and the business community.

The talent must carefully review the background and quality of the product, as he or she quickly becomes identified with the product in the public's eye. To be identified with a shoddy product, or a product considered unhealthy or unreliable, may severely damage the reputation of the talent. Likewise, the client reviews the talent's background thoroughly, searching for skeletons that could jump out of a closet and sabotage a multimillion dollar advertising campaign, causing often irreparable economic damage to its product. It will review the talent's political position, history with drugs, scandals, and other embarrassing past incidents that could affect, and potentially damage, the image of the product in the public's mind.

In an industry where millions of dollars are spent on research and development of a product, the client tends to select spokespersons with great care. Likewise, the talent who has spent years training and carefully developing an artistic career is highly selective of the product he or she chooses to endorse.

## CREATIVE CONTROL

In most circumstances, the client maintains control over the final look and feel of the commercials and printed ads, since the client is considered to have the necessary expertise in developing the marketing strategy to most effectively exploit the endorsement. In addition, absent a specific clause in the agreement, the client is entitled to use any or all portions of the work product for the purpose of promoting the product.

## RIGHT OF OWNERSHIP OF WORK PRODUCT

Since the talent is generally, by contract, an employee for hire, the work product of the endorsement is usually the property of the client. This agreement typically clarifies that all advertising material produced by the client remains the absolute property of the client in perpetuity. In addition, the talent may give up any claim to any right, title, or interest of any kind in the endorsement, or to any component part, tape, element, character, or characterization used in the endorsement.

## MERCHANDISING

An area subject to potential difficulties is that of merchandising the talent's likeness and image. The client may demand the limited right to promote and use the client's image, name, and likeness in various merchandising ways, such as posters, calendars, pens, mugs, and the like. The agreement may state that such merchandising should not interfere with any merchandising arrangements the talent may have outside of the agreement.

There is generally a fine line between the right to merchandise the talent's image and likeness as it relates to the endorsement and the so-called merchandising right retained by the talent in other contexts of the talent's career in the entertainment industry.

The endorsement agreement should address the issue of surplus publicity material. From the talent's point of view, if such material is not destroyed, it may have a negative impact on future merchandising agreements, since the talent will not make any royalties from such publicity material if such material enters general circulation subsequent to the termination of the endorsement campaign.

## UNION MEMBERSHIP

The Screen Actors Guild (SAG) and the American Federation of Television and Radio Artists (AFTRA) are the two primary unions representing performers on television. Often, the jurisdiction of each union is unclear. It is generally agreed that the talent, at his or her sole expense, be a member in good standing of either SAG or AFTRA, as required by the by-laws of the unions.

If a talent is a member of either AFTRA or SAG, the contract generally includes the stipulation that nothing contained in the endorsement agreement should be construed so as to require the violation of the appropriate union agreements in effect at the time of the signing of the endorsement agreement. Moreover, the contract may state that wherever there is any conflict between any provision of the agreement and the appropriate union agreement, the latter shall prevail, but only to the extent necessary to permit compliance with the AFTRA or SAG agreements.

## INSURANCE

The production of a television commercial is a costly venture that often relies on the health and well-being of a few key individuals. A star performer's sudden illness can cost a client dearly, depending on the urgency of the campaign and how it relates to general marketing strategy. Likewise, a director's presence and vision are, at times, pivotal to the success of some commercials.

The client, in order to insure investments and interests, will often require the talent to submit to the examinations required by an insurer. The beneficiary of such insurance is usually the client. The client may consider this clause to be essential and will usually terminate the talent's agreement if unable to obtain insurance at reasonable rates.

## OPTION TO RENEW

An endorsement agreement may grant a client the option to continue using the services of the talent, upon proper notice of its intention, to exercise the option, so long as the option is exercised within a designated time prior to the termination of the preceding term.

Unless stipulated otherwise, the provisions of the option are usually prestated in the initial agreement. It is to the benefit of the talent to maximize income while minimizing effort. Conversely, the client may attempt, in keeping costs down, to maintain the same basic provisions as the original agreement.

If the client requires that the services agreed to in the option are needed in advance of the option, this clause may provide that the option may be executed prior to the expiration of the basic agreement. In such a situation, however, the talent usually insists that the second agreement be extended in direct proportion to the amount of time deleted from the initial agreement. For example, if the initial term of the agreement is in its tenth month and the client decides to execute the option starting on the eleventh month, instead of the option year being twelve months, the terms of the second option will be for fourteen months to offset the loss of the original two months.

Depending on the type of endorsement—television commercials or print—the client may decide to update a commercial or change the advertising campaign completely. Consequently, the contract generally provides that the client, during its subsequent option periods, reserves the right to reshoot or redo any new material. Conversely, if the advertising campaign is doing better than expected in the market place, the client may decide to use the spots for an indefinite period of time. The contract may grant the client the option to extend the use of the commercial or endorsement, upon the proper payment of additional compensation, for a simultaneous option period, effective upon notice.

In the event the client decides to institute a new campaign or update an older campaign, the agreement typically states that the basic terms and conditions, including options for renewals, would remain the same except for the issue of compensation. With respect to income, both parties generally stipulate that they will bargain in good faith, usually within a fixed period during the preceding term. If the bargaining is fruitless, the contract may provide that either the talent or client may give notice to the other party of its intention to decline entering into the following option period.

## COMPENSATION

Compensation is typically the cornerstone of any contract. Depending on the status or track record of the talent, the agreement may be relatively simple or complex. Where tax factors are paramount, this aspect of the contract may include deferred compensation arrangements in order to maximize income and minimize tax liabilities.

Typically, the compensation clause reaffirms the specified duties to be compensated under the terms of the agreement. They may include the right of the client to use the talent's services, name, likeness, and image in the production of commercials on television, radio, and other electronic media, in relation to the client's product.

If the talent retains the uppermost bargaining position, he or she may demand full payment at the time of signing. However, the agreement usually provides for a partial payment, in advance, to the talent. The amount due and owing the talent under the terms of the agreement is usually paid according to an agreed schedule detailed in the agreement. In addition, the talent may be entitled to receive an agreed residual payment upon the successful completion of a determined performance cycle.

Moreover, the agreement usually outlines in detail the amount of payments due the talent upon the execution and acceptance of each additional option period. An alternative method is to negotiate the terms of each option within an agreed upon period of time preceding the termination of the initial option period. If a specific amount is stated in the options clause of the endorsement agreement, then the agreement usually defines and outlines the time frame for the payment of such additional monies.

The agreement may also state that, in the event the client requires extended production calls – whether they be still shoots, audio recordings, additional film or video footage, or other types of advertising or publicity materials – due to circumstances beyond the control of the talent, the talent will receive additional compensation on a per diem basis for the performance of such services. The agreement may also state that the additional compensation will be deposited to the account of the talent or paid directly to the talent or a representative within an agreed upon number of business days.

These are detailed deal points that must be negotiated on a case-by-case basis. Since an endorsement is usually made by a well-known personality, it is highly unlikely that union minimum scales will be prevalent, unless the endorsement is related to a nonprofit charitable organization, and the talent agrees to work for the minimum amount required under the union or guild agreements.

At times, the endorsement contract is based on a pilot marketing project, in which case only certain test markets are used. If the client foresees the possible use of additional markets for the endorsements, a compensation scale typically includes such possible contingencies. The contract may state that, in the event an additional number of cities or markets are used, the talent's compensation will be increased by an agreed amount.

### Pay or Play

One area to be negotiated heavily between the talent and the client is the pay or play clause.[5] Without such a clause, the client may be free to cancel the planned advertising or endorsement campaign without the obligation to the talent. Without the pay or play clause, the client would, under most circumstances, be free to disregard the entire work product and pay the talent only for work actually completed (e.g., the client may be responsible to the talent only for the time actually spent preparing the endorsement).

Under most pay or play clauses, the talent is guaranteed full payment for the full value of the contract, whether or not the material is actually filmed, shot, used, or broadcast. The inclusion of the pay or play clause usually depends on the talent's bargaining strength and market demand.

## HEALTH AND PENSION BENEFITS

Another aspect of the endorsement agreement deals with union health and pension benefits. Typically, the client is required to contribute to the talent's health and pension benefits. In the event the endorsement is intended to be aired and presented across the full range of media—television, radio, or print—the talent may require the client to allocate health and pension donations to various union funds. For example, if the endorsement takes the form of a music video, payments may go to AFM, to SAG, and to AFTRA.

## WARRANTIES AND PERFORMANCE DUTIES

The performance clause generally reiterates that the talent is ready, willing, and able to perform according to the terms of the contract, which includes complying with the client's instructions as related to the script, director, and all creative decisions. This clause typically reaffirms that the talent will use his or her right of approval, if the talent has won that contested point, on a reasonable basis, that the talent will not withhold permission unreasonably, and that the talent will maintain a willingness to negotiate such a difference of opinion.

The talent may also warrant that he or she will perform services in a professional and artistic manner, to the best of the talent's ability. Moreover, the talent may agree to be subject to the client's approval, direction, and control. The talent may also agree to comply with whatever reasonable instructions, suggestions, and recommendations the client may give in connection with the rendition of the talent's services under this agreement.

If, as part of the endorsement, the talent agrees to use the client's service or product exclusively, the agreement may state that the talent agrees to use the product or service in a prudent and reasonable manner, and that if the talent discontinues using the product, he or she must notify the client in writing within a predetermined length of time. Moreover, the client usually retains the right, at its sole discretion, to cancel and nullify the endorsement agreement, with the pay or play provision ineffective if the talent foregoes obligations under the agreement.

## *FORCE MAJEURE*

The endorsement agreement is generally limited in time. Since this contract is for a specific performance where time may be of the essence, it is generally important to provide a clause that accommodates unforeseen difficulties if events external to the control of the client or talent make the performance impossible or impractical. The *force majeure* clause[6] covers unforseen events that may require the suspension of the performance obligation. This clause avoids a breach of contract and provides a cure for the resumption of the obligation as soon as the event triggering the clause is declared gone.

This clause should include a termination provision that is mutually beneficial and will have the effect of, under certain contracted conditions, avoiding an indefinite suspension of the agreement.

## TERMINATION

The client generally indicates in the contract that it may terminate the agreement at any time after the occurrence of a specified disability and the talent's inability to perform. The talent is likewise granted the right to terminate the agreement if the client's disability results in a suspension of compensation for a specified period of time. Naturally, the amount of time and how such written notice is to be delivered is to be negotiated between the parties prior to the signing of the agreement. The carefully drafted contract should, however, include a clause enabling either the talent or the client to effect a cure if the other executes the right to terminate the agreement. The amount of time required to notify the talent of the cure is negotiable.

## FAILURE TO PERFORM

If either the talent or client does not fulfill obligations and responsibilities under the agreement, the wronged party must, if agreed, bring that failure to the attention of the other in writing. This puts the parties on notice that the defaulting party has a reasonable period of time within which to right the wrong. If after that period the wrong has not been cured, the agreement may be severed without liability, if the wrong is considered a major breach.

## UNENFORCEABILITY

In the event one condition is ruled to be unenforceable by a change in the law, or by an interpretation of the courts, the parties can agree to let the rest of the contract remain in full force and effect. This will insure consistency in the performance of the terms of the contract without having one error void the whole agreement and nullify fruits of labor.

## INCORPORATION BY PERFORMER

In the event the talent incorporates, the client may request the assurance that the new corporation will enter into an identical agreement with the agency, especially if the contract has several options attached to it. The client and talent, by agreeing to this clause, are usually able to continue their working relationship, no matter what business format their organizations take in the future.

## JURISDICTION

The agreement usually clarifies which state within the United States has jurisdiction[7] over disputes. The most convenient and least costly state in the event of litigation is generally the one where both parties maintain their business.

### Arbitration

The parties may agree to settle their disputes by arbitration regulated by the rules of the AAA. Arbitration proceedings are less formal than civil proceedings and the decision of the arbitrator is final and enforceable by the courts. Resolving a dispute through arbitration is often a less lengthy process and thereby less costly than litigation. There is generally more leniency in the arbitration proceeding, and the arbitrators are often peers in the industry rather than judges.[8]

Unlike conventional trial judges whose expertise may not necessarily be in the advertising field, the typical arbitrator is an expert in the contested field. In many instances the arbitrators may not be attorneys, but working members of the field.

Typically, it is agreed in the contract that both parties have the right to select one of the arbitrators. The odd member of the arbitration team is typically chosen by an independent third party.

A perceived advantage of the arbitration process is that the arbitrators do not necessarily have to follow the more stringent legal procedures, including the Federal Rules of Evidence. Arbitration is a more informal process in which there is less emphasis on formality and structure and more on actual dispute settlement. Therefore, evidence that may not be acceptable in a formal court setting could possibly be acceptable in arbitration.

## REMEDIES AND BREACHES

The agreement generally states that no casual or inadvertent failure to comply with the provisions of the endorsement agreement will be deemed a breach by the client. The agreement usually stipulates that the talent recognize and confirm that, in the event of a failure or omission by the client that would constitute a breach of the client's obligations under the terms of the agreement, any damages the talent feels has resulted from this breach are not irreparable or sufficient enough to entitle the talent to injunctive or other equitable relief. This clause may be important for the client, since it may prevent the talent from obtaining a court injunction demanding the client cease and desist from distributing the commercial in the case of a reparable error on the client's part.

The agreement generally stipulates that the talent is entitled to legal remedies (usually damages in money). However, the money damages to which the talent may be entitled may be difficult to measure.

The services rendered by the performer are generally considered to be unique, irreplaceable, and extraordinary. The client may claim that the loss of the talent's services will cause them irreparable injury and damage, a loss that could not be adequately compensated in a legal action. The client typically requires a clause be included in the agreement permitting injunctive or other equitable relief against the talent to prevent a breach.[9] Such injunctive relief ordinarily prevents the talent from working elsewhere, at least in making endorsements.

## NEGATIVE COVENANTS

The client may wish to control the dissemination of news items to the press to coincide with a planned press release. The talent is usually restricted from issuing news stories or publicity relating to the commercial or endorsement unless directed to do so by the agency or until such time as client shall decide to commence the release of publicity.

## TALENT'S INCAPACITY

As a key member of the creative team, the talent must be available for the job as required by the production schedule. A protracted illness or accident may put the entire project in jeopardy. Consequently, the employment contract between the client and the talent should provide for such a contingency.

The agreement generally states that, if by reason of mental or physical disability the talent is incapacitated and prevented from performing the duties agreed to in the contract for more than a negotiated amount of days in a row or a negotiated amount of days over an aggregate period of time, the client has the right to terminate the services of the talent pending written notice to the performer of such termination.

As a concession to the talent, the clause may also stipulate that the talent will be granted an opportunity to cure this disability. This would avoid the need of the client to find a replacement performer.

## BREACH OF CONTRACT AND DEFAULTS

The endorsement agreement usually states that if the talent fails or refuses to comply with any of the material terms or conditions of the contract as a whole, then the client may reserve the right to terminate the contract and replace the talent, providing that advance written notice is provided to the performer. A talent with enough bargaining strength may insist on including a subclause that would allow the talent to cure the breach within a reasonable amount of time.

The term material breach is generally used to soften the potential harshness of the contract. In that case, what may be characterized as a harmless or nonmaterial breach of some technical aspect of the contract should not be used as a vehicle for voiding an agreement that would otherwise be valid.

Depending on the nature of the endorsement and its relative value to the client, the contract may, as an alternative to termination, provide for the temporary suspension of the talent's services without pay. The contract typically states that any incapacity or default of the talent will be deemed to continue until the client receives a written notice that talent is ready, willing, and able to perform the services required under the contract.

Since this provision postpones the responsibility of the talent from carrying out the commitment to the agency or client, this clause may also stipulate that the talent will not render services for any person, firm, or corporation other than the client. The contract may also state that, in the event the talent is suspended without pay and subsequently reinstated, the term of the entire contract may be extended in the same ratio as was the suspension.

If the talent is of sufficient caliber and stature, he or she may insist on the insertion of a clause stating that the talent shall have the right to render services to third parties during any period of suspension based upon a client's disability, subject, however, to the client's right to require the talent to resume services upon prior notice.

# 15

---

# INDEPENDENT PRODUCTION FINANCING

The production of motion pictures by independent producers represents a substantial portion of film production in the United States. Independent productions can keep costs under control by maintaining a firm grip on above-the-line and below-the-line costs. Independents usually keep their overhead low, pay less wages than major studio-financed productions and often negotiate approved low-budget contracts with the various unions.

When the costs of production are controlled, the break-even point is often easier to achieve. Even a picture with minor theatrical appeal that has been filmed as a low- or medium-budget project, may return a profit to the producer through ancillary sales. Licensing the home video, free and pay television, pay-per-view and foreign markets usually return to the producer and distributor a substantial proportion of the revenues of a motion picture.

Independent production companies must generally raise private financing in order to produce motion pictures. Conventional sources include prelicensing of inherent property rights (such as foreign rights or home video rights), bank loans, and credit lines. A more difficult and costlier approach is that of raising funds on the capital markets, either through private placements or public offerings.

In the event the private placement method is used, the producer typically offers the investor a portion of the net profits earned from the exploitation of the film in all media. If, on the other hand, the producer offers corporate underwriting, dividends are usually paid based on the company's overall profitability. In either instance, the production team must abide by the securities laws of federal and state governments.

In order to issue securities to individual investors, a person or business entity must first register those securities with the federal SEC (Securities and Exchange Commission). Registration can be a costly and lengthy process.

An investor interested in a public offering of securities should review, among other considerations, the number of offerees of the securities, the relationship of the offerees to each other and to the offerer, the number of units being offered, and the manner in which they are being offered.

The federal government has allowed exemptions under the law permitting producers to raise monies under the private placement structure for the production of motion pictures, without the requirement of registering with the SEC.

## EXEMPTIONS FROM SEC FILINGS

Section 4(2) of the Securities Act of 1933, as amended, allows for the producer, or issuer of securities, to make a sale of securities to a specific person or persons without the requirement of registration. The SEC will typically permit this exemption to apply in those situations where the investor is considered sufficiently informed to make a sophisticated investment decision. Bank loans, institutions, or investments by a few closely related persons in exchange for securities usually also fall under this exemption. Unsophisticated and uninformed investors are specifically excluded from this exemption.

The exemption may apply under the following circumstances:

- Where there are a limited amount of investors
- Where the investors have full access to all investment information
- Where the investors are sophisticated business people, considered to be familiar with finance
- Where the investors state, in a signed written document, that they can afford the loss of their investment
- Where the amount of money to be raised by the offering is limited
- Where the producer, or issuer, has contacted the investors directly, without public advertising or solicitation

This narrow and limited exemption is normally used for relatively low-budget film productions or as a means of raising the start-up capital necessary to launch a venture.

### Regulation D

The SEC also instituted the exception commonly referred to as Regulation D (Reg D). Certain requirements must be met in order to qualify for this exemption: There can be no open solicitation of the offered private placement, the offered placement cannot extend over a regulated period, and the producer/offerer of securities must supply to the potential investor a full disclosure of information regarding the offering and the venture.

Disclosure documents known as private placement memoranda are presented to the offerees prior to the sale of any securities. The offerer must also be available to supply the investor with answers to all questions regarding the offering.

It is important, and required, that the information in the memorandum be accurate and updated. If a memorandum is amended, the amended circular must be supplied to all potential investors, as well as investors who have already committed to the offering. If the amended memorandum contains information that is prejudicial against investors who have already purchased or contracted to buy such securities, these investors are allowed to withdraw their investments without penalty.

The information supplied in the private placement memorandum should be as honest and blunt as possible, even to the point of discouraging potential investors from making an investment. The memorandum should clearly disclose the negative and risk potential of the agreement. Such disclosures generally serve as notice and a means of protecting the producer/offerer from charges of misrepresentation.

The private placement memorandum generally contains the following information:

- company overview
- financial data
- description of the offering
- detailed information on the company's business
- manner in which the proceeds will be used
- equity capital held by the company and the debt structure, both prior to and following the offering
- pro forma capital structure, before and after the offering
- any legal proceedings instituted or pending against the company or officers or directors of the company
- any film properties, literary properties, copyrights, and real estate owned by the company
- description of the securities registered, including the title, dividends, voting rights, right to liquidate, and warrant terms
- information on the underwriting company, if applicable
- legal and accounting opinions
- financial statements, including accountants' reports, audited balance sheets, and audited statements of income

- relevant contracts, by-laws and other required documentation
- risks, business and tax, of investing in the particular motion picture venture
- background and experience of the principals (officers, management team, directors)
- compensation due the principals and officers of the corporation
- capitalization, including a review of pro forma capitalization using recent balance sheets, any debts and obligations, leases, bank loans, contingent liabilities, and percentage and equity ownership by officers, directors, and majority shareholders
- manner in which the funds raised will be used
- conflicts of interest of any of the principals
- nature of the entertainment industry
- manner in which the motion picture, when produced, can be exploited (theatrical distribution, television, foreign licensing, home video licensing)
- all financial information on the producer/offerer
- additional means of financing for the project or projects
- terms under which the investment will be returned to the investor
- nature of the competition in the entertainment industry
- financial data, including income statements, balance sheets, changes in financial conditions over the recent past, company acquisitions, operating capital budget, and long-range plans
- projections of returns to the investors at estimated revenue levels
- total amount of funds to be raised by the offering and the amount of commissions and fees to be paid to attorneys, accountants, and underwriters
- explanation of the completion bond guarantee, if in place
- all other information necessary for the investors to make an educated evaluation of the risks involved in the investment

Securities acquired under the Reg D offering typically do not have a ready trading market and, thus, the purchasers must be made aware that no likely public demand will be available and that the stocks may have severely restricted covenants against their liquidation.

The regulations allow the producer to offer the securities to accredited (sophisticated) investors as well as nonaccredited investors.

Rule 501 of Reg D defines an accredited or sophisticated investor as a person or business entity that complies with one of the following requirements:

- banks, insurance companies, investment companies, business development companies, or other companies that meet the tests of Reg D;
- director, general partner, or executive officer of the offerer of the securities being sold;

- any person or entity who purchases in excess of $150,000 of the securities offered, as long as the investor's total purchase price does not exceed 20 percent of the investor's net worth (or joint net worth of the investor and the investor's spouse) at the time of the acquisition of the securities;
- if the net worth of the investor, individually or jointly with the investor's spouse, exceeds $1,000,000 at the time of the acquisition of the securities; or
- if the income of the investor over the past two years exceeded $200,000, and if there is a reasonable expectation that the investor's income will exceed $200,000 the current year.

A questionnaire supplied with the memorandum offered the investors determines if they comply with the SEC's accepted definition of accredited investor.

Under Reg D, there are three distinct exemptions from the federal filing requirements of the SEC:

1. *Rule 504: Exemption for limited offers and sales of securities not exceeding $500,000.* The offerer can generally offer and sell a maximum of $500,000 in securities to an unlimited number of investors during the regulated period. While Rule 504 does not specifically require an offering memorandum, one is generally drawn up and presented to the offeree to prevent a possible claim of fraud and misrepresentation by the investors.

2. *Rule 505: Exemption for limited offers and sales of securities not exceeding $5,000,000.* The offerer may solicit the sale of securities during the regulated period to an unlimited number of accredited investors and to a maximum of thirty-five nonaccredited investors. According to the regulations, the offering memorandum must be distributed to nonaccredited investors, though the offering memorandum is usually presented to all investors, making future claims of fraud and misrepresentation more difficult to substantiate.

3. *Rule 506: Exemption for limited offers and sales without any limitation of the dollar amount of securities offered.* The offerer may offer the sale of securities to an unlimited number of accredited investors and to a maximum of thirty-five nonaccredited investors. An offering memorandum must be presented to all nonaccredited investors. But, again, it is advisable to present the offering memorandum to all investors.

### Regulation A

Another means of issuing securities for the purpose of raising motion picture financing, is under the guidelines of Regulation A (Reg A). The offerer of securities under Reg A must abide by the following requirements:

- Reg A is limited to a maximum of a $1,500,000 offering.
- The offering memorandum, a notification statement, and exhibits required by the SEC must be filed at least ten days prior to the sale of any offering.

- The potential investor, in most circumstances, must be given the offering memorandum prior to the offer of sale, or actual sale, of the offered securities.
- There is a regulated time limit after the initial offering memorandum in which the offerer must prepare, file, and use an updated offering memorandum.
- Advertising and general solicitation is permitted under the following restrictions: The SEC filing requirements must be completed, and the offerer must provide its name and title, the amount of securities being offered, the public price of the securities offered to the public, the type of business the offerer is engaged in, and a brief statement of the general character of the offerer's property.

The federal government has imposed these strict regulations in the hopes of protecting the investor from risky ventures. It is important, in order to lessen the possibility of legal liability, to discuss all the filing requirements under Reg D and Reg A with an SEC specialized attorney and accountant, as the rules are stringent and complicated and the penalty for noncompliance is severe and costly. Litigation and civil sentences can arise from failure to abide by SEC requirements.

The above description, and all explanations in this chapter regarding investments, securities, and requirements under federal, state, and local laws are intended only as general description and should not be considered legal advice.

## PUBLIC OFFERINGS

By issuing an initial public offering (IPO), the entertainment company offers for sale to the public, through underwriters and broker/dealers, shares of stock. The company by going public hopes to raise needed investment capital from a broad range of investors. A public company is held accountable to its shareholders for all its actions. The company must operate within the strict guidelines of both SEC and individual state regulatory bodies (the "blue sky" procedure) in the states where such stock is offered for sale.

In order to make the offering more attractive to prospective shareholders, a start-up company may decide to issue units composed of common stock plus warrants entitling the shareholder an option to purchase additional common shares of the stock at a determined price within a designated term of years.

Generally, these warrants are negotiable or openly traded as securities, separate and apart from their underlying stock. If the market price is greater than the option price, the difference between the option price and the market price at the time the warrants are executed by the original unit purchaser represents additional income to the investor.

This type of unit offering must comply with SEC and state regulations regarding reporting and disclosure requirements. It attracts investors who may be more apt to buy into the smaller, start-up company because of the additional shares of stock available at a determined price and the exercise of the warrant.

### Public Disclosure of Accounts

The company must disclose its operations to the public through annual shareholder reports, quarterly financial reports (Form 10-Q), annual financial reports (Form 10-K), audited financial statements, and other pertinent reports.

Going public is generally an expensive procedure that requires ample initial funding and time to organize. Specialized attorneys should be retained to review the corporate by-laws of the company intending to go public, and to assess company financial matters such as loans, lease agreements, outstanding debts, employment contracts, and all other documentation that would be required to satisfy the SEC's disclosure requirements.

An underwriting firm with a good reputation and a broad syndication network should be selected and terms should be negotiated prior to signing the underwriters' agreement.

### Prospectus

An offering prospectus, which supplies information required by the SEC, is prepared and distributed to underwriters and prospective investors. The prospectus is filed with the SEC, which evaluates the registration statement and issues comments. The SEC may require some changes to be made prior to issuing its approval. All such changes must be complied with before shares can be issued and publicly sold.

### DEBT FINANCING

If the entertainment company would rather maintain complete ownership and control of its operations without any obligation to shareholders or limited partners, it may choose to finance its operation through debt financing. The company generally must show a history of revenue, earnings stability and a secure cash flow which is sufficient to cover the interest payments and the principal.

The company securing debt financing typically agrees to repay the loan, with interest, over a fixed period of years. Normally, lenders are in a preferred or guaranteed first position for repayment in the event of bankruptcy or liquidation.

There are several forms capital financing can take:

- long-term loans, which may be at or near prime rate

- short-term or bridge loans, which are structured to carry the company through interim periods and whose interest rates are normally higher than those in the more standard long-term loan
- bank-issued credit line, which will guarantee the availability of a designated sum of capital, based on an agreed upon collateral as well as the designation of management as credit worthy

Due to the highly risky nature of film production, the production company, in borrowing substantial debt financing, may be required, corporately or individually, to pledge or collateralize personal or the company's assets (real estate, distribution contracts, receivables, publishing rights, intellectual property rights, etc.).

Financial institutions, banks, and venture capital firms that normally make loans usually look for stable borrowers with an operational history of professional management, growing share of the market place, monthly cash flow, and the promise of additional or soon to be realized profits and cash flow.

Private companies are not required to report any such loans to the public in general, although individual partners or private shareholders are typically entitled to such information. Publicly traded corporations and limited partnerships, which may also be traded on the major stock exchanges, must make this information available to shareholders in their quarterly and annual financial reports.

## VENTURE CAPITAL

Private investors, investment bankers, or venture capital corporations that are knowledgeable about the entertainment industry may fund a portion of the capital necessary to start up a motion picture production company. For example, in return for risk taking in supporting a project, the venture capitalist generally requires a substantial return on investment in profit participation, sizeable ownership of the company, film credit (typically as executive producer), and veto power.

Often, entertainment companies use venture capital for front money to acquire the rights of a particular property and to develop a motion picture. The venture capitalist usually looks at the project and the personnel attached to it (producer, director, actors, etc.) before making a decision to invest. The most common source of venture capitalists for initial phases of a start-up company is friends, family, and businesspeople with prior experience investing in entertainment projects.

## PRESALE FINANCING

A binding distribution agreement for licensing a motion picture through international distributors to the various territories of the world is another means of financing the production of motion pictures. Such presale arrangements often provide for an advance payment to the producer. In addition, licensing the motion picture to the different media (home video, pay television, free television, pay-per-view, etc.) and the advance payment to the producer in exchange for the granting of the various licenses typically helps defray a portion of the costs of the production.

## BANK LOANS BASED ON GUARANTEED DISTRIBUTION AGREEMENTS

A bank lender may be more apt to issue a loan for the production of the picture if it can secure the loan against the guaranteed distribution of the completed film through the various media. Domestic and international theatrical distribution, free, pay, and cable television, pay-per-view and home video are the usual distribution outlets for a completed picture.

A major motion picture distribution company may guarantee the domestic, foreign, or worldwide distribution of a film based solely on the stars and director involved. It will commit to spending for prints and advertising and to wide scale distribution in an agreed market. With such a strong guarantee from a reputable company, banks may be willing to offer a loan at a favorable interest rate to the production company to cover the costs of production.

## COMPLETION BONDS

Independent producers who rely on independent financing to produce a film must often lessen the risk of investing in such a speculative venture by guaranteeing to their investors (banks, limited partners, venture capitalists, etc.) that the actual filming will be completed within the budget presented. The producer must insure the completion of the film or the return of the investment. Completion bonds are guarantors insuring that, in the event the production exceeds its budget, the guarantor will either supply the financing, and often replace the management, to complete the picture that goes over budget, or repay the investors the money they committed.

### The Premium

The completion bond has become a routine part of any budget, and, often, distributors and investors will not finance the production of a picture unless the producer obtains the bond. The premium for this bond is usually 4 percent to 6 percent of the production budget.

Of course, the premium is not fixed. If a producer requires completion bonds for several motion pictures, or if the producer has a history of completing productions within the allocated budget, the completion bond guarantor will often lower premiums.

The guarantor often returns to the producer a rebate of 1 percent to 2 percent of the amount of the premium, if it had not been called on to step in and take over the production or to supplement the budget. This rebate, and the refusal to cede production responsibility to the completion bond guarantor, is often enticement enough for a producer to seek additional funds from sources other than the bond guarantor in the event the production goes over budget.

## Evaluation of the Project

The completion bond guarantor generally reviews and evaluates the risk of each project presented. The guarantor typically rejects a majority of them as bad risks, and considers several factors to decide on what projects to chose.

The creative personnel are given close scrutiny, especially the director, producer, and leading members of the cast. The guarantor reviews their contracts to determine whether they are restricted to a particular shooting schedule. In addition, the guarantor often considers whether individual cast members have creative control.

The script, budget, and shooting schedule are evaluated. The guarantor must decide if the film can actually be completed on schedule with the cast contracted. Often, the guarantor requires the producer to guarantee in a written statement that the production will be completed as scheduled.

The guarantor generally has the capacity to demand that specific approved crew and business personnel (e.g., set accountant) are used during the production. The guarantor also generally insists on an insurance policy for all staff and management.

## Limiting the Guarantor's Responsibility

While the guarantor insures much of the production, there are many aspects of the production over which the guarantor usually does not assume responsibility. The guarantor generally exempts itself paying such costs as for:

- reshooting a scene after the production staff has moved locations
- damages to film negatives during shipping
- producer's bankruptcy
- unpaid insurance claims because of inaction by the insurer

- negligence of the producer
- replacing the cast members
- costs in excess of budget, including trailers and changes in the screenplay

## Supervising the Finances

The completion bond guarantor generally insists on keeping an eye on the finances of the production by reviewing all production reports, countersigning production checks, approving the scheduled financing, and requesting the right of approval for changes in the budget and shooting schedule. The guarantor also provides a representative of the bonding company on the set to oversee finances and production flow.

## Duties of the Guarantor

In the event the cost of production exceeds the approved budget, the guarantor may choose to take control of the production from the producer. This step is deemed a necessary action in order to protect the vested interests of the bond guarantor. The guarantor then typically has the right to hire a new producer, director, and, if necessary, even cast members. He is also able to rearrange the shooting schedule and sign, singularly, all production checks. The completion bond guarantor, under these circumstances becomes, in effect, the production company and completes the production of the motion picture as inexpensively and efficiently as possible.

# 16

## The Attorney and the Accountant

The writer, actor, director, or producer, or any member of the entertainment industry who stands alone, is vulnerable to the entangling, often confusing, nuances of the entertainment business deal. The film industry in particular is a business that requires a special knowledge of the customs, practices, and definitions unique to it. A misinterpretation of a contract clause, or a lack of understanding of a royalty term in a compensation clause, for example, can result in a substantial loss of income for the talent. The entertainment attorney and accountant play special roles in the entertainment industry and are uniquely vital to the success of the client.

### THE ATTORNEY

The entertainment attorney is a corporate attorney – a specialist who understands the intricacies of a movie deal, from the accepted pay for a first-time writer, to the gross participation employment agreement acceptable to a proven box office actor. The attorney's clients, whether they be writers, actors, directors, or producers, require personal and corporate service on a continual basis.

The services the entertainment attorney offers is broad based and covers the entire gamut of the legal profession. The client usually enters a relationship with an attorney after an initial consultation and the signing of a retainer agreement. The agreement usually clarifies the services the attorney will perform and the hourly fees to be charged, including the initial retainer payment, which is a fee paid in advance for legal services to be rendered.

First and foremost, the entertainment attorney understands the movie business. The contracts, as they are drafted by the personal or corporate attorney, must reflect an in-depth knowledge and familiarization with the terms specific to this field. Such terms, unique to the entertainment industry, hold a significant meaning within the film or music business but may go unheeded by an attorney who has not had the experience or training in entertainment law situations.

A writer, for example, who performs unique service as an employee of a production company, may at times not remain the owner of the work he or she has written. Ownership may depend on the contractual relationship between writer and producer. In another situation, the writer may not be aware that, by writing about an individual resembling a person who had recently died, the writer may be infringing on the privacy rights of the deceased. The attorney should be able to clarify those and many other twists unique to the entertainment industry.

The entertainment lawyer, along with the manager and agent, helps negotiate an agreement for the talent that will be equitable and just, considering the talent's position within the pecking order of the entertainment field.[1] The attorney generally draws up and revises the contract as negotiations progress.

The legal adviser should review contracts submitted to the client, judging them for fairness and reasonableness within the industry and often suggesting changes or clarification.

Moreover, a talented entertainment lawyer constantly keeps the interests of the client paramount. The attorney has pledged to counsel clients to the best of his or her ability. The attorney must recall that obligations as an attorney do not disappear as the attorney broadens his or her practice to include business transactions, such as production, management, or agency representation.[2]

In the event of a dispute between a client and a third party, the attorney can negotiate a settlement. The attorney should forcefully state the client's case and request fulfillment of the obligations, whether they be payment of monies owed or the performance of services. Persuasive argument showing that justice should be served usually initiates a resolution without arbitration or litigation.

If settlement discussions fail to resolve a dispute, the matter can be decided by arbitration or litigation. The attorney's knowledge of contracts, the client's credits, as well as the customs and practices of the entertainment industry are generally helpful if arbitration is requested by either party. Arbitration is binding dispute settlement officiated by members of the AAA, peers within the entertainment industry who hear both sides of a dispute and judge where equity lies. The rules of the arbitrator are typically more lenient than those of the court, yet the findings of the arbitrators are binding and will be upheld by a court of law.

Litigation, the act of deciding a matter in a court of law, is another service the attorney performs for the client by pleading the client's case to a jury or to a judge. Litigation is a complex matter requiring detailed knowledge of the technicalities that allow the court systems to move forward systematically.

Litigation, as a form of dispute resolution, also requires an accumulation of facts and issues to be used by the attorney to prove the rightness or legitimacy of the client's claim. In litigation matters it is especially important that the attorney be familiar with the custom and practice of the entertainment industry, since there are precedents unique to the industry. The positioning of credits and the distribution of net profit income are only two examples of business matters that separate entertainment practice from other forms of corporate law.

Using interviews with the client and information learned from discovery and interrogatory proceedings with the opposing party, the case is prepared for the courts, to try the issues and decide the outcome.

In other matters, the attorney is often called upon to give counsel and perform legal services when the client accumulates real estate. The attorney performs the closings of coops, condominiums, or single-family home for the client. The attorney aids in the legal requirement faced when the client accumulates real property for investment and proceeds to sell those properties for profit.

The attorney is generally by the client's side in the event of marital problems, helps the client reach an equitable divorce settlement, and answers questions related to tax matters. Much of the time, the attorney helps the client incorporate or form a partnership.

The entertainment attorney is an integral partner in the growth, success, and stability of an entertainer's career, and will perform any service that benefits and is required by the client.

## THE ACCOUNTANT

The CPA performs a service that is a necessity in the entertainment industry. The CPA understands the intricate aspects of the Internal Revenue Service code that are unique to the entertainment industry, and will advise the actor, director, producer, or writer whether certain income is deemed earned income or a deductible business expense. For example, can clothes be deducted as a business expense if those clothes were purchased for the express use by a model in a little-publicized marketing campaign? Are phone calls made from pay phones legitimate expenses for actors calling their answering service? Can a writer's rental apartment be considered a place of business if that is the location he or she uses to write screenplays? Does the situation change if those screenplays are not sold? What is the definition, from a tax point of view, of an actor or writer?

With the passage of tax reform many new questions have arisen concerning the precise meanings and interpretations of the new law and the regulations derived from the reformed code. It will be the role of the CPA and tax lawyer (often, the same party) to not only keep informed of the changes but also their ramifications on the movie industry, and to communicate such information to their clients.

Questions relating to a client's savings are always of paramount importance. The CPA will, within the bounds of permissible deductions, help the client retain as much as allowable.

As the client becomes more successful, the accountant's job extends beyond a yearly tax filing. Often the CPA keeps clients' ledgers and records; records assets, liabilities, and earnings of the client; and calculates the net profits earned by the client.

If the client intends to initiate a private placement or limited partnership or solicit investments, an outside auditor/CPA usually performs an audit of the company, ascertaining profits or losses, making projections of future income, and, in general, stating an opinion on the offering.

Likewise, if the client intends to invest in other companies or ventures, or expresses interest in the feasibility of acquiring another company, the CPA is generally called upon to evaluate the other firm's business records and accounting books and provide an opinion regarding the financial health of the other company.

Most contracts entered into by talent allow for review of the other party's books and records by a CPA (if the agreements are based on net or gross profit, such review should be a requirement). The CPA reviews those books in order to determine if the client is due any monies as per the contractual agreement.

The entertainment industry over a period of years has developed its own accounting terms, which may not be familiar to the actor or to an accountant inexperienced in the field. In the entertainment industry, clues may be hard to find for an unsophisticated eye. An accountant is an entertainer's financial advisor and helps protect the monies he or she has worked so hard to earn.

An entertainment CPA may be able to trace improper allocation costs that a CPA who is not an entertainment specialist would miss (e.g., a producer improperly using the income of the client's film to offset the overhead of several other motion pictures produced by the same company). The accountant must know what clues to look for when reviewing the books and records of an entertainment company.

# Appendix A

## Copyright Registration Forms

# Filling Out Application Form VA

*Detach and read these instructions before completing this form. Make sure all applicable spaces have been filled in before you return this form.*

## BASIC INFORMATION

**When to Use This Form:** Use Form VA for copyright registration of published or unpublished works of the visual arts. This category consists of "pictorial, graphic, or sculptural works," including two-dimensional and three-dimensional works of fine, graphic, and applied art, photographs, prints and art reproductions, maps, globes, charts, technical drawings, diagrams, and models.

**What Does Copyright Protect?** Copyright in a work of the visual arts protects those pictorial, graphic, or sculptural elements that, either alone or in combination, represent an "original work of authorship." The statute declares: "In no case does copyright protection for an original work of authorship extend to any idea, procedure, process, system, method of operation, concept, principle, or discovery, regardless of the form in which it is described, explained, illustrated, or embodied in such work."

**Works of Artistic Craftsmanship and Designs:** "Works of artistic craftsmanship" are registrable on Form VA, but the statute makes clear that protection extends to "their form" and not to "their mechanical or utilitarian aspects." The "design of a useful article" is considered copyrightable "only if, and only to the extent that, such design incorporates pictorial, graphic, or sculptural features that can be identified separately from, and are capable of existing independently of, the utilitarian aspects of the article."

**Labels and Advertisements:** Works prepared for use in connection with the sale or advertisement of goods and services are registrable if they contain "original work of authorship." Use Form VA if the copyrightable material in the work you are registering is mainly pictorial or graphic; use Form TX if it consists mainly of text. NOTE: Words and short phrases such as names, titles, and slogans cannot be protected by copyright, and the same is true of standard symbols, emblems, and other commonly used graphic designs that are in the public domain. When used commercially, material of that sort can sometimes be protected under state laws of unfair competition or under the Federal trademark laws. For information about trademark registration, write to the Commissioner of Patents and Trademarks, Washington, D.C. 20231.

**Deposit to Accompany Application:** An application for copyright registration must be accompanied by a deposit consisting of copies representing the en-

tire work for which registration is to be made.

**Unpublished Work:** Deposit one complete copy.

**Published Work:** Deposit two complete copies of the best edition.

**Work First Published Outside the United States:** Deposit one complete copy of the first foreign edition.

**Contribution to a Collective Work:** Deposit one complete copy of the best edition of the collective work.

**The Copyright Notice:** For published works, the law provides that a copyright notice in a specified form "shall be placed on all publicly distributed copies from which the work can be visually perceived." Use of the copyright notice is the responsibility of the copyright owner and does not require advance permission from the Copyright Office. The required form of the notice for copies generally consists of three elements: (1) the symbol "©", or the word "Copyright," or the abbreviation "Copr."; (2) the year of first publication; and (3) the name of the owner of copyright. For example: © 1981 Constance Porter." The notice is to be affixed to the copies "in such manner and location as to give reasonable notice of the claim of copyright."

For further information about copyright registration, notice, or special questions relating to copyright problems, write:

Information and Publications Section, LM-455
Copyright Office, Library of Congress, Washington, D.C. 20559

# LINE-BY-LINE INSTRUCTIONS

## 1 SPACE 1: Title

**Title of This Work:** Every work submitted for copyright registration must be given a title to identify that particular work. If the copies of the work bear a title (or an identifying phrase that could serve as a title), transcribe that wording *completely* and *exactly* on the application. Indexing of the registration and future identification of the work will depend on the information you give here.

**Previous or Alternative Titles:** Complete this space if there are any additional titles for the work under which someone searching for the registration might be likely to look, or under which a document pertaining to the work might be recorded.

**Publication as a Contribution:** If the work being registered is a contribution to a perodical, serial, or collection, give the title of the contribution in the "Title of This Work" space. Then, in the line headed "Publication as a Contribution," give information about the collective work in which the contribution appeared.

**Nature of This Work:** Briefly describe the general nature or character of the pictorial, graphic, or sculptural work being registered for copyright. Examples: "Oil Painting"; "Charcoal Drawing"; "Etching"; "Sculpture"; "Map"; "Photograph"; "Scale Model"; "Lithographic Print"; "Jewelry Design"; "Fabric Design."

## 2 SPACE 2: Author(s)

**General Instructions:** After reading these instructions, decide who are the "authors" of this work for copyright purposes. Then, unless the work is a "collective work," give the requested information about every "author" who contributed any appreciable amount of copyrightable matter to this version of the work. If you need further space, request additional Continuation Sheets. In the case of a collective work, such as a catalog of paintings or collection of cartoons by various authors, give information about the author of the collective work as a whole.

**Name of Author:** The fullest form of the author's name should be given. Unless the work was "made for hire," the individual who actually created the work is its "author." In the case of a work made for hire, the statute provides that "the employer or other person for whom the work was prepared is considered the author."

**What is a "Work Made for Hire"?** A "work made for hire" is defined as: (1) "a work prepared by an employee within the scope of his or her employment"; or (2) "a work specially ordered or commissioned for use as a contribution to a collective work, as a part of a motion picture or other audiovisual work, as a translation, as a supplementary work, as a compilation, as an instructional text, as a test, as answer material for a test, or as an atlas, if the parties expressly agree in a written instrument signed by them that the work shall be considered a work made for hire." If you have checked "Yes" to indicate that the work was "made for hire," you must give the full legal name of the employer (or other person for whom the work was prepared). You may also include the name of the employee along with the name of the employer (for example: "Elster Publishing Co., employer for hire of John Ferguson").

**"Anonymous" or "Pseudonymous" Work:** An author's contribution to a work is "anonymous" if that author is not identified on the copies or phonorecords of the work. An author's contribution to a work is "pseudonymous" if that author is identified on the copies or phonorecords under a fictitious name. If the work is "anonymous" you may: (1) leave the line blank; or (2) state "anonymous" on the line; or (3) reveal the author's identity. If the work is "pseudonymous" you may: (1) leave the line blank; or (2) give the pseudonym and identify it as such (for example: "Huntley Haverstock, pseudonym"); or (3) reveal the author's name, making clear which is the real name and which is the pseudonym (for example: "Henry Leek, whose pseudonym is Priam Farrel"). However, the citizenship or domicile of the author **must** be given in all cases.

**Dates of Birth and Death:** If the author is dead, the statute requires that the year of death be included in the application unless the work is anonymous or pseudonymous. The author's birth date is optional, but is useful as a form of identification. Leave this space blank if the author's contribution was a "work made for hire."

tive work as a whole.

**Author's Nationality or Domicile:** Give the country of which the author is a citizen, or the country in which the author is domiciled. Nationality or domicile **must** be given in all cases.

**Nature of Authorship:** Give a brief general statement of the nature of this particular author's contribution to the work. Examples: "Painting"; "Photograph"; "Silk Screen Reproduction"; "Co-author of Cartographic Material"; "Technical Drawing"; "Text and Artwork."

# 3 SPACE 3: Creation and Publication

**General Instructions:** Do not confuse "creation" with "publication." Every application for copyright registration must state "the year in which creation of the work was completed." Give the date and nation of first publication only if the work has been published.

**Creation:** Under the statute, a work is "created" when it is fixed in a copy or phonorecord for the first time. Where a work has been prepared over a period of time, the part of the work existing in fixed form on a particular date constitutes the created work on that date. The date you give here should be the year in which the author completed the particular version for which registration is now being sought, even if other versions exist or if further changes or additions are planned.

**Publication:** The statute defines "publication" as "the distribution of copies or phonorecords of a work to the public by sale or other transfer of ownership, or by rental, lease, or lending"; a work is also "published" if there has been an "offering to distribute copies or phonorecords to a group of persons for purposes of further distribution, public performance, or public display." Give the full date (month, day, year) when, and the country where, publication first occurred. If first publication took place simultaneously in the United States and other countries, it is sufficient to state "U.S.A."

# 4 SPACE 4: Claimant(s)

**Name(s) and Address(es) of Copyright Claimant(s):** Give the name(s) and address(es) of the copyright claimant(s) in this work even if the claimant is the same as the author. Copyright in a work belongs initially to the author of the work (including, in the case of a work made for hire, the employer or other person for whom the work was prepared). The copyright claimant is either the author of the work or a person or organization to whom the copyright initially belonging to the author has been transferred.

one other than the author is identified as copyright claimant in the earlier registration, and the author is now seeking registration in his or her own name. If either of these two exceptions apply, check the appropriate box and give the earlier registration number and date. Otherwise, do not submit Form VA; instead, write the Copyright Office for information about supplementary registration or recordation of transfers of copyright ownership.

**Changed Version:** If the work has been changed, and you are now seeking registration to cover the additions or revisions, check the last box in space 5, give the earlier registration number and date, and complete both parts of space 6 in accordance with the instructions below.

**Previous Registration Number and Date:** If more than one previous registration has been made for the work, give the number and date of the latest registration.

# 6 SPACE 6: Derivative Work or Compilation

**General Instructions:** Complete space 6 if this work is a "changed version," "compilation," or "derivative work," and if it incorporates one or more earlier works that have already been published or registered for copyright, or that have fallen into the public domain. A "compilation" is defined as "a work formed by the collection and assembling of preexisting materials or of data that are selected, coordinated, or arranged in such a way that the resulting work as a whole constitutes an original work of authorship." A "derivative work" is "a work based on one or more preexisting works." Examples of derivative works include reproductions of works of art, sculptures based on drawings, lithographs based on paintings, maps based on previously published sources, or "any other form in which a work may be recast, transformed, or adapted." Derivative works also include works "consisting of editorial revisions, annotations, or other modifications" if these changes, as a whole, represent an original work of authorship.

**Preexisting Material (space 6a):** Complete this space **and** space 6b for derivative works. In this space identify the preexisting work that has been recast, transformed, or adapted. Examples of preexisting material might be "Grunewald Altarpiece"; or "19th century quilt design." Do not complete this space for compilations.

**Material Added to This Work (space 6b):** Give a brief, general statement of the **additional** new material covered by the copyright claim for which registration is sought. In the case of a derivative work, identify this new material. Examples: "Adaptation of design and additional artistic work"; "Reproduction of painting by photolithography"; "Additional cartographic material"; "Com-

Transfer: The statute provides that, if the copyright claimant is not the author, the application for registration must contain "a brief statement of how the claimant obtained ownership of the copyright." If any copyright claimant named in space 4 is not an author named in space 2, give a brief, general statement summarizing the means by which that claimant obtained ownership of the copyright. Examples: "By written contract"; "Transfer of all rights by author"; "Assignment"; "By will." Do not attach transfer documents or other attachments or riders.

# 5 SPACE 5: Previous Registration

General Instructions: The questions in space 5 are intended to find out whether an earlier registration has been made for this work and, if so, whether there is any basis for a new registration. As a rule, only one basic copyright registration can be made for the same version of a particular work.

Same Version: If this version is substantially the same as the work covered by a previous registration, a second registration is not generally possible unless: (1) the work has been registered in unpublished form and a second registration is now being sought to cover this first published edition; or (2) some-

pilation of photographs." If the work is a compilation, give a brief, general statement describing both the material that has been compiled and the compilation itself. Example: "Compilation of 19th Century Political Cartoons."

# 7,8,9 SPACE 7, 8, 9: Fee, Correspondence, Certification, Return Address

Deposit Account: If you maintain a Deposit Account in the Copyright Office, identify it in space 7. Otherwise leave the space blank and send the fee of $10 with your application and deposit.

Correspondence (space 7): This space should contain the name, address, area code, and telephone number of the person to be consulted if correspondence about this application becomes necessary.

Certification (space 8): The application cannot be accepted unless it bears the date and the handwritten signature of the author or other copyright claimant, or of the owner of exclusive right(s), or of the duly authorized agent of the author, claimant, or owner of exclusive right(s).

Address for Return of Certificate (space 9): The address box must be completed legibly since the certificate will be returned in a window envelope.

# MORE INFORMATION

## Form of Deposit for Works of the Visual Arts

Exceptions to General Deposit Requirements: As explained on the reverse side of this page, the statutory deposit requirements (generally one copy for unpublished works and two copies for published works) will vary for particular kinds of works of the visual arts. The copyright law authorizes the Register of Copyrights to issue regulations specifying "the administrative classes into which works are to be placed for purposes of deposit and registration, and the nature of the copies or phonorecords to be deposited in the various classes specified." For particular classes, the regulations may require or permit "the deposit of identifying material instead of copies or phonorecords," or "the deposit of only one copy or phonorecord where two would normally be required."

What Should You Deposit? The detailed requirements with respect to the kind of deposit to accompany an application on Form VA are contained in the Copyright Office Regulations. The following does not cover all of the deposit requirements, but is intended to give you some general guidance.

For an Unpublished Work, the material deposited should represent the entire copyrightable content of the work for which registration is being sought.

For a Published Work, the material deposited should generally consist of two complete copies of the best edition. Exceptions: (1) For certain types of works, one complete copy may be deposited instead of two. These include greeting cards, postcards, stationery, labels, advertisements, scientific drawings, and globes; (2) For most three-dimensional sculptural works, and for certain two-dimensional works, the Copyright Office Regulations require deposit of identifying material (photographs or drawings in a specified form) rather than copies; and (3) Under certain circumstances, for works published in five copies or less or in limited, numbered editions, the deposit may consist of one copy or of identifying reproductions.

# FORM VA
UNITED STATES COPYRIGHT OFFICE

REGISTRATION NUMBER

VA     VAU

EFFECTIVE DATE OF REGISTRATION

Month    Day    Year

**DO NOT WRITE ABOVE THIS LINE. IF YOU NEED MORE SPACE, USE A SEPARATE CONTINUATION SHEET.**

**1**   **TITLE OF THIS WORK ▼**

NATURE OF THIS WORK ▼ See instructions

**PREVIOUS OR ALTERNATIVE TITLES ▼**

**PUBLICATION AS A CONTRIBUTION** If this work was published as a contribution to a periodical, serial, or collection, give information about the collective work in which the contribution appeared.    **Title of Collective Work ▼**

If published in a periodical or serial give: **Volume ▼**    **Number ▼**    **Issue Date ▼**    **On Pages ▼**

**2**   **NAME OF AUTHOR ▼**

a.

Was this contribution to the work a "work made for hire"?
☐ Yes
☐ No

**AUTHOR'S NATIONALITY OR DOMICILE**
Name of Country
OR { Citizen of ▶
Domiciled in ▶

**DATES OF BIRTH AND DEATH**
Year Born ▼    Year Died ▼

**WAS THIS AUTHOR'S CONTRIBUTION TO THE WORK**
Anonymous?    ☐ Yes ☐ No
Pseudonymous?    ☐ Yes ☐ No

If the answer to either of these questions is "Yes," see detailed instructions.

**NATURE OF AUTHORSHIP** Briefly describe nature of the material created by this author in which copyright is claimed. ▶

**NOTE**

Under the law, the "author" of a "work made for hire" is generally the employer, not the employee (see instructions). For any part of this work that was "made for hire" check "Yes" in the space provided, give the employer (or other person for whom the work was prepared) as "Author" of that part, and leave the space for dates of birth and death blank.

See instructions before completing this space.

**2**

**NAME OF AUTHOR ▼**

b

Was this contribution to the work a "work made for hire"?
☐ Yes
☐ No

**AUTHOR'S NATIONALITY OR DOMICILE**
Name of country
OR { Citizen of ▶ _____
Domiciled in ▶ _____

**DATES OF BIRTH AND DEATH**
Year Born ▼        Year Died ▼

**WAS THIS AUTHOR'S CONTRIBUTION TO THE WORK**
Anonymous?     ☐ Yes ☐ No
Pseudonymous?  ☐ Yes ☐ No
If the answer to either of these questions is "Yes," see detailed instructions.

**NATURE OF AUTHORSHIP** Briefly describe nature of the material created by this author in which copyright is claimed. ▼

**NAME OF AUTHOR ▼**

c

Was this contribution to the work a "work made for hire"?
☐ Yes
☐ No

**AUTHOR'S NATIONALITY OR DOMICILE**
Name of Country
OR { Citizen of ▶ _____
Domiciled in ▶ _____

**DATES OF BIRTH AND DEATH**
Year Born ▼        Year Died ▼

**WAS THIS AUTHOR'S CONTRIBUTION TO THE WORK**
Anonymous?     ☐ Yes ☐ No
Pseudonymous?  ☐ Yes ☐ No
If the answer to either of these questions is "Yes," see detailed instructions.

**NATURE OF AUTHORSHIP** Briefly describe nature of the material created by this author in which copyright is claimed. ▼

**3**

**YEAR IN WHICH CREATION OF THIS WORK WAS COMPLETED** This information must be given in all cases.
◀ Year

**DATE AND NATION OF FIRST PUBLICATION OF THIS PARTICULAR WORK**
Complete this information  Month ▶ _____ Day ▶ _____ Year ▶ _____
ONLY if this work
has been published.      ◀ Nation

**4**

**COPYRIGHT CLAIMANT(S)** Name and address must be given even if the claimant is the same as the author given in space 2.▼

**TRANSFER** If the claimant(s) named here in space 4 are different from the author(s) named in space 2, give a brief statement of how the claimant(s) obtained ownership of the copyright.▼

**MORE ON BACK ▶** • Complete all applicable spaces (numbers 5-9) on the reverse side of this page.
• See detailed instructions.                • Sign the form at line 8.

DO NOT WRITE HERE
Page 1 of _____ pages

EXAMINED BY _____

CHECKED BY _____

☐ CORRESPONDENCE
Yes

☐ DEPOSIT ACCOUNT
FUNDS USED

FOR
COPYRIGHT
OFFICE
USE
ONLY

FORM VA

**DO NOT WRITE ABOVE THIS LINE. IF YOU NEED MORE SPACE, USE A SEPARATE CONTINUATION SHEET.**

**PREVIOUS REGISTRATION** Has registration for this work, or for an earlier version of this work, already been made in the Copyright Office?

☐ **Yes** ☐ **No** If your answer is "Yes," why is another registration being sought? (Check appropriate box) ▼

☐ This is the first published edition of a work previously registered in unpublished form.

☐ This is the first application submitted by this author as copyright claimant.

☐ This is a changed version of the work, as shown by space 6 on this application.

If your answer is "Yes," give: **Previous Registration Number** ▼          **Year of Registration** ▼

**5**

**DERIVATIVE WORK OR COMPILATION**   Complete both space 6a & 6b for a derivative work; complete only 6b for a compilation.

a.  **Preexisting Material**  Identify any preexisting work or works that this work is based on or incorporates. ▼

_____

b.  **Material Added to This Work**   Give a brief, general statement of the material that has been added to this work and in which copyright is claimed. ▼

_____

See instructions
before completing
this space.

**6**

**DEPOSIT ACCOUNT**   If the registration fee is to be charged to a Deposit Account established in the Copyright Office, give name and number of Account.

**Name** ▼                          **Account Number** ▼

**7**

**CORRESPONDENCE** Give name and address to which correspondence about this application should be sent. Name/Address/Apt/City/State/Zip ▼

Area Code & Telephone Number ►

Be sure to
give your
daytime phone
◄ number

**8**

**CERTIFICATION\*** I, the undersigned, hereby certify that I am the

Check only one ▼

☐ author
☐ other copyright claimant
☐ owner of exclusive right(s)
☐ authorized agent of _____
Name of author or other copyright claimant, or owner of exclusive right(s) ▲

of the work identified in this application and that the statements made
by me in this application are correct to the best of my knowledge.

Typed or printed name and date ▼ If this is a published work, this date must be the same as or later than the date of publication given in space 3.

_____ date ►  _____

👉 Handwritten signature (X) ▼

**MAIL CERTIFI-CATE TO**

**Certificate will be mailed in window envelope**

Name ▼

Number/Street/Apartment Number ▼

City/State/ZIP ▼

**9**

**Have you:**
• Completed all necessary spaces?
• Signed your application in space 8?
• Enclosed check or money order for $10 payable to *Register of Copyrights*?
• Enclosed your deposit material with the application and fee?
**MAIL TO:** Register of Copyrights, Library of Congress, Washington, D.C. 20559.

\* 17 U.S.C. § 506(e): Any person who knowingly makes a false representation of a material fact in the application for copyright registration provided for by section 409, or in any written statement filed in connection with the application, shall be fined not more than $2,500.

☆U.S. GOVERNMENT PRINTING OFFICE: 1988—241-428/80,010

November 1988—25,000

195

# Filling Out Application Form PA

*Detach and read these instructions before completing this form. Make sure all applicable spaces have been filled in before you return this form.*

## BASIC INFORMATION

**When to Use This Form:** Use Form PA for registration of published or unpublished works of the performing arts. This class includes works prepared for the purpose of being "performed" directly before an audience or indirectly "by means of any device or process." Works of the performing arts include: (1) musical works, including any accompanying words; (2) dramatic works, including any accompanying music; (3) pantomimes and choreographic works; and (4) motion pictures and other audiovisual works.

**Deposit to Accompany Application:** An application for copyright registration must be accompanied by a deposit consisting of copies or phonorecords representing the entire work for which registration is to be made. The following are the general deposit requirements as set forth in the statute:

**Unpublished Work:** Deposit one complete copy (or phonorecord).

**Published Work:** Deposit two complete copies (or phonorecords) of the best edition.

**Work First Published Outside the United States:** Deposit one complete copy (or phonorecord) of the first foreign edition.

**Contribution to a Collective Work:** Deposit one complete copy (or phonorecord) of the best edition of the collective work.

**Motion Pictures:** Deposit *both* of the following: (1) a separate written description of the contents of the motion picture; and (2) for a published work, one complete copy of the best edition of the motion picture; or, for an unpublished work, one complete copy of the motion picture or identifying material. Identifying material may be either an audiorecording of the entire soundtrack or one frame enlargement or similar visual print from each 10-minute segment.

**The Copyright Notice:** For published works, the law provides that a copyright notice in a specified form "shall be placed on all publicly distributed copies from which the work can be visually perceived." Use of the copyright notice is the responsibility of the copyright owner and does not require advance permission from the Copyright Office. The required form of the notice for copies generally consists of three elements: (1) the symbol "©", or the word "Copyright," or the abbreviation "Copr."; (2) the year of first publication; and (3) the name of the owner of copyright. For example: "© 1981 Constance Porter." The notice is to be affixed to the copies "in such manner and location as to give reasonable notice of the claim of copyright."

For further information about copyright registration, notice, or special questions relating to copyright problems, write:

Information and Publications Section, LM-455
Copyright Office
Library of Congress
Washington, D.C. 20559

# LINE-BY-LINE INSTRUCTIONS

## 1 SPACE 1: Title

**Title of This Work:** Every work submitted for copyright registration must be given a title to identify that particular work. If the copies or phonorecords of the work bear a title (or an identifying phrase that could serve as a title), transcribe that wording *completely* and *exactly* on the application. Indexing of the registration and future identification of the work will depend on the information you give here. If the work you are registering is an entire "collective work" (such as a collection of plays or songs), give the overall title of the collection. If you are registering one or more individual contributions to a collective work, give the title of each contribution, followed by the title of the collective work, preceded by the title of the collective work, followed by the title of the collection. Example: *"A Song for Elinda" in Old and New Ballads for Old and New People."*

**Previous or Alternative Titles:** Complete this space if there are any additional titles for the work under which someone searching for the registration might be likely to look, or under which a document pertaining to the work might be recorded.

**Nature of This Work:** Briefly describe the general nature or character of the work being registered for copyright. Examples: "Music"; "Song Lyrics"; "Words and Music"; "Drama"; "Musical Play"; "Choreography"; "Pantomime"; "Motion Picture"; "Audiovisual Work."

## 2 SPACE 2: Author(s)

**General Instructions:** After reading these instructions, decide who are the "authors" of this work for copyright purposes. Then, unless the work is a "collective work," give the requested information about every "author" who contributed any appreciable amount of copyrightable matter to this version of the work. If you need further space, request additional Continuation Sheets. In the case of a collective work, such as a songbook or a collection of plays, give information about the author of the collective work as a whole.

**Name of Author:** The fullest form of the author's name should be given. Unless the work was "made for hire," the individual who actually created the work is its "author." In the case of a work made for hire, the statute provides

---

that "the employer or other person for whom the work was prepared is considered the author."

**What is a "Work Made for Hire"?** A "work made for hire" is defined as: (1) "a work prepared by an employee within the scope of his or her employment"; or (2) "a work specially ordered or commissioned for use as a contribution to a collective work, as a part of a motion picture or other audiovisual work, as a translation, as a supplementary work, as a compilation, as an instructional text, as a test, as answer material for a test, or as an atlas, if the parties expressly agree in a written instrument signed by them that the work shall be considered a work made for hire." If you have checked "Yes" to indicate that the work was "made for hire," you must give the full legal name of the employer (or other person for whom the work was prepared). You may also include the name of the employee along with the name of the employer (for example: "Elster Music Co., employer for hire of John Ferguson").

**"Anonymous" or "Pseudonymous" Work:** An author's contribution to a work is "anonymous" if that author is not identified on the copies or phonorecords of the work. An author's contribution to a work is "pseudonymous" if that author is identified on the copies or phonorecords under a fictitious name. If the work is "anonymous" you may: (1) leave the line blank; or (2) state "anonymous" on the line; or (3) reveal the author's identity. If the work is "pseudonymous" you may: (1) leave the line blank; or (2) give the pseudonym and identify it as such (for example: "Huntley Haverstock, pseudonym"); or (3) reveal the author's name, making clear which is the real name and which is the pseudonym (for example: "Judith Barton, whose pseudonym is Madeline Elster"). However, the citizenship or domicile of the author **must** be given in all cases.

**Dates of Birth and Death:** If the author is dead, the statute requires that the year of death be included in the application unless the work is anonymous or pseudonymous. The author's birth date is optional, but is useful as a form of identification. Leave this space blank if the author's contribution was a "work made for hire."

**Author's Nationality or Domicile:** Give the country of which the author is a citizen, or the country in which the author is domiciled. Nationality or domicile **must** be given in all cases.

**Nature of Authorship:** Give a brief general statement of the nature of this particular author's contribution to the work. Examples: "Words"; "Co-Author of Music"; "Words and Music"; "Arrangement"; "Co-Author of Book and Lyrics"; "Dramatization"; "Screen Play"; "Compilation and English Translation"; "Editorial Revisions."

earlier registration number and date. Otherwise, do not submit Form PA; instead, write the Copyright Office for information about supplementary registration or recordation of transfers of copyright ownership.

**Changed Version:** If the work has been changed, and you are now seeking registration to cover the additions or revisions, check the last box in space 5, give the earlier registration number and date, and complete both parts of space 6 in accordance with the instructions below.

**Previous Registration Number and Date:** If more than one previous registration has been made for the work, give the number and date of the latest registration.

# 3 SPACE 3: Creation and Publication

**General Instructions:** Do not confuse "creation" with "publication." Every application for copyright registration must state "the year in which creation of the work was completed." Give the date and nation of first publication only if the work has been published.

**Creation:** Under the statute, a work is "created" when it is fixed in a copy or phonorecord for the first time. Where a work has been prepared over a period of time, the part of the work existing in fixed form on a particular date constitutes the created work on that date. The date you give here should be the year in which the author completed the particular version for which registration is now being sought, even if other versions exist or if further changes or additions are planned.

**Publication:** The statute defines "publication" as "the distribution of copies or phonorecords of a work to the public by sale or other transfer of ownership, or by rental, lease, or lending"; a work is also "published" if there has been an "offering to distribute copies or phonorecords to a group of persons for purposes of further distribution, public performance, or public display." Give the full date (month, day, year) when, and the country where, publication first occurred. If first publication took place simultaneously in the United States and other countries, it is sufficient to state "U.S.A."

# 4 SPACE 4: Claimant(s)

**Name(s) and Address(es) of Copyright Claimant(s):** Give the name(s) and address(es) of the copyright claimant(s) in this work even if the claimant is the same as the author. Copyright in a work belongs initially to the author of the work (including, in the case of a work made for hire, the employer or other person for whom the work was prepared). The copyright claimant is either the author of the work or a person or organization to whom the copyright initially belonging to the author has been transferred.

**Transfer:** The statute provides that, if the copyright claimant is not the author, the application for registration must contain "a brief statement of how the claimant obtained ownership of the copyright." If any copyright claimant named in space 4 is not an author named in space 2, give a brief, general statement summarizing the means by which that claimant obtained ownership of the copyright. Examples: "By written contract"; "Transfer of all rights by author"; "Assignment"; "By will." Do not attach transfer documents or other attachments or riders.

# 6 SPACE 6: Derivative Work or Compilation

**General Instructions:** Complete space 6 if this work is a "changed version," "compilation," or "derivative work," and if it incorporates one or more earlier works that have already been published or registered for copyright, or that have fallen into the public domain. A "compilation" is defined as "a work formed by the collection and assembling of preexisting materials or of data that are selected, coordinated, or arranged in such a way that the resulting work as a whole constitutes an original work of authorship." A "derivative work" is "a work based on one or more preexisting works." Examples of derivative works include musical arrangements, dramatizations, translations, abridgments, condensations, motion picture versions, or "any other form in which a work may be recast, transformed, or adapted." Derivative works also include works "consisting of editorial revisions, annotations, or other modifications" if these changes, as a whole, represent an original work of authorship.

**Preexisting Material (space 6a):** Complete this space and space 6b for derivative works. In this space identify the preexisting work that has been recast, transformed, or adapted. For example, the preexisting material might be: "French version of Hugo's 'Le Roi s'amuse.'" Do not complete this space for compilations.

**Material Added to This Work (space 6b):** Give a brief, general statement of the additional new material covered by the copyright claim for which registration is sought. In the case of a derivative work, identify this new material. Examples: "Arrangement for piano and orchestra"; "Dramatization for television"; "New film version"; "Revisions throughout; Act III completely new." If the work is a compilation, give a brief, general statement describing both the material that has been compiled and the compilation itself. Example: "Compilation of 19th Century Military Songs."

# 5 SPACE 5: Previous Registration

**General Instructions:** The questions in space 5 are intended to find out whether an earlier registration has been made for this work and, if so, whether there is any basis for a new registration. As a general rule, only one basic copyright registration can be made for the same version of a particular work.

**Same Version:** If this version is substantially the same as the work covered by a previous registration, a second registration is not generally possible unless: (1) the work has been registered in unpublished form and a second registration is now being sought to cover this first published edition; or (2) someone other than the author is identified as copyright claimant in the earlier registration, and the author is now seeking registration in his or her own name. If either of these two exceptions apply, check the appropriate box and give the

# 7,8,9 SPACE 7, 8, 9: Fee, Correspondence, Certification, Return Address

**Deposit Account:** If you maintain a Deposit Account in the Copyright Office, identify it in space 7. Otherwise leave the space blank and send the fee of $10 with your application and deposit.

**Correspondence** (space 7): This space should contain the name, address, area code, and telephone number of the person to be consulted if correspondence about this application becomes necessary.

**Certification** (space 8): The application cannot be accepted unless it bears the date and the **handwritten signature** of the author or other copyright claimant, or of the owner of exclusive right(s), or of the duly authorized agent of the author, claimant, or owner of exclusive right(s).

**Address for Return of Certificate** (space 9): The address box must be completed legibly since the certificate will be returned in a window envelope.

---

# MORE INFORMATION

---

**How To Register a Recorded Work:** If the musical or dramatic work that you are registering has been recorded (as a tape, disk, or cassette), you may choose either copyright application Form PA or Form SR, Performing Arts or Sound Recordings, depending on the purpose of the registration.

Form PA should be used to register the underlying musical composition or dramatic work. Form SR has been developed specifically to register a "sound recording" as defined by the Copyright Act—a work resulting from the "fixation of a series of sounds," separate and distinct from the underlying musical or dramatic work. Form SR should be used when the copyright claim is limited to the sound recording itself. (In one instance, Form SR may also be used to file for a copyright registration for both kinds of works—see (4) below.) Therefore:

**(1)** File **Form PA** if you are seeking to register the musical or dramatic work, not the "sound recording," even though what you deposit for copyright purposes may be in the form of a phonorecord.

**(2)** File **Form PA** if you are seeking to register the audio portion of an audiovisual work, such as a motion picture soundtrack; these are considered integral parts of the audiovisual work.

**(3)** File **Form SR** if you are seeking to register the "sound recording" itself, that is, the work that results from the fixation of a series of musical, spoken, or other sounds, but not the underlying musical or dramatic work.

**(4)** File **Form SR** if you are the copyright claimant for both the underlying musical or dramatic work and the sound recording, *and* you prefer to register both on the same form.

**(5)** File **both forms PA and SR** if the copyright claimant for the underlying work and sound recording differ, or you prefer to have separate registration for them.

**"Copies" and "Phonorecords":** To register for copyright, you are required to deposit "copies" or "phonorecords." These are defined as follows:

Musical compositions may be embodied (fixed) in "copies," objects from which a work can be read or visually perceived, directly or with the aid of a machine or device, such as manuscripts, books, sheet music, film, and videotape. They may also be fixed in "phonorecords," objects embodying fixations of sounds, such as tapes and phonograph disks, commonly known as phonograph records. For example, a song (the work to be registered) can be reproduced in sheet music ("copies") or phonograph records ("phonorecords"), or both.

**DO NOT WRITE ABOVE THIS LINE. IF YOU NEED MORE SPACE, USE A SEPARATE CONTINUATION SHEET.**

**1** TITLE OF THIS WORK ▼

PREVIOUS OR ALTERNATIVE TITLES ▼

NATURE OF THIS WORK ▼  See instructions

**2** NAME OF AUTHOR ▼

a

Was this contribution to the work a "work made for hire"?
☐ Yes
☐ No

AUTHOR'S NATIONALITY OR DOMICILE
Name of Country
OR { Citizen of ▶ _____
     Domiciled in ▶ _____

DATES OF BIRTH AND DEATH
Year Born ▼        Year Died ▼

WAS THIS AUTHOR'S CONTRIBUTION TO THE WORK
Anonymous?     ☐ Yes ☐ No
Pseudonymous?  ☐ Yes ☐ No

If the answer to either of these questions is "Yes," see detailed instructions.

NATURE OF AUTHORSHIP  Briefly describe nature of the material created by this author in which copyright is claimed. ▼

**NOTE**

Under the law, the "author" of a "work made for hire" is generally the employer, not the employee (see instructions). For any part of this work that was "made for hire" check "Yes" in the space provided, give the employer (or other person for whom the work was prepared) as "Author" of that part, and leave the space for dates of birth and death blank.

**a** NAME OF AUTHOR ▼

DATES OF BIRTH AND DEATH
Year Born ▼          Year Died ▼

Was this contribution to the work a "work made for hire"?
☐ Yes
☐ No

AUTHOR'S NATIONALITY OR DOMICILE
Name of country
OR { Citizen of ▶ _____
{ Domiciled in ▶ _____

WAS THIS AUTHOR'S CONTRIBUTION TO THE WORK
Anonymous?    ☐ Yes  ☐ No
Pseudonymous?  ☐ Yes  ☐ No
If the answer to either of these questions is "Yes," see detailed instructions

NATURE OF AUTHORSHIP  Briefly describe nature of the material created by this author in which copyright is claimed. ▼

**b** NAME OF AUTHOR ▼

DATES OF BIRTH AND DEATH
Year Born ▼          Year Died ▼

Was this contribution to the work a "work made for hire"?
☐ Yes
☐ No

AUTHOR'S NATIONALITY OR DOMICILE
Name of Country
OR { Citizen of ▶ _____
{ Domiciled in ▶ _____

WAS THIS AUTHOR'S CONTRIBUTION TO THE WORK
Anonymous?    ☐ Yes  ☐ No
Pseudonymous?  ☐ Yes  ☐ No
If the answer to either of these questions is "Yes," see detailed instructions

NATURE OF AUTHORSHIP  Briefly describe nature of the material created by this author in which copyright is claimed. ▼

**3** YEAR IN WHICH CREATION OF THIS WORK WAS COMPLETED  This information must be given in all cases.
◀ Year

DATE AND NATION OF FIRST PUBLICATION OF THIS PARTICULAR WORK
Complete this information Month ▶ _____ Day ▶ _____ Year ▶ _____
ONLY if this work has been published.
◀ Nation

**4** COPYRIGHT CLAIMANT(S)  Name and address must be given even if the claimant is the same as the author given in space 2. ▼

See instructions before completing this space.

TRANSFER If the claimant(s) named here in space 4 are different from the author(s) named in space 2, give a brief statement of how the claimant(s) obtained ownership of the copyright. ▼

APPLICATION RECEIVED

ONE DEPOSIT RECEIVED

TWO DEPOSITS RECEIVED

REMITTANCE NUMBER AND DATE

DO NOT WRITE HERE
OFFICE USE ONLY

MORE ON BACK ▶  • Complete all applicable spaces (numbers 5-9) on the reverse side of this page.
• See detailed instructions  • Sign the form at line 8

DO NOT WRITE HERE
Page 1 of _____ pages

201

EXAMINED BY

**FORM PA**

CHECKED BY

☐ CORRESPONDENCE
Yes

☐ DEPOSIT ACCOUNT
FUNDS USED

FOR
COPYRIGHT
OFFICE
USE
ONLY

**5**

**DO NOT WRITE ABOVE THIS LINE. IF YOU NEED MORE SPACE, USE A SEPARATE CONTINUATION SHEET.**

**PREVIOUS REGISTRATION** Has registration for this work, or for an earlier version of this work, already been made in the Copyright Office?
☐ **Yes** ☐ **No** If your answer is "Yes," why is another registration being sought? (Check appropriate box) ▼
☐ This is the first published edition of a work previously registered in unpublished form.
☐ This is the first application submitted by this author as copyright claimant.
☐ This is a changed version of the work, as shown by space 6 on this application.
If your answer is "Yes," give: **Previous Registration Number** ▼          **Year of Registration** ▼

**6**

**DERIVATIVE WORK OR COMPILATION** Complete both space 6a & 6b for a derivative work; complete only 6b for a compilation.
a. **Preexisting Material** Identify any preexisting work or works that this work is based on or incorporates. ▼

See instructions
before completing
this space.

b. **Material Added to This Work** Give a brief, general statement of the material that has been added to this work and in which copyright is claimed. ▼

**7**

**DEPOSIT ACCOUNT** If the registration fee is to be charged to a Deposit Account established in the Copyright Office, give name and number of Account.
**Name** ▼          **Account Number** ▼

202

**CORRESPONDENCE** Give name and address to which correspondence about this application should be sent. Name/Address/Apt/City/State/Zip ▼

_____

_____

Area Code & Telephone Number ▶

**8**

**CERTIFICATION\*** I, the undersigned, hereby certify that I am the

Check only one ▼

☐ author
☐ other copyright claimant
☐ owner of exclusive right(s)
☐ authorized agent of _____
　　　　　Name of author or other copyright claimant, or owner of exclusive right(s) ▲

of the work identified in this application and that the statements made
by me in this application are correct to the best of my knowledge.

Typed or printed name and date ▼ If this is a published work, this date must be the same as or later than the date of publication given in space 3.

_____ date ▶ _____

✋ Handwritten signature (X) ▼

_____

**9**

**MAIL CERTIFI-CATE TO**

**Certificate will be mailed in window envelope**

| Name ▼ |
| --- |
| Number/Street/Apartment Number ▼ |
| City/State/ZIP ▼ |

**Have you:**
● Completed all necessary spaces?
● Signed your application in space 8?
● Enclosed check or money order for $10 payable to _Register of Copyrights?_
● Enclosed your deposit material with the application and fee?

**MAIL TO:** Register of Copyrights, Library of Congress, Washington, D.C. 20559

☆U.S. GOVERNMENT PRINTING OFFICE: 1985: 461-584/20,003

July 1985—200,000

# Filling Out Application Form TX

*Detach and read these instructions before completing this form. Make sure all applicable spaces have been filled in before you return this form.*

## BASIC INFORMATION

**When to Use This Form:** Use Form TX for registration of published or unpublished non-dramatic literary works, excluding periodicals or serial issues. This class includes a wide variety of works: fiction, non-fiction, poetry, textbooks, reference works, directories, catalogs, advertising copy, compilations of information, and computer programs. For periodicals and serials, use Form SE.

**Deposit to Accompany Application:** An application for copyright registration must be accompanied by a deposit consisting of copies or phonorecords representing the entire work for which registration is to be made. The following are the general deposit requirements as set forth in the statute:

**Unpublished Work:** Deposit one complete copy (or phonorecord).

**Published Work:** Deposit two complete copies (or phonorecords) of the best edition.

**Work First Published Outside the United States:** Deposit one complete copy (or phonorecord) of the first foreign edition.

**Contribution to a Collective Work:** Deposit one complete copy (or phonorecord) of the best edition of the collective work.

**The Copyright Notice:** For published works, the law provides that a copyright notice in a specified form "shall be placed on all publicly distributed copies from which the work can be visually perceived." Use of the copyright notice is the responsibility of the copyright owner and does not require advance permission from the Copyright Office. The required form of the notice for copies generally consists of three elements: (1) the symbol "©", or the word "Copyright," or the abbreviation "Copr."; (2) the year of first publication; and (3) the name of the owner of copyright. For example: "© 1981 Constance Porter." The notice is to be affixed to the copies "in such manner and location as to give reasonable notice of the claim of copyright."

For further information about copyright registration, notice, or special questions relating to copyright problems, write:

Information and Publications Section, LM-455
Copyright Office
Library of Congress
Washington, D.C. 20559

**PRIVACY ACT ADVISORY STATEMENT**
**Required by the Privacy Act of 1974 (Public Law 93-579)**

AUTHORITY FOR REQUESTING THIS INFORMATION:
● Title 17, U.S.C., Secs. 409 and 410

FURNISHING THE REQUESTED INFORMATION IS:
● Voluntary

BUT IF THE INFORMATION IS NOT FURNISHED:
● It may be necessary to delay or refuse registration
● You may not be entitled to certain relief, remedies, and benefits provided in chapters 4 and 5 of title 17, U.S.C.

PRINCIPAL USES OF REQUESTED INFORMATION
● Establishment and maintenance of a public record
● Examination of the application for compliance with legal requirements

OTHER ROUTINE USES:
● Public inspection and copying
● Preparation of public indexes
● Preparation of public catalogs of copyright registrations
● Preparation of search reports upon request

NOTE:
● No other advisory statement will be given you in connection with this application
● Please keep this statement and refer to it if we communicate with you regarding this application

# LINE-BY-LINE INSTRUCTIONS

## 1 SPACE 1: Title

**Title of This Work:** Every work submitted for copyright registration must be given a title to identify that particular work. If the copies or phonorecords of the work bear a title (or an identifying phrase that could serve as a title), transcribe that wording *completely* and *exactly* on the application. Indexing of the registration and future identification of the work will depend on the information you give here.

**Previous or Alternative Titles:** Complete this space if there are any additional titles for the work under which someone searching for the registration might be likely to look, or under which a document pertaining to the work might be recorded.

**Publication as a Contribution:** If the work being registered is a contribution to a periodical, serial, or collection, give the title of the contribution in the "Title of this Work" space. Then, in the line headed "Publication as a Contribution," give information about the collective work in which the contribution appeared.

## 2 SPACE 2: Author(s)

**General Instructions:** After reading these instructions, decide who are the "authors" of this work for copyright purposes. Then, unless the work is a "collective work," give the requested information about every "author" who contributed any appreciable amount of copyrightable matter to this version of the work. If you need further space, request additional Continuation sheets. In the case of a collective work, such as an anthology, collection of essays, or encyclopedia, give information about the author of the collective work as a whole.

**Name of Author:** The fullest form of the author's name should be given. Unless the work was "made for hire," the individual who actually created the work is its "author." In the case of a work made for hire, the statute provides that "the employer or other person for whom the work was prepared is considered the author."

**What is a "Work Made for Hire"?** A "work made for hire" is defined as: (1) "a work prepared by an employee within the scope of his or her employment"; or (2) "a work specially ordered or commissioned for use as a contribution to a collective work, as a part of a motion picture or other audiovisual work, as a translation, as a supplementary work, as a compilation, as an instructional text, as a test, as answer material for a test, or as an atlas, if the parties expressly agree in a written instrument signed by them that the work shall be considered a work made for hire." If you have checked "Yes" to indicate that the work was "made for hire," you must give the full legal name of the employer (or other person for whom the work was prepared). You may also include the name of the employee along with the name of the employer (for example: "Elster Publishing Co., employer for hire of John Ferguson").

**"Anonymous" or "Pseudonymous" Work:** An author's contribution to a work is "anonymous" if that author is not identified on the copies or phonorecords of the work. An author's contribution to a work is "pseudonymous" if that author is identified on the copies or phonorecords under a fictitious name. If the work is "anonymous" you may: (1) leave the line blank; or (2) state "anonymous" on the line; or (3) reveal the author's identity. If the work is "pseudonymous" you may: (1) leave the line blank; or (2) give the pseudonym and identify it as such (for example: "Huntley Haverstock, pseudonym"); or (3) reveal the author's name, making clear which is the real name and which is the pseudonym (for example: "Judith Barton, whose pseudonym is Madeline Elster"). However, the citizenship or domicile of the author **must** be given in all cases.

**Dates of Birth and Death:** If the author is dead, the statute requires that the year of death be included in the application unless the work is anonymous or pseudonymous. The author's birth date is optional, but is useful as a form of identification. Leave this space blank if the author's contribution was a "work made for hire."

**Author's Nationality or Domicile:** Give the country of which the author is a citizen, or the country in which the author is domiciled. Nationality or domicile **must** be given in all cases.

**Nature of Authorship:** After the words "Nature of Authorship" give a brief general statement of the nature of this particular author's contribution to the work. Examples: "Entire text"; "Coauthor of entire text"; "Chapters 11-14"; "Editorial revisions"; "Compilation and English translation"; "New text."

205

a whole constitutes an original work of authorship. A "derivative work" is "a work based on one or more preexisting works." Examples of derivative works include translations, fictionalizations, abridgments, condensations, or "any other form in which a work may be recast, transformed, or adapted." Derivative works also include works "consisting of editorial revisions, annotations, or other modifications" if these changes, as a whole, represent an original work of authorship.

Preexisting Material (space 6a): For derivative works, complete this space and space 6b. In space 6a identify the preexisting work that has been recast, transformed, or adapted. An example of preexisting material might be: "Russian version of Goncharov's 'Oblomov'." Do not complete space 6a for compilations.

Material Added to This Work (space 6b): Give a brief, general statement of the new material covered by the copyright claim for which registration is sought. Derivative work examples include: "Foreword, editing, critical annotations"; "Translation"; "Chapters 11-17." If the work is a compilation, describe both the compilation itself and the material that has been compiled. Example: "Compilation of certain 1917 Speeches by Woodrow Wilson." A work may be both a derivative work and compilation, in which case a sample statement might be: "Compilation and additional new material."

# 7 SPACE 7: Manufacturing Provisions

Due to the expiration of the Manufacturing Clause of the copyright law on June 30, 1986, this space has been deleted.

# 3 SPACE 3: Creation and Publication

General Instructions: Do not confuse "creation" with "publication." Every application for copyright registration must state "the year in which creation of the work was completed." Give the date and nation of first publication only if the work has been published.

Creation: Under the statute, a work is "created" when it is fixed in a copy or phonorecord for the first time. Where a work has been prepared over a period of time, the part of the work existing in fixed form on a particular date constitutes the created work on that date. The date you give here should be the year in which the author completed the particular version for which registration is now being sought, even if other versions exist or if further changes or additions are planned.

Publication: The statute defines "publication" as "the distribution of copies or phonorecords of a work to the public by sale or other transfer of ownership, or by rental, lease, or lending"; a work is also "published" if there has been an "offering to distribute copies or phonorecords to a group of persons for purposes of further distribution, public performance, or public display." Give the full date (month, day, year) when, and the country where, publication first occurred. If first publication took place simultaneously in the United States and other countries, it is sufficient to state "U.S.A."

# 4 SPACE 4: Claimant(s)

Name(s) and Address(es) of Copyright Claimant(s): Give the name(s) and address(es) of the copyright claimant(s) in this work even if the claimant is the same as the author. Copyright in a work belongs initially to the author of the work (including, in the case of a work made for hire, the employer or other person for whom the work was prepared). The copyright claimant is either the author of the work or a person or organization to whom the copyright initially belonging to the author has been transferred.

Transfer: The statute provides that, if the copyright claimant is not the author, the application for registration must contain "a brief statement of how the claimant obtained ownership of the copyright." If any copyright claimant named in space 4 is not an author named in space 2, give a brief, general statement summarizing the means by which that claimant obtained ownership of the copyright. Examples: "By written contract"; "Transfer of all rights by author"; "Assignment"; "By will." Do not attach transfer documents or other attachments or riders.

# 5 SPACE 5: Previous Registration

**General Instructions:** The questions in space 5 are intended to find out whether an earlier registration has been made for this work and, if so, whether there is any basis for a new registration. As a general rule, only one basic copyright registration can be made for the same version of a particular work.

**Same Version:** If this version is substantially the same as the work covered by a previous registration, a second registration is not generally possible unless: (1) the work has been registered in unpublished form and a second registration is now being sought to cover this first published edition; or (2) someone other than the author is identified as copyright claimant in the earlier registration, and the author is now seeking registration in his or her own name. If either of these two exceptions apply, check the appropriate box and give the earlier registration number and date. Otherwise, do not submit Form TX; instead, write the Copyright Office for information about supplementary registration or recordation of transfers of copyright ownership.

**Changed Version:** If the work has been changed, and you are now seeking registration to cover the additions or revisions, check the last box in space 5, give the earlier registration number and date, and complete both parts of space 6 in accordance with the instructions below.

**Previous Registration Number and Date:** If more than one previous registration has been made for the work, give the number and date of the latest registration.

# 6 SPACE 6: Derivative Work or Compilation

**General Instructions:** Complete space 6 if this work is a "changed version," "compilation," or "derivative work," and if it incorporates one or more earlier works that have already been published or registered for copyright, or that have fallen into the public domain. A "compilation" is defined as "a work formed by the collection and assembling of preexisting materials or of data that are selected, coordinated, or arranged in such a way that the resulting work as

# 8 SPACE 8: Reproduction for Use of Blind or Physically Handicapped Individuals

**General Instructions:** One of the major programs of the Library of Congress is to provide Braille editions and special recordings of works for the exclusive use of the blind and physically handicapped. In an effort to simplify and speed up the copyright licensing procedures that are a necessary part of this program, section 710 of the copyright statute provides for the establishment of a voluntary licensing system to be tied in with copyright registration. Copyright Office regulations provide that you may grant a license for such reproduction and distribution solely for the use of persons who are certified by competent authority as unable to read normal printed material as a result of physical limitations. The license is entirely voluntary, nonexclusive, and may be terminated upon 90 days notice.

**How to Grant the License:** If you wish to grant it, check one of the three boxes in space 8. Your check in one of these boxes, together with your signature in space 10, will mean that the Library of Congress can proceed to reproduce and distribute under the license without further paperwork. For further information, write for Circular R63.

# 9,10,11 SPACE 9, 10, 11: Fee, Correspondence, Certification, Return Address

**Deposit Account:** If you maintain a Deposit Account in the Copyright Office, identify it in space 9. Otherwise leave the space blank and send the fee of $10 with your application and deposit.

**Correspondence** (space 9): This space should contain the name, address, area code, and telephone number of the person to be consulted if correspondence about this application becomes necessary.

**Certification** (space 10): The application can not be accepted unless it bears the date and the **handwritten signature** of the author or other copyright claimant, or of the owner of exclusive right(s), or of the duly authorized agent of author, claimant, or owner of exclusive right(s).

**Address for Return of Certificate** (space 11): The address box must be completed legibly since the certificate will be returned in a window envelope.

# FORM TX

UNITED STATES COPYRIGHT OFFICE

REGISTRATION NUMBER

TX                    TXU

EFFECTIVE DATE OF REGISTRATION

_____    _____    _____
Month                    Day                    Year

---

**DO NOT WRITE ABOVE THIS LINE. IF YOU NEED MORE SPACE, USE A SEPARATE CONTINUATION SHEET.**

**1** TITLE OF THIS WORK ▼

PREVIOUS OR ALTERNATIVE TITLES ▼

PUBLICATION AS A CONTRIBUTION   If this work was published as a contribution to a periodical, serial, or collection, give information about the
collective work in which the contribution appeared.   **Title of Collective Work** ▼

If published in a periodical or serial give: **Volume** ▼          **Number** ▼                    **Issue Date** ▼          **On Pages** ▼

**2** NAME OF AUTHOR ▼

a

Was this contribution to the work a
"work made for hire"?
☐ Yes
☐ No

**AUTHOR'S NATIONALITY OR DOMICILE**
Name of Country
OR { Citizen of ▶ _____
      Domiciled in ▶ _____

**DATES OF BIRTH AND DEATH**
Year Born ▼          Year Died ▼

**WAS THIS AUTHOR'S CONTRIBUTION TO
THE WORK**                          If the answer to either
Anonymous?      ☐ Yes  ☐ No        of these questions is
Pseudonymous?  ☐ Yes  ☐ No        "Yes," see detailed
                                    instructions.

NATURE OF AUTHORSHIP   Briefly describe nature of the material created by this author in which copyright is claimed. ▼

# NOTE

Under the law, the "author" of a "work made for hire" is generally the employer, not the employee (see instructions). For any part of this work that was "made for hire" check "Yes" in the space provided, give the employer (or other person for whom the work was prepared) as "Author" of that part, and leave the space for dates of birth and death blank.

See instructions before completing this space.

## NAME OF AUTHOR ▼

**D**

Was this contribution to the work a "work made for hire"?
☐ Yes
☐ No

**DATES OF BIRTH AND DEATH**
Year Born ▼          Year Died ▼

**AUTHOR'S NATIONALITY OR DOMICILE**
Name of country
OR { Citizen of ▶ _____
{ Domiciled in ▶ _____

**WAS THIS AUTHOR'S CONTRIBUTION TO THE WORK**
Anonymous?        ☐ Yes ☐ No
Pseudonymous?     ☐ Yes ☐ No
If the answer to either of these questions is "Yes," see detailed instructions.

**NATURE OF AUTHORSHIP**  Briefly describe nature of the material created by this author in which copyright is claimed. ▼

## NAME OF AUTHOR ▼

**C**

Was this contribution to the work a "work made for hire"?
☐ Yes
☐ No

**DATES OF BIRTH AND DEATH**
Year Born ▼          Year Died ▼

**AUTHOR'S NATIONALITY OR DOMICILE**
Name of Country
OR { Citizen of ▶ _____
{ Domiciled in ▶ _____

**WAS THIS AUTHOR'S CONTRIBUTION TO THE WORK**
Anonymous?        ☐ Yes ☐ No
Pseudonymous?     ☐ Yes ☐ No
If the answer to either of these questions is "Yes," see detailed instructions.

**NATURE OF AUTHORSHIP**  Briefly describe nature of the material created by this author in which copyright is claimed. ▼

## 3

**YEAR IN WHICH CREATION OF THIS WORK WAS COMPLETED** This information must be given in all cases.
_____ ◀ Year

**DATE AND NATION OF FIRST PUBLICATION OF THIS PARTICULAR WORK**
Complete this information  Month ▶ _____ Day ▶ _____ Year ▶ _____  ◀ Nation
ONLY if this work has been published.

## 4

**COPYRIGHT CLAIMANT(S)** Name and address must be given even if the claimant is the same as the author given in space 2.▼

**TRANSFER** If the claimant(s) named here in space 4 are different from the author(s) named in space 2, give a brief statement of how the claimant(s) obtained ownership of the copyright. ▼

**MORE ON BACK ▶** • Complete all applicable spaces (numbers 5-11) on the reverse side of this page.
• See detailed instructions.          • Sign the form at line 10.

DO NOT WRITE HERE
Page 1 of _____ pages

EXAMINED BY

FORM TX

CHECKED BY

☐ CORRESPONDENCE
Yes

☐ DEPOSIT ACCOUNT
FUNDS USED

FOR
COPYRIGHT
OFFICE
USE
ONLY

**DO NOT WRITE ABOVE THIS LINE. IF YOU NEED MORE SPACE, USE A SEPARATE CONTINUATION SHEET.**

**PREVIOUS REGISTRATION** Has registration for this work, or for an earlier version of this work, already been made in the Copyright Office?

☐ **Yes** ☐ **No** If your answer is "Yes," why is another registration being sought? (Check appropriate box) ▼

☐ This is the first published edition of a work previously registered in unpublished form.

☐ This is the first application submitted by this author as copyright claimant.

☐ This is a changed version of the work, as shown by space 6 on this application.

If your answer is "Yes," give: **Previous Registration Number** ▼          **Year of Registration** ▼

**5**

**DERIVATIVE WORK OR COMPILATION** Complete both space 6a & 6b for a derivative work; complete only 6b for a compilation.

a. **Preexisting Material** Identify any preexisting work or works that this work is based on or incorporates. ▼

b. **Material Added to This Work** Give a brief, general statement of the material that has been added to this work and in which copyright is claimed. ▼

**6**

See instructions
before completing
this space

—space deleted—

**7**

210

**8** REPRODUCTION FOR USE OF BLIND OR PHYSICALLY HANDICAPPED INDIVIDUALS    A signature on this form at space 10, and a check in one of the boxes here in space 8, constitutes a non-exclusive grant of permission to the Library of Congress to reproduce and distribute solely for the blind and physically handicapped and under the conditions and limitations prescribed by the regulations of the Copyright Office: (1) copies of the work identified in space 1 of this application in Braille (or similar tactile symbols); or (2) phonorecords embodying a fixation of a reading of that work; or (3) both.

a ☐ Copies and Phonorecords          b ☐ Copies Only          c ☐ Phonorecords Only          See instructions.

**9** DEPOSIT ACCOUNT    If the registration fee is to be charged to a Deposit Account established in the Copyright Office, give name and number of Account.

Name ▼                                                                          Account Number ▼

CORRESPONDENCE    Give name and address to which correspondence about this application should be sent.    Name/Address/Apt/City/State/Zip ▼

Area Code & Telephone Number ▼

Be sure to
give your
daytime phone
▼number

**10** CERTIFICATION*    I, the undersigned, hereby certify that I am the

Check one ▶
☐ author
☐ other copyright claimant
☐ owner of exclusive right(s)
☐ authorized agent of _____
                       Name of author or other copyright claimant, or owner of exclusive right(s) ▲

of the work identified in this application and that the statements made
by me in this application are correct to the best of my knowledge.

Typed or printed name and date ▼ If this is a published work, this date must be the same as or later than the date of publication given in space 3.

_____  date ▶ _____

Handwritten signature (X) ▼

_____

**11** MAIL
CERTIFI-
CATE TO

Name ▼

Number/Street/Apartment Number ▼

City/State/ZIP ▼

Certificate
will be
mailed in
window
envelope

YOU MUST:
• Complete all necessary spaces
• Sign your application in space 10

SEND ALL 3 ELEMENTS
IN THE SAME PACKAGE:
1. Application form
2. Non-refundable $10 filing fee
   in check or money order
   payable to Register of Copyrights
3. Deposit material

MAIL TO:
Register of Copyrights
Library of Congress
Washington, D.C. 20559

* 17 U.S.C. § 506(e): Any person who knowingly makes a false representation of a material fact in the application for copyright registration provided for by section 409, or in any written statement filed in connection with the application, shall be fined not more than $2,500.

U.S. GOVERNMENT PRINTING OFFICE 1988—241-428 80,009          February 1989—65,000

# Filling Out Application Form SR

*Detach and read these instructions before completing this form. Make sure all applicable spaces have been filled in before you return this form.*

## BASIC INFORMATION

**When to Use This Form:** Use Form SR for copyright registration of published or unpublished sound recordings. It should be used where the copyright claim is limited to the sound recording itself, and it may also be used where the same copyright claimant is seeking simultaneous registration of the underlying musical, dramatic, or literary work embodied in the phonorecord.

With one exception, "sound recordings" are works that result from the fixation of a series of musical, spoken, or other sounds. The exception is for the audio portions of audiovisual works, such as a motion picture soundtrack or an audio cassette accompanying a filmstrip; these are considered a part of the audiovisual work as a whole.

**Deposit to Accompany Application:** An application for copyright registration of a sound recording must be accompanied by a deposit consisting of phonorecords representing the entire work for which registration is to be made.

**Unpublished Work:** Deposit one complete phonorecord.

**Published Work:** Deposit two complete phonorecords of the best edition, together with "any printed or other visually perceptible material" published with the phonorecords.

**Work First Published Outside the United States:** Deposit one complete phonorecord of the first foreign edition.

**Contribution to a Collective Work:** Deposit one complete phonorecord of the best edition of the collective work.

**The Copyright Notice:** For published sound recordings, the law provides that a copyright notice in a specified form "shall be placed on all publicly distributed phonorecords of the sound recording." Use of the copyright notice is the responsibility of the copyright owner and does not require advance permission from the Copyright Office. The required form of the notice for phonorecords of sound recordings consists of three elements: (1) the symbol "℗" (the letter "P" in a circle); (2) the year of first publication of the sound recording; and (3) the name of the owner of copyright. For example: "℗ 1981 Rittenhouse Record Co." The notice is to be "placed on the surface of the phonorecord, or on the label or container, in such manner and location as to give reasonable notice of the claim of copyright." For further information about copyright, write: Information and Publications Section, LM-455 Copyright Office, Library of Congress, Washington, D.C. 20559

# LINE-BY-LINE INSTRUCTIONS

## 1 SPACE 1: Title

**Title of This Work:** Every work submitted for copyright registration must be given a title to identify that particular work. If the phonorecords or any accompanying printed material bear a title (or an identifying phrase that could serve as a title), transcribe that wording completely and exactly on the application. Indexing of the registration and future identification of the work may depend on the information you give here.

**Nature of Material Recorded:** Indicate the general type or character of the works or other material embodied in the recording. The box marked "Literary" should be checked for nondramatic spoken material of all sorts, including narration, interviews, panel discussions, and training material. If the material recorded is not musical, dramatic, or literary in nature, check "Other" and briefly describe the type of sounds fixed in the recording. For example: "Sound Effects"; "Bird Calls"; "Crowd Noises."

**Previous or Alternative Titles:** Complete this space if there are any additional titles for the work under which someone searching for the registration might be likely to look, or under which a document pertaining to the work might be recorded.

## 2 SPACE 2: Author(s)

**General Instructions:** After reading these instructions, decide who are the "authors" of this work for copyright purposes. Then, unless the work is a "collective work," give the requested information about every "author" who contributed any appreciable amount of copyrightable matter to this version of the work. If you need further space, request additional Continuation Sheets. In the case of a collective work, such as a collection of previously published or registered sound recordings, give information about the author of the collective work as a whole. If you are submitting this Form SR to cover the recorded musical, dramatic, or literary work as well as the sound recording itself, it is important for space 2 to include full information about the various authors of all of the material covered by the copyright claim, making clear the nature of each author's contribution.

**Name of Author:** The fullest form of the author's name should be given. Unless the work was "made for hire," the individual who actually created the work is its "author." In the case of a work made for hire, the statute provides that "the employer or other person for whom the work was prepared is considered the author."

**What is a "Work Made for Hire"?** A "work made for hire" is defined as: (1) "a work prepared by an employee within the scope of his or her employment"; or (2) "a work specially ordered or commissioned for use as a contribution to a collective work, as a part of a motion picture or other audiovisual work, as a translation, as a supplementary work, as a compilation, as an instructional text, as a test, as answer material for a test, or as an atlas, if the parties expressly agree in a written instrument signed by them that the work shall be considered a work made for hire." If you have checked "Yes" to indicate that the work was "made for hire," you must give the full legal name of the employer (or other person for whom the work was prepared). You may also include the name of the employee along with the name of the employer (for example: "Elster Record Co., employer for hire of John Ferguson").

**"Anonymous" or "Pseudonymous" Work:** An author's contribution to a work is "anonymous" if that author is not identified on the copies or phonorecords of the work. An author's contribution to a work is "pseudonymous" if that author is identified on the copies or phonorecords under a fictitious name. If the work is "anonymous" you may: (1) leave the line blank; or (2) state "anonymous" on the line; or (3) reveal the author's identity. If the work is "pseudonymous" you may: (1) leave the line blank; or (2) give the pseudonym and identify it as such (for example: "Huntley Haverstock, pseudonym"); or (3) reveal the author's name, making clear which is the real name and which is the pseudonym (for example: "Judith Barton, whose pseudonym is Madeline Elster"). However, the citizenship or domicile of the author must be given in all cases.

**Dates of Birth and Death:** If the author is dead, the statute requires that the year of death be included in the application unless the work is anonymous or pseudonymous. The author's birth date is optional, but is useful as a form of identification. Leave this space blank if the author's contribution was a "work made for hire."

**Author's Nationality or Domicile:** Give the country of which the author is a citizen, or the country in which the author is domiciled. Nationality or domicile **must** be given in all cases.

**Nature of Authorship:** Give a brief general statement of the nature of this particular author's contribution to the work. If you are submitting this Form SR to cover both the sound recording and the underlying musical, dramatic, or literary work, make sure that the precise nature of each author's contribution is reflected here. Examples where the authorship pertains to the recording: "Sound Recording"; "Performance and Recording"; "Compilation and Remixing of Sounds." Examples where the authorship pertains to both the recording and the underlying work: "Words, Music, Performance, Recording"; "Arrangement of Music and Recording"; "Compilation of Poems and Reading."

## 3 SPACE 3: Creation and Publication

**General Instructions:** Do not confuse "creation" with "publication." Every application for copyright registration must state "the year in which creation of the work was completed." Give the date and nation of first publication only if the work has been published.

**Creation:** Under the statute, a work is "created" when it is fixed in a copy or phonorecord for the first time. Where a work has been prepared over a period of time, the part of the work existing in fixed form on a particular date constitutes the created work on that date. The date you give here should be the year in which the author completed the particular version for which registration is now being sought, even if other versions exist or if further changes or additions are planned.

**Publication:** The statute defines "publication" as "the distribution of copies or phonorecords of a work to the public by sale or other transfer of ownership, or by rental, lease, or lending"; a work is also "published" if there has been an "offering to distribute copies or phonorecords to a group of persons for purposes of further distribution, public performance, or public display." Give the full date (month, day, year) when, and the country where, publication first occurred. If first publication took place simultaneously in the United States and other countries, it is sufficient to state "U.S.A."

## 4 SPACE 4: Claimant(s)

**Name(s) and Address(es) of Copyright Claimant(s):** Give the name(s) and address(es) of the copyright claimant(s) in this work even if the claimant is the same as the author. Copyright in a work belongs initially to the author or of the work (including, in the case of a work made for hire, the employer or other person for whom the work was prepared). The copyright claimant is either the author of the work or a person or organization to whom the copyright initially belonging to the author has been transferred.

**Transfer:** The statute provides that, if the copyright claimant is not the author, the application for registration must contain "a brief statement of how the claimant obtained ownership of the copyright." If any copyright claimant named in space 4 is not an author named in space 2, give a brief, general statement summarizing the means by which that claimant obtained ownership of the copyright. Examples: "By written contract"; "Transfer of all rights by author"; "Assignment"; "By will." Do not attach transfer documents or other attachments or riders.

**Changed Version:** If the work has been changed, and you are now seeking registration to cover the additions or revisions, check the last box in space 5, give the earlier registration number and date, and complete both parts of space 6 in accordance with the instructions below.

**Previous Registration Number and Date:** If more than one previous registration has been made for the work, give the number and date of the latest registration.

## 6 SPACE 6: Derivative Work or Compilation

**General Instructions:** Complete space 6 if this work is a "changed version," "compilation," or "derivative work," and if it incorporates one or more earlier works that have already been published or registered for copyright, or that have fallen into the public domain, or sound recordings that were fixed before February 15, 1972. A "compilation" is defined as "a work formed by the collection and assembling of preexisting materials or of data that are selected, coordinated, or arranged in such a way that the resulting work as a whole constitutes an original work of authorship." A "derivative work" is "a work based on one or more preexisting works." Examples of derivative works include recordings reissued with substantial editorial revisions or abridgments of the recorded sounds, and recordings republished with new recorded material, or "any other form in which a work may be recast, transformed, or adapted." Derivative works also include works "consisting of editorial revisions, annotations, or other modifications" if these changes, as a whole, represent an original work of authorship.

**Preexisting Material (space 6a):** Complete this space and space 6b for derivative works. In this space identify the preexisting work that has been recast, transformed, or adapted. For example, the preexisting material might be: "1970 recording by Sperryville Symphony of Bach Double Concerto." Do not complete this space for compilations.

**Material Added to This Work (space 6b):** Give a brief, general statement of the additional new material covered by the copyright claim for which registration is sought. In the case of a derivative work, identify this new material. Examples: "Recorded performances on bands 1 and 3"; "Remixed sounds from original multitrack sound sources"; "New words, arrangement, and additional sounds." If the work is a compilation, give a brief, general statement describing both the material that has been compiled and the compilation itself. Example: "Compilation of 1938 Recordings by various swing bands."

# 5 SPACE 5: Previous Registration

**General Instructions:** The questions in space 5 are intended to find out whether an earlier registration has been made for this work and, if so, whether there is any basis for a new registration. As a rule, only one basic copyright registration can be made for the same version of a particular work.

**Same Version:** If this version is substantially the same as the work covered by a previous registration, a second registration is not generally possible unless: (1) the work has been registered in unpublished form and a second registration is now being sought to cover this first published edition; or (2) someone other than the author is identified as copyright claimant in the earlier registration, and the author is now seeking registration in his or her own name. If either of these two exceptions apply, check the appropriate box and give the earlier registration number and date. Otherwise, do not submit Form SR; instead, write the Copyright Office for information about supplementary registration or recordation of transfers of copyright ownership.

# 7,8,9 SPACE 7, 8, 9: Fee, Correspondence, Certification, Return Address

**Deposit Account:** If you maintain a Deposit Account in the Copyright Office, identify it in space 7. Otherwise leave the space blank and send the fee of $10 with your application and deposit.

**Correspondence (space 7):** This space should contain the name, address, area code, and telephone number of the person to be consulted if correspondence about this application becomes necessary.

**Certification (space 8):** The application cannot be accepted unless it bears the date and the **handwritten signature** of the author or other copyright claimant, or of the owner of exclusive right(s), or of the duly authorized agent of the author, claimant, or owner of exclusive right(s).

**Address for Return of Certificate (space 9):** The address box must be completed legibly since the certificate will be returned in a window envelope.

# MORE INFORMATION

**"Works":** "Works" are the basic subject matter of copyright; they are what authors create and copyright protects. The statute draws a sharp distinction between the "work" and "any material object in which the work is embodied."

**"Copies" and "Phonorecords":** These are the two types of material objects in which "works" are embodied. In general, "copies" are objects from which a work can be read or visually perceived, directly or with the aid of a machine or device, such as manuscripts, books, sheet music, film, and videotape. "**Phonorecords**" are objects embodying fixations of sounds, such as audio tapes and phonograph disks. For example, a song (the "work") can be reproduced in sheet music ("copies") or phonograph disks ("phonorecords"), or both.

**"Sound Recordings":** These are "works," not "copies" or "phonorecords." "Sound recordings" are "works that result from the fixation of a series of musical, spoken, or other sounds, but not including the sounds accompanying a motion picture or other audiovisual work."Example:When a record company issues a new release, the release will typically involve two distinct "works": the "musical work" that has been recorded, and the "sound recording" as a separate work in itself. The material objects that the record company sends out are "phonorecords": physical reproductions of both the "musical work" and the "sound recording."

## Should You File More Than One Application? 

If your work consists of a recorded musical, dramatic, or literary work, and both that "work," and the sound recording as a separate "work," are eligible for registration, the application form you should file depends on the following:

**File Only Form SR if:** The copyright claimant is the same for both the musical, dramatic, or literary work and for the sound recording, and you are seeking a single registration to cover both of these "works."

**File Only Form PA (or Form TX) if:** You are seeking to register only the musical, dramatic, or literary work, not the sound recording. Form PA is appropriate for works of the performing arts; Form TX is for nondramatic literary works.

**Separate Applications Should Be Filed on Form PA (or Form TX) and on Form SR if:** (1) The copyright claimant for the musical, dramatic, or literary work is different from the copyright claimant for the sound recording; or (2) You prefer to have separate registrations for the musical, dramatic, or literary work and for the sound recording.

# FORM SR

UNITED STATES COPYRIGHT OFFICE

REGISTRATION NUMBER

SR     SRU

EFFECTIVE DATE OF REGISTRATION

Month    Day    Year

**DO NOT WRITE ABOVE THIS LINE. IF YOU NEED MORE SPACE, USE A SEPARATE CONTINUATION SHEET.**

**1**   **TITLE OF THIS WORK ▼**

**PREVIOUS OR ALTERNATIVE TITLES ▼**

**NATURE OF MATERIAL RECORDED ▼** See instructions
☐ Musical   ☐ Musical-Dramatic
☐ Dramatic   ☐ Literary
☐ Other _____

**2**   **NAME OF AUTHOR ▼**

a

Was this contribution to the work a "work made for hire"?
☐ Yes
☐ No

**AUTHOR'S NATIONALITY OR DOMICILE**
Name of Country
OR { Citizen of ▶ _____
     Domiciled in ▶ _____

**DATES OF BIRTH AND DEATH**
Year Born ▼    Year Died ▼

**WAS THIS AUTHOR'S CONTRIBUTION TO THE WORK**
Anonymous?   ☐ Yes   ☐ No
Pseudonymous?   ☐ Yes   ☐ No
If the answer to either of these questions is "Yes," see detailed instructions

**NATURE OF AUTHORSHIP** Briefly describe nature of the material created by this author in which copyright is claimed. ▼

# NOTE

Under the law, the "author" of a "work made for hire" is generally the employer, not the employee (see instructions). For any part of this work that was "made for hire" check "Yes" in the space provided, give the employer (or other person for whom the work was prepared) as "Author" of that part, and leave the space for dates of birth and death blank.

**2**

**NAME OF AUTHOR ▼**

**DATES OF BIRTH AND DEATH**
Year Born ▼   Year Died ▼

Was this contribution to the work a "work made for hire"?
☐ Yes
☐ No

**AUTHOR'S NATIONALITY OR DOMICILE**
Name of country
OR { Citizen of ▶
Domiciled in ▶

**WAS THIS AUTHOR'S CONTRIBUTION TO THE WORK**
Anonymous?   ☐ Yes ☐ No
Pseudonymous?   ☐ Yes ☐ No
If the answer to either of these questions is "Yes," see detailed instructions.

**NATURE OF AUTHORSHIP**   Briefly describe nature of the material created by this author in which copyright is claimed. ▼

**NAME OF AUTHOR ▼**

**DATES OF BIRTH AND DEATH**
Year Born ▼   Year Died ▼

Was this contribution to the work a "work made for hire"?
☐ Yes
☐ No

**AUTHOR'S NATIONALITY OR DOMICILE**
Name of Country
OR { Citizen of ▶
Domiciled in ▶

**WAS THIS AUTHOR'S CONTRIBUTION TO THE WORK**
Anonymous?   ☐ Yes ☐ No
Pseudonymous?   ☐ Yes ☐ No
If the answer to either of these questions is "Yes," see detailed instructions.

**NATURE OF AUTHORSHIP**   Briefly describe nature of the material created by this author in which copyright is claimed. ▼

**3**

See instructions before completing this space

**YEAR IN WHICH CREATION OF THIS WORK WAS COMPLETED** This information must be given in all cases.
◀ Year

**DATE AND NATION OF FIRST PUBLICATION OF THIS PARTICULAR WORK**
Complete this information ONLY if this work has been published.
Month ▶   Day ▶   Year ▶   ◀ Nation

**4**

**COPYRIGHT CLAIMANT(S)** Name and address must be given even if the claimant is the same as the author given in space 2. ▼

**TRANSFER** If the claimant(s) named here in space 4 are different from the author(s) named in space 2, give a brief statement of how the claimant(s) obtained ownership of the copyright. ▼

**MORE ON BACK ▶**
• Complete all applicable spaces (numbers 5-9) on the reverse side of this page.
• See detailed instructions.
• Sign the form at line 8

DO NOT WRITE HERE

Page 1 of _____ pages

217

**FORM SR**

EXAMINED BY

CHECKED BY

☐ CORRESPONDENCE
Yes

☐ DEPOSIT ACCOUNT
FUNDS USED

FOR
COPYRIGHT
OFFICE
USE
ONLY

**5**

**DO NOT WRITE ABOVE THIS LINE. IF YOU NEED MORE SPACE, USE A SEPARATE CONTINUATION SHEET.**

**PREVIOUS REGISTRATION** Has registration for this work, or for an earlier version of this work, already been made in the Copyright Office?
☐ **Yes** ☐ **No** If your answer is "Yes," why is another registration being sought? (Check appropriate box) ▼
☐ This is the first published edition of a work previously registered in unpublished form.
☐ This is the first application submitted by this author as copyright claimant.
☐ This is a changed version of the work, as shown by space 6 on this application.
If your answer is "Yes," give: **Previous Registration Number** ▼          **Year of Registration** ▼

**6**

**DERIVATIVE WORK OR COMPILATION** Complete both space 6a & 6b for a derivative work; complete only 6b for a compilation.
a. **Preexisting Material** Identify any preexisting work or works that this work is based on or incorporates. ▼

b. **Material Added to This Work** Give a brief, general statement of the material that has been added to this work and in which copyright is claimed. ▼

See instructions
before completing
this space

**7**

**DEPOSIT ACCOUNT** If the registration fee is to be charged to a Deposit Account established in the Copyright Office, give name and number of Account.
**Name** ▼          **Account Number** ▼

**CORRESPONDENCE** Give name and address to which correspondence about this application should be sent. Name/Address/Apt/City/State/Zip ▼

Area Code & Telephone Number ▶

Be sure to
give your
daytime phone
▶ number

**8**

**CERTIFICATION\*** I, the undersigned, hereby certify that I am the

Check one ▼

☐ author
☐ other copyright claimant
☐ owner of exclusive right(s)
☐ authorized agent of _____
    Name of author or other copyright claimant, or owner of exclusive right(s) ▲

of the work identified in this application and that the statements made
by me in this application are correct to the best of my knowledge.

**Typed or printed name and date ▼** If this is a published work, this date must be the same as or later than the date of publication given in space 3.

_____ date▶ _____

   ☞    Handwritten signature (X) ▼

**MAIL
CERTIFI-
CATE TO**

Name ▼

**Certificate
will be
mailed in
window
envelope**

Number/Street/Apartment Number ▼

City/State/ZIP ▼

**9**

**Have you:**
● Completed all necessary
  spaces?
● Signed your application in space
  8?
● Enclosed check or money order
  for $10 payable to *Register of
  Copyrights?*
● Enclosed your deposit material
  with the application and fee?

**MAIL TO:** Register of Copyrights.
Library of Congress. Washington.
D.C. 20559

U.S. GOVERNMENT PRINTING OFFICE: 1987—181—531 60.005

August 1987—60.000

# Filling Out Application Form SE

*Detach and read these instructions before completing this form. Make sure all applicable spaces have been filled in before you return this form.*

## BASIC INFORMATION

**When To Use This Form:** Use a separate Form SE for registration of each individual issue of a serial, Class SE. A serial is defined as a work issued or intended to be issued in successive parts bearing numerical or chronological designations and intended to be continued indefinitely. This class includes a variety of works: periodicals; newspapers; annuals; the journals, proceedings, transactions, etc., of societies. Do not use Form SE to register an individual contribution to a serial. Request Form TX for such contributions.

**Deposit to Accompany Application:** An application for copyright registration must be accompanied by a deposit consisting of copies or phonorecords representing the entire work for which registration is to be made. The following are the general deposit requirements as set forth in the statute:

**Unpublished Work:** Deposit one complete copy (or phonorecord).

**Published Work:** Deposit two complete copies (or phonorecords) of the best edition.

**Work First Published Outside the United States:** Deposit one complete copy (or phonorecord) of the first foreign edition.

**Mailing Requirements:** It is important that you send the application, the deposit copy or copies, and the $10 fee together in the same envelope or package. The Copyright Office cannot process them unless they are received together. Send to: *Register of Copyrights, Library of Congress, Washington, D.C. 20559.*

**The Copyright Notice:** For published works, the law provides that a copyright notice in a specified form "shall be placed on all publicly distributed copies from which the work can be visually perceived." Use of the copyright notice is the responsibility of the copyright owner and does not require advance permission from the Copyright Office. The required form of the notice for copies generally consists of three elements: (1) the symbol "©"; or the word "Copyright," or the abbreviation "Copr."; (2) the year of first publication; and (3) the name of the owner of copyright. For example: "© 1981 National News Publishers, Inc." The notice is to be affixed to the copies "in such manner and location as to give reasonable notice of the claim of copyright." For further information about copyright registration, notice, or special questions relating to copyright problems, write:

> Information and Publications Section, LM-455
> Copyright Office, Library of Congress, Washington, D.C. 20559

# LINE-BY-LINE INSTRUCTIONS

## 1 SPACE 1: Title

**Title of This Serial:** Every work submitted for copyright registration must be given a title to identify that particular work. If the copies or phonorecords of the work bear a title (or an identifying phrase that could serve as a title), give the volume copy that wording *completely* and *exactly* on the application. Give the volume and number of the periodical issue for which you are seeking registration. The "Date on copies" in space 1 should be the date appearing on the actual copies (for example: "June 1981," "Winter 1981"). Indexing of the registration and future identification of the work will depend on the information you give here.

**Previous or Alternative Titles:** Complete this space only if there are any additional titles for the serial under which someone searching for the registration might be likely to look, or under which a document pertaining to the work might be recorded.

## 2 SPACE 2: Author(s)

**General Instructions:** After reading these instructions, decide who are the "authors" of this work for copyright purposes. In the case of a serial issue, the person for whom the work was prepared is considered the author." If this issue is a "work made for hire," the author's name will be the full legal name of the hiring organization, corporation, or individual. The title of the periodical should not ordinarily be listed as "author" because the title itself does not usually correspond to a legal entity capable of authorship. When an individual creates an issue of a serial independently and not as an "employee" of an organization or corporation, that individual should be listed as the "author."

**Author's Nationality or Domicile:** Give the country of which the author is a citizen, or the country in which the author is domiciled. Nationality or domicile **must** be given in all cases. The citizenship of an organization formed under United States Federal or state law should be stated as "U.S.A."

**What is a "Work Made for Hire"?** A "work made for hire" is defined as: (1) "a work prepared by an employee within the scope of his or her employment"; or (2) "a work specially ordered or commissioned for use as a contribution to a collective work, as a part of a motion picture or other audiovisual work, as a translation, as a supplementary work, as a compilation, as an instructional text, as a test, as answer material for a test, or as an atlas, if the parties expressly agree in a written instrument signed by them that the work shall be considered a work made for hire." An organization that uses the efforts of volunteers in the creation of a "collective work" (see "Nature of Authorship") may also be considered the author of a "work made for hire" even though those volunteers were not specifically paid by the organization. In the case of a "work made for hire," give the full legal name of the employer and check "Yes" to indicate that the work was made for hire. You may also include the name of the employee along with the name of the employer (for example: "Elster Publishing Co., employer for hire of John Ferguson").

**"Anonymous" or "Pseudonymous" Work:** Leave this space **blank** if the serial is a "work made for hire." An author's contribution to a work is "anonymous" if that author is not identified on the copies or phonorecords of the work. An author's contribution to a work is "pseudonymous" if that author is identified on the copies or phonorecords under a fictitious name. If the work is "anonymous" you may: (1) leave the line blank; or (2) state "anonymous" on the line; or (3) reveal the author's identity. If the work is "pseudonymous" you may: (1) leave the line blank; or (2) give the pseudonym and identify it as such (for example: "Huntley Haverstock, pseudonym"); or (3) reveal the author's name, making clear which is the real name and which is the pseudonym (for example: "Judith Barton, whose pseudonym is Madeline Elster"). However, the citizenship or domicile of the author **must** be given in all cases.

**Dates of Birth and Death:** Leave this space blank if the author's contribution was a "work made for hire." If the author is dead, the statute requires that the year of death be included in the application unless the work is anonymous or pseudonymous. The author's birth date is optional, but is useful as a form of identification.

**Nature of Authorship:** Give a brief statement of the nature of the particular author's contribution to the work. If an organization directed, controlled, and supervised the creation of the serial issue as a whole, check the box "collective work." The term "collective work" means that the author is responsible for compilation and editorial revision, and may also be responsible for certain individual contributions to the serial issue. Further examples of "Authorship" which may apply both to organizational and to individual authors are "Entire text"; "Entire text and/or illustrations"; "Editorial revision, compilation, plus additional new material."

## 3 SPACE 3: Creation and Publication

**General Instructions:** Do not confuse "creation" with "publication." Every application for copyright registration must state "the year in which creation of the work was completed." Give the date and nation of first publication only if the work has been published.

**Creation:** Under the statute, a work is "created" when it is fixed in a copy or phonorecord for the first time. Where a work has been prepared over a period of time, the part of the work existing in fixed form on a particular date constitutes the created work on that date. The date you give here should be the year in which this particular issue was completed.

**Publication:** The statute defines "publication" as "the distribution of copies or phonorecords of a work to the public by sale or other transfer of ownership, or by rental, lease, or lending"; a work is also "published" if there has been an "offering to distribute copies or phonorecords to a group of persons for purposes of further distribution, public performance, or public display." Give the full date (month, day, year) when, and the country where, publication of this particular issue first occurred. If first publication took place simultaneously in the United States and other countries, it is sufficient to state "U.S.A."

## 4 SPACE 4: Claimant(s)

**Name(s) and Address(es) of Copyright Claimant(s):** This space must be completed. Give the name(s) and address(es) of the copyright claimant(s) of this work even if the claimant is the same as the author named in space 2. Copyright in a work belongs initially to the author of the work (including, in the case of a work made for hire, the employer or other person for whom the work was prepared). The copyright claimant is either the author of the work or a person or organization to whom the copyright initially belonging to the author has been transferred.

**Transfer:** The statute provides that, if the copyright claimant is not the author, the application for registration must contain "a brief statement of how the claimant obtained ownership of the copyright." A transfer of copyright ownership (other than one brought about by operation of law) must be in writing. If any copyright claimant named in space 4 is not an author named in space 2, give a brief, general statement describing the means by which that claimant obtained ownership of the copyright from the original author. Examples: "By written contract"; "Inherited by will." Do not attach the actual document of transfer or other attachments or riders.

lected, coordinated, or arranged in such a way that the resulting work as a whole constitutes an original work of authorship." A "derivative work" is "a work based on one or more preexisting works." Examples of derivative works include translations, fictionalizations, abridgments, condensations, or "any other form in which a work may be recast, transformed, or adapted." Derivative works also include works "consisting of editorial revisions, annotations, or other modifications" if these changes, as a whole, represent an original work of authorship.

**Preexisting Material (space 6a):** For derivative works, complete this space and space 6b. In space 6a identify the preexisting work that has been recast, transformed, adapted, or updated. Example: "1978 Morgan Co. Sales Catalog." Do not complete space 6a for compilations.

**Material Added to This Work (space 6b):** Give a brief, general statement of the new material covered by the copyright claim for which registration is sought. **Derivative work** examples include: "Editorial revisions and additions to the Catalog"; "Translation"; "Additional material." If a periodical issue is a **compilation,** describe both the compilation itself and the material that has been compiled. Examples: "Compilation of previously published journal articles"; "Compilation of previously published data." An issue may be both a derivative work and a compilation, in which case a sample statement might be: "Compilation of [describe] and additional new material."

## 7 SPACE 7: Manufacturing Provisions

**Due to the expiration of the Manufacturing Clause of the copyright law on June 30, 1986, this space has been deleted.**

# 5 SPACE 5: Previous Registration

**General Instructions:** This space applies only rarely to serials. Complete space 5 if this particular issue has been registered earlier or if it contains a substantial amount of material that has been previously registered. Do not complete this space if the previous registrations are simply those made for earlier issues.

**Previous Registration:**

**a. Check this box** if this issue has been registered in unpublished form and a second registration is now sought to cover the first published edition.

**b. Check this box** if someone other than the author is identified as copyright claimant in the earlier registration and the author is now seeking registration in his or her own name. If the work in question is a contribution to a collective work, as opposed to the issue as a whole, file Form TX, not Form SE.

**c. Check this box** (and complete space 6) if this particular issue, or a substantial portion of the material in it, has been previously registered and you are now seeking registration for the additions and revisions which appear in this issue for the first time.

**Previous Registration Number and Date:** Complete this line if you checked one of the boxes above. If more than one previous registration has been made for the issue or for material in it, give only the number and year date for the latest registration.

# 6 SPACE 6: Derivative Work or Compilation

**General Instructions:** Complete space 6 if this issue is a "changed version," "compilation," or "derivative work," which incorporates one or more earlier works that have already been published or registered for copyright, or that have fallen into the public domain. Do not complete space 6 for an issue consisting of entirely new material appearing for the first time, such as a new issue of a continuing serial. A "compilation" is defined as "a work formed by the collection and assembling of preexisting materials or of data that are se-

# 8 SPACE 8: Reproduction for Use of Blind or Physically Handicapped Individuals

**General Instructions:** One of the major programs of the Library of Congress is to provide Braille editions and special recordings of works for the exclusive use of the blind and physically handicapped. In an effort to simplify and speed up the copyright licensing procedures that are a necessary part of this program, section 710 of the copyright statute provides for the establishment of a voluntary licensing system to be tied in with copyright registration. Copyright Office regulations provide that you may grant a license for such reproduction and distribution solely for the use of persons who are certified by competent authority as unable to read normal printed material as a result of physical limitations. The license is entirely voluntary, nonexclusive, and may be terminated upon 90 days notice.

**How to Grant the License:** If you wish to grant it, check one of the three boxes in space 8. Your check in one of these boxes, together with your signature in space 10, will mean that the Library of Congress can proceed to reproduce and distribute under the license without further paperwork. For further information, write for Circular R63.

# 9,10,11 SPACE 9, 10, 11: Fee, Correspondence, Certification, Return Address

**Deposit Account:** If you maintain a Deposit Account in the Copyright Office, identify it in space 9. Otherwise leave the space blank and send the fee of $10 with your application and deposit.

**Correspondence** (space 9): This space should contain the name, address, area code, and telephone number of the person to be consulted if correspondence about this application becomes necessary.

**Certification** (space 10): The application cannot be accepted unless it bears the date and the **handwritten signature** of the author or other copyright claimant, or of the owner of exclusive right(s), or of the duly authorized agent of the author, claimant, or owner of exclusive right(s).

**Address for Return of Certificate** (space 11): The address box must be completed legibly since the certificate will be returned in a window envelope.

223

# FORM SE
UNITED STATES COPYRIGHT OFFICE

REGISTRATION NUMBER

U

EFFECTIVE DATE OF REGISTRATION

Month     Day     Year

---

**DO NOT WRITE ABOVE THIS LINE. IF YOU NEED MORE SPACE, USE A SEPARATE CONTINUATION SHEET.**

**1**    **TITLE OF THIS SERIAL** ▼

Volume ▼     Number ▼     Date on Copies ▼     Frequency of Publication ▼

**PREVIOUS OR ALTERNATIVE TITLES** ▼

**2**    **NAME OF AUTHOR** ▼

Was this contribution to the work a "work made for hire"?

☐ Yes
☐ No

**AUTHOR'S NATIONALITY OR DOMICILE**
Name of Country

OR { Citizen of ▶ _____
     Domiciled in ▶ _____

**DATES OF BIRTH AND DEATH**
Year Born ▼     Year Died ▼

**WAS THIS AUTHOR'S CONTRIBUTION TO THE WORK**

Anonymous?   ☐ Yes   ☐ No
Pseudonymous?   ☐ Yes   ☐ No

If the answer to either of these questions is "Yes," see detailed instructions.

**NATURE OF AUTHORSHIP**   Briefly describe nature of the material created by this author in which copyright is claimed. ▼

☐ Collective Work     Other:

**NOTE**

Under the law, the "author" of a "work made for hire" is generally the employer, not the employee (see instructions). For any part of this work that was "made for hire" check "Yes" in the space provided, give the employer (or other person for whom the work was prepared) as "Author" of that part, and leave the space for dates of birth and death blank.

See instructions before completing this space.

**NAME OF AUTHOR ▼**

b

Was this contribution to the work a "work made for hire"?
☐ Yes
☐ No

**NATURE OF AUTHORSHIP**   ☐ Collective Work   Other:

**NAME OF AUTHOR ▼**

c

Was this contribution to the work a "work made for hire"?
☐ Yes
☐ No

**NATURE OF AUTHORSHIP**   ☐ Collective Work   Other:

**DATES OF BIRTH AND DEATH**
Year Born ▼     Year Died ▼

**AUTHOR'S NATIONALITY OR DOMICILE**
Name of country
OR { Citizen of ▶ _____
    Domiciled in ▶ _____

**WAS THIS AUTHOR'S CONTRIBUTION TO THE WORK**
Anonymous?    ☐ Yes   ☐ No
Pseudonymous?  ☐ Yes   ☐ No
If the answer to either of these questions is "Yes," see detailed instructions.

Briefly describe nature of the material created by this author in which copyright is claimed. ▼

**DATES OF BIRTH AND DEATH**
Year Born ▼     Year Died ▼

**AUTHOR'S NATIONALITY OR DOMICILE**
Name of Country
OR { Citizen of ▶ _____
    Domiciled in ▶ _____

**WAS THIS AUTHOR'S CONTRIBUTION TO THE WORK**
Anonymous?    ☐ Yes   ☐ No
Pseudonymous?  ☐ Yes   ☐ No
If the answer to either of these questions is "Yes," see detailed instructions.

Briefly describe nature of the material created by this author in which copyright is claimed. ▼

**3** **YEAR IN WHICH CREATION OF THIS ISSUE WAS COMPLETED**   This information must be given in all cases.
◀ Year

**DATE AND NATION OF FIRST PUBLICATION OF THIS PARTICULAR ISSUE**
Complete this information   Month ▶ _____   Day ▶ _____   Year ▶ _____
ONLY if this work
has been published.                                                      ◀ Nation

**4** **COPYRIGHT CLAIMANT(S)** Name and address must be given even if the claimant is the same as the author given in space 2.▼

See instructions before completing this space.

**TRANSFER** If the claimant(s) named here in space 4 are different from the author(s) named in space 2, give a brief statement of how the claimant(s) obtained ownership of the copyright.▼

**DO NOT WRITE HERE**
**OFFICE USE ONLY**

APPLICATION RECEIVED

ONE DEPOSIT RECEIVED

TWO DEPOSITS RECEIVED

REMITTANCE NUMBER AND DATE

**MORE ON BACK ▶**   • Complete all applicable spaces (numbers 5-11) on the reverse side of this page.
• See detailed instructions.     • Sign the form at line 10

**DO NOT WRITE HERE**
Page 1 of _____ pages

EXAMINED BY

FORM SE

CHECKED BY

☐ CORRESPONDENCE
Yes

☐ DEPOSIT ACCOUNT
FUNDS USED

FOR
COPYRIGHT
OFFICE
USE
ONLY

**5**

**DO NOT WRITE ABOVE THIS LINE. IF YOU NEED MORE SPACE, USE A SEPARATE CONTINUATION SHEET.**

**PREVIOUS REGISTRATION** Has registration for this issue, or for an earlier version of this particular issue, already been made in the Copyright Office?

☐ **Yes** ☐ **No** If your answer is "Yes," why is another registration being sought? (Check appropriate box) ▶

**a.** ☐ This is the first published version of an issue previously registered in unpublished form.

**b.** ☐ This is the first application submitted by this author as copyright claimant.

**c.** ☐ This is a changed version of this issue, as shown by space 6 on this application.

If your answer is "Yes," give: **Previous Registration Number** ▶          **Year of Registration** ▶

**DERIVATIVE WORK OR COMPILATION**    Complete both space 6a & 6b for a derivative work; complete only 6b for a compilation.

**a. Preexisting Material**  Identify any preexisting work or works that this work is based on or incorporates. ▶

**6**

**b. Material Added to This Work**  Give a brief, general statement of the material that has been added to this work and in which copyright is claimed. ▶

See instructions
before completing
this space.

**7**

—space deleted—

226

**8** REPRODUCTION FOR USE OF BLIND OR PHYSICALLY HANDICAPPED INDIVIDUALS     A signature on this form at space 10, and a check in one of the boxes here in space 8, constitutes a non-exclusive grant of permission to the Library of Congress to reproduce and distribute solely for the blind and physically handicapped and under the conditions and limitations prescribed by the regulations of the Copyright Office: (1) copies of the work identified in space 1 of this application in Braille (or similar tactile symbols); or (2) phonorecords embodying a fixation of a reading of that work; or (3) both.

a ☐ Copies and Phonorecords          b ☐ Copies Only          c ☐ Phonorecords Only          See instructions

**9** DEPOSIT ACCOUNT   If the registration fee is to be charged to a Deposit Account established in the Copyright Office, give name and  number of Account.

Name ▼                    Account Number ▼

CORRESPONDENCE   Give name and address to which correspondence about this application should be sent.   Name/Address/Apt/City/State/Zip ▼

Area Code & Telephone Number ▶

Be sure to
give your
daytime phone
◀ number.

**10** CERTIFICATION*   I, the undersigned, hereby certify that I am the

Check one ▶

☐ author
☐ other copyright claimant
☐ owner of exclusive right(s)
☐ authorized agent of _____
   Name of author or other copyright claimant, or owner of exclusive right(s) ▲

of the work identified in this application and that the statements made
by me in this application are correct to the best of my knowledge.

Typed or printed name and date ▼ If this is a published work, this date must be the same as or later than the date of publication given in space 3.

_____ date ▶

☞ Handwritten signature (X) ▼

**11** MAIL CERTIFI- CATE TO

Name ▼

Number Street Apartment Number ▼

City State ZIP ▼

Certificate
will be
mailed in
window
envelope

**Have you:**
• Completed all necessary spaces?
• Signed your application in space 10?
• Enclosed check or money order for $10 payable to *Register of Copyrights*?
• Enclosed your deposit material with the application and fee?

**MAIL TO:** Register of Copyrights, Library of Congress, Washington, D.C. 20559.

* 17 U.S.C. § 506(e)  Any person who knowingly makes a false representation of a material fact in the application for copyright registration provided for by section 409, or in any written statement filed in connection with the application, shall be fined not more than $2,500.

July 1988—30,000

U.S. GOVERNMENT PRINTING OFFICE: 1988—202-133.80,005

227

# APPLICATION FOR
## *Renewal Registration*

## HOW TO REGISTER A RENEWAL CLAIM:

- **First:** Study the information on this page and make sure you know the answers to two questions:

  (1) What are the renewal time limits in your case?

  (2) Who can claim the renewal?

- **Second:** Turn this page over and read through the specific instructions for filling out Form RE. Make sure, before starting to complete the form, that the copyright is now eligible for renewal, that you are authorized to file a renewal claim, and that you have all of the information about the copyright you will need.

- **Third:** Complete all applicable spaces on Form RE, following the line-by-line instructions on the back of this page. Use typewriter, or print the information in dark ink.

- **Fourth:** Detach this sheet and send your completed Form RE to: Register of Copyrights, Library of Congress, Washington, D.C. 20559. Unless you have a Deposit Account in the Copyright Office, your application must be accompanied by a check or money order for $6, payable to: *Register of Copyrights*. Do not send copies, phonorecords, or supporting documents with your renewal application.

**WHAT IS RENEWAL OF COPYRIGHT?** For works originally copyrighted between January 1, 1950 and December 31, 1977, the statute now in effect provides for a first term of copyright protection lasting for 28 years, with the possibility of renewal for a second term of 47 years. If a valid renewal registration is made for a work, its total copyright term is 75 years (a first term of 28 years, plus a renewal term of 47 years). Example:

To determine the time limits for renewal in your case:

(1) First, find out the date of original copyright for the work. (In the case of works originally registered in unpublished form, the date of copyright is the date of registration; for published works, copyright begins on the date of first publication.)

For a work copyrighted in 1960, the first term will expire in 1988, but if renewed at the proper time the copyright will last through the end of 2035.

## SOME BASIC POINTS ABOUT RENEWAL:

(1) There are strict time limits and deadlines for renewing a copyright.

(2) Only certain persons who fall into specific categories named in the law can claim renewal.

(3) The new copyright law does away with renewal requirements for works first copyrighted after 1977. However, copyrights that were already in their first copyright term on January 1, 1978 (that is, works originally copyrighted between January 1, 1950 and December 31, 1977) **still have to be renewed** in order to be protected for a second term.

**TIME LIMITS FOR RENEWAL REGISTRATION:** The new copyright statute provides that, in order to renew a copyright, the renewal application and fee must be received in the Copyright Office "within one year prior to the expiration of the copyright." It also provides that all terms of copyright will run through the end of the year in which they would otherwise expire. Since all copyright terms will expire on December 31st of their last year, all periods for renewal registration will run from December 31st of the 27th year of the copyright, and will end on December 31st of the following year.

(2) Then add 28 years to the year the work was originally copyrighted.

Your answer will be the calendar year during which the copyright will be eligible for renewal, and December 31st of that year will be the renewal deadline. Example: a work originally copyrighted on April 19, 1957, will be eligible for renewal between December 31, 1984, and December 31, 1985.

**WHO MAY CLAIM RENEWAL:** Renewal copyright may be claimed only by those persons specified in the law. Except in the case of four specific types of works, the law gives the right to claim renewal to the individual author of the work, regardless of who owned the copyright during the original term. If the author is dead, the statute gives the right to claim renewal to certain of the author's beneficiaries (widow and children, executors, or next of kin, depending on the circumstances). The present owner (proprietor) of the copyright is entitled to claim renewal only in four specified cases, as explained in more detail on the reverse of this page.

**CAUTION:** Renewal registration is possible only if an acceptable application and fee are **received** in the Copyright Office during the renewal period and before the renewal deadline. If an acceptable application and fee are not received before the renewal deadline, the work falls into the public domain and the copyright cannot be renewed. The Copyright Office has no discretion to extend the renewal time limits.

# INSTRUCTIONS FOR COMPLETING FORM RE

## SPACE 1: RENEWAL CLAIM(S)

- **General Instructions:** In order for this application to result in a valid renewal, space 1 must identify one or more of the persons who are entitled to renew the copyright under the statute. Give the full name and address of each claimant, with a statement of the basis of each claim, using the wording given in these instructions.

- **Persons Entitled to Renew:**

A. The following persons may claim renewal in all types of works except those enumerated in Paragraph B, below:

1. The author, if living. State the claim as: *the author.*
2. The widow, widower, and/or children of the author, if the author is not living. State the claim as: *the widow (widower) of the author* . . . . . . . . . . (Name of author) and/or *the child (children) of the deceased author* . . . . . . . . . . . . (Name of author)

3. The author's executor(s), if the author left a will and if there is no surviving widow, widower, or child. State the claim as: *the executor(s) of the author* . . . . . . . . . . . . (Name of author)

4. The next of kin of the author, if the author left no will and if there is no surviving widow, widower, or child. State the claim as: *the next of kin of the deceased author* . . . . . . . . . . . . *there being no will.* (Name of author)

B. In the case of the following four types of works, the proprietor (owner of the copyright at the time of the renewal registration) may claim renewal:

1. Posthumous work (a work as to which no copyright assignment or other contract for exploitation has occurred during the author's lifetime). State the claim as: *proprietor of copyright in a posthumous work.*

2. Periodical, cyclopedic, or other composite work. State the claim as: *proprietor of copyright in a composite work.*

3. "Work copyrighted by a corporate body otherwise than as assignee or licensee of the individual author." State the claim as: *proprietor of copyright in a work copyrighted by a corporate body otherwise than as assignee or licensee of the individual author.* (This type of claim is considered appropriate in relatively few cases.)

4. Work copyrighted by an employer for whom such work was made for hire. State the claim as: *proprietor of copyright in a work made for hire.*

## SPACE 2: WORK RENEWED

- **General Instructions:** This space is to identify the particular work being renewed. The information given here should agree with that appearing in the certificate of original registration.

- **Title:** Give the full title of the work, together with any subtitles or descriptive wording included with the title in the original registration. In the case of a musical composition, give the specific instrumentation of the work.

- **Renewable Matter:** Copyright in a new version of a previous work (such as an arrangement, translation, dramatization, compilation, or work republished with new matter) covers only the additions, changes, or other new material appearing for the first time in that version. If this work was a new version, state in general the new matter upon which copyright was claimed.

- **Contribution to Periodical, Serial, or other Composite Work:** Separate renewal registration is possible for a work published as a contribution to a periodical, serial, or other composite work, whether the contribution was copyrighted independently or as part of the larger work in which it appeared. Each contribution published in a separate issue ordinarily requires a separate renewal registration. However, the new law provides an alternative, permitting groups of periodical contributions by the same individual author to be combined under a single renewal application and fee in certain cases.

If this renewal application covers a single contribution, give all of the requested information in space 2. If you are seeking to renew a group of contributions, include a reference such as "See space 5" in space 2 and give the requested information about all of the contributions in space 5.

230

# SPACE 3: AUTHOR(S)

• *General Instructions:* The copyright secured in a new version of a work is independent of any copyright protection in material published earlier. The only "authors" of a new version are those who contributed copyrightable matter to it. Thus, for renewal purposes, the person who wrote the original version on which the new work is based cannot be regarded as an "author" of the new version, unless that person also contributed to the new matter.

• *Authors of Renewable Matter:* Give the full names of all authors who contributed copyrightable matter to this particular version of the work.

# SPACE 4: FACTS OF ORIGINAL REGISTRATION

• *General Instructions:* Each item in space 4 should agree with the information appearing in the original registration for the work. If the work being renewed is a single contribution to a periodical or composite work that was not separately registered, give information about the particular issue in which the contribution appeared. You may leave this space blank if you are completing space 5.

• *Original Registration Number:* Give the full registration number, which is a series of numerical digits, preceded by one or more letters. The registration number appears in the upper right hand corner of the certificate of registration.

• *Original Copyright Claimant:* Give the name in which ownership of the copyright was claimed in the original registration.

• *Date of Publication or Registration:* Give only one date. If the original registration gave a publication date, it should be transcribed here; otherwise the registration was for an unpublished work, and the date of registration should be given.

# SPACE 5: GROUP RENEWALS

• *General Instructions:* A single renewal registration can be made for a group of works if all of the following statutory conditions are met: (1) all of the works were written by the same author, who is named in space 3 and who is or was an individual (not an employer for hire); (2) all of the works were first published as contributions to periodicals (including newspapers) and were copyrighted on their first publication; (3) the renewal claimant or claimants, and the basis of claim or claims, as stated in space 1, is the same for all of the works; (4) the renewal application and fee are "received not more than 28 or less than 27 years after the 31st day of December of the calendar year in which all of the works were first published"; and (5) the renewal application identifies each work separately, including the periodical containing it and the date of first publication.

*Time Limits for Group Renewals:* To be renewed as a group, all of the contributions must have been first published during the same calendar year. For example, suppose six contributions by the same author were published on April 1, 1960, July 1, 1960, November 1, 1960, February 1, 1961, July 1, 1961, and March 1, 1962. The three 1960 copyrights can be combined and renewed at any time during 1988, and the two 1961 copyrights can be renewed as a group during 1989, but the 1962 copyright must be renewed by itself, in 1990.

*Identification of Each Work:* Give all of the requested information for each contribution. The registration number should be that for the contribution itself if it was separately registered, and the registration number for the periodical issue if it was not.

# SPACES 6, 7 AND 8: FEE, MAILING INSTRUCTIONS, AND CERTIFICATION

• *Deposit Account and Mailing Instructions (Space 6):* If you maintain a Deposit Account in the Copyright Office, identify it in space 6. Otherwise, you will need to send the renewal registration fee of $6 with your form. The space headed "Correspondence" should contain the name and address of the person to be consulted if correspondence about the form becomes necessary

• *Certification (Space 7):* The renewal application is not acceptable unless it bears the handwritten signature of the renewal claimant or the duly authorized agent of the renewal claimant.

• *Address for Return of Certificate (Space 8):* The address box must be completed legibly, since the certificate will be returned in a window envelope.

# FORM RE

UNITED STATES COPYRIGHT OFFICE

REGISTRATION NUMBER

EFFECTIVE DATE OF RENEWAL REGISTRATION

..........  ..........  ..........
(Month)     (Day)      (Year)

---

DO NOT WRITE ABOVE THIS LINE.    FOR COPYRIGHT OFFICE USE ONLY

---

RENEWAL CLAIMANT(S), ADDRESS(ES), AND STATEMENT OF CLAIM: (See Instructions)

| ① Renewal Claimant(s) | 1 | Name .................................................................... <br> Address ................................................................. <br> Claiming as ........................................................... <br> (Use appropriate statement from instructions) |
|---|---|---|
| | 2 | Name .................................................................... <br> Address ................................................................. <br> Claiming as ........................................................... <br> (Use appropriate statement from instructions) |
| | 3 | Name .................................................................... <br> Address ................................................................. <br> Claiming as ........................................................... <br> (Use appropriate statement from instructions) |

**② Work Renewed**

**TITLE OF WORK IN WHICH RENEWAL IS CLAIMED:**

**RENEWABLE MATTER:**

**CONTRIBUTION TO PERIODICAL OR COMPOSITE WORK:**

Title of periodical or composite work: ...........................................

If a periodical or other serial, give: Vol. ............... No. ............... Issue Date ...............

**③ Author(s)**

**AUTHOR(S) OF RENEWABLE MATTER:**

**④ Facts of Original Registration**

**ORIGINAL REGISTRATION NUMBER:**

..............................................

**ORIGINAL COPYRIGHT CLAIMANT:**

**ORIGINAL DATE OF COPYRIGHT:**

• If the original registration for this work was made in published form,

give:

DATE OF PUBLICATION: ...............  ...............  ...............
　　　　　　　　　　　　　　(Month)　　(Day)　　(Year)

OR

• If the original registration for this work was made in unpublished form,

give:

DATE OF REGISTRATION: ...............  ...............  ...............
　　　　　　　　　　　　　　(Month)　　(Day)　　(Year)

233

**DO NOT WRITE ABOVE THIS LINE. FOR COPYRIGHT OFFICE USE ONLY**

**RENEWAL FOR GROUP OF WORKS BY SAME AUTHOR:** To make a single registration for a group of works by the same individual author published as contributions to periodicals (see instructions). give full information about each contribution. If more space is needed, request continuation sheet (Form RE/CON).

**5** Renewal for Group of Works

| | | |
|---|---|---|
| **1** | Title of Contribution: .......... | |
| | Title of Periodical: .......... Vol. .... No. .... Issue Date .... | |
| | Date of Publication: .......... Registration Number: .... | |
| | (Month) (Day) (Year) | |
| **2** | Title of Contribution: .......... | |
| | Title of Periodical: .......... Vol. .... No. .... Issue Date .... | |
| | Date of Publication: .......... Registration Number: .... | |
| | (Month) (Day) (Year) | |
| **3** | Title of Contribution: .......... | |
| | Title of Periodical: .......... Vol. .... No. .... Issue Date .... | |
| | Date of Publication: .......... Registration Number: .... | |
| | (Month) (Day) (Year) | |
| **4** | Title of Contribution: .......... | |
| | Title of Periodical: .......... Vol. .... No. .... Issue Date .... | |
| | Date of Publication: .......... Registration Number: .... | |
| | (Month) (Day) (Year) | |
| **5** | Title of Contribution: .......... | |
| | Title of Periodical: .......... Vol. .... No. .... Issue Date .... | |
| | Date of Publication: .......... Registration Number: .... | |
| | (Month) (Day) (Year) | |

234

|   | Title of Contribution: . . . . . . . . . . . . . . . . . . . . . . . . . . . . . . . . . . . . . . . . . . . . . . . . . . . . . . . . . . . . . . . . . . |
|---|---|
| 6 | Title of Periodical: . . . . . . . . . . . . . . . . . . . . . . . . . Vol. . . . . . . No. . . . . . . Issue Date . . . . . . . |
|   | Date of Publication: . . . . . . . . . . . . . . . . . . . . . . . . . . . . . . . . . . . . . . Registration Number: . . . . . . |
|   | (Month) (Day) (Year) |
|   | Title of Contribution: . . . . . . . . . . . . . . . . . . . . . . . . . . . . . . . . . . . . . . . . . . . . . . . . . . . . . . . . . . . |
| 7 | Title of Periodical: . . . . . . . . . . . . . . . . . . . . . . . . . Vol. . . . . . . No. . . . . . . Issue Date . . . . . . . |
|   | Date of Publication: . . . . . . . . . . . . . . . . . . . . . . . . . . . . . . . . . . . . . . Registration Number: . . . . . . |
|   | (Month) (Day) (Year) |

**(6)**
Fee and Correspond-ence

**DEPOSIT ACCOUNT:** (If the registration fee is to be charged to a Deposit Account established in the Copyright Office, give name and number of Account.)

Name: . . . . . . . . . . . . . . . . . . . . . . . . . . . . . . . . . . . . . . . . . . . . . . . . . . . . . . . . . .

Account Number: . . . . . . . . . . . . . . . . . . . . . . . . . . . . . . . . . . . . . . . . . . . . . . . . . .

**CORRESPONDENCE:** (Give name and address to which correspond-ence about this application should be sent.)

Name: . . . . . . . . . . . . . . . . . . . . . . . . . . . . . . . . . . . . . . . . . . . . . . . . . . . . . . . . . . . .

Address: . . . . . . . . . . . . . . . . . . . . . . . . . . . . . . . . . . . . . . . . . . . . . . (Apt.) . . . . .

. . . . . . . . . . . . . . . . . . . . . . . . . . . . . . . . . . . . . . . . . . . . . . . . . . . . . . . . . . . . . . . .

(City) (State) (ZIP)

**(7)**
Certification (Application must be signed)

**CERTIFICATION:** I, the undersigned, hereby certify that I am the: (Check one)

☐ renewal claimant      ☐ duly authorized agent of: . . . . . . . . . . . . . . . . . . . . . . . . . . .

(Name of renewal claimant)

of the work identified in this application, and that the statements made by me in this application are correct to the best of my knowledge.

Handwritten signature: (X) . . . . . . . . . . . . . . . . . . . . . . . . . . . . . . . . . . . . . . . . . . . . . . . . .

Typed or printed name . . . . . . . . . . . . . . . . . . . . . . . . . . . . . Date: . . . . . . . . . . . . . . . . . .

**(8)**
Address for Return of Certificate

**MAIL CERTIFICATE TO**

(Certificate will be mailed in window envelope)

. . . . . . . . . . . . . . . . . . . . . . . . . . . . . . . . . . . . . . . . . . . . . . . . . . . . . . . . . . . . . . . . .
(Name)

. . . . . . . . . . . . . . . . . . . . . . . . . . . . . . . . . . . . . . . . . . . . . . . . . . . . . . . . . . . . . . . . .
(Number, Street and Apartment Number)

. . . . . . . . . . . . . . . . . . . . . . . . . . . . . . . . . . . . . . . . . . . . . . . . . . . . . . . . . . . . . . . . .
(City) (State) (ZIP code)

★ U.S. GOVERNMENT PRINTING OFFICE: 1987—181—531/40,019

March 1987—30,000

## FORM CA

UNITED STATES COPYRIGHT OFFICE
LIBRARY OF CONGRESS
WASHINGTON, D.C. 20559

# Application for
# Supplementary Copyright Registration

To Correct or Amplify Information Given in the
Copyright Office Record of an Earlier Registration

**USE THIS FORM WHEN:**

- An earlier registration has been made in the Copyright Office; and

- Some of the facts given in that registration are incorrect or incomplete; and

- You want to place the correct or complete facts on record.

**What is "Supplementary Copyright Registration"?** Supplementary registration is a special type of copyright registration provided for in section 408(d) of the copyright law.

**Purpose of Supplementary Registration.** As a rule, only one basic copyright registration can be made for the same work. To take care of cases where information in the basic registration turns out to be incorrect or incomplete, the law provides for "the filing of an application for supplementary registration, to correct an error in a copyright registration or to amplify the information given in a registration."

**How to Apply for Supplementary Registration:**

*First:* Study the information on this page to make sure that filing an application on Form CA is the best procedure to follow in your case.

*Second:* Turn this page over and read through the specific instructions for filling out Form CA. Make sure, before starting to complete the form, that you have all of the detailed information about the basic registration you will need.

236

**Earlier Registration Necessary.** Supplementary registration can be made only if a basic copyright registration for the same work has already been completed.

**Who May File.** Once basic registration has been made for a work, any author or other copyright claimant, or owner of any exclusive right in the work, who wishes to correct or amplify the information given in the basic registration, may submit Form CA.

**Please Note:**

- Do not use Form CA to correct errors in statements on the copies or phonorecords of the work in question, or to reflect changes in the content of the work. If the work has been changed substantially, you should consider making an entirely new registration for the revised version to cover the additions or revisions.

- Do not use Form CA as a substitute for renewal registration. For works originally copyrighted between January 1, 1950 and December 31, 1977, registration of a renewal claim within strict time limits is necessary to extend the first 28-year copyright term to the full term of 75 years. This cannot be done by filing Form CA.

- Do not use Form CA as a substitute for recording a transfer of copyright or other document pertaining to rights under a copyright. Recording a document under section 205 of the statute gives all persons constructive notice of the facts stated in the document and may have other important consequences in cases of infringement or conflicting transfers. Supplementary registration does not have that legal effect.

***Third:*** Complete all applicable spaces on this form, following the line-by-line instructions on the back of this page. Use typewriter, or print the information in dark ink.

***Fourth:*** Detach this sheet and send your completed Form CA to: Register of Copyrights, Library of Congress, Washington, D.C. 20559. Unless you have a Deposit Account in the Copyright Office, your application must be accompanied by a non-refundable filing fee in the form of a check or money order for $10 payable to: *Register of Copyrights.* Do not send copies, phonorecords, or supporting documents with your application, since they cannot be made part of the record of a supplementary registration.

**What Happens When a Supplementary Registration is Made?** When a supplementary registration is completed, the Copyright Office will assign it a new registration number in the appropriate registration category, and issue a certificate of supplementary registration under that number. The basic registration will not be expunged or cancelled, and the two registrations will both stand in the Copyright Office records. The supplementary registration will have the effect of calling the public's attention to a possible error or omission in the basic registration, and of placing the correct facts or the additional information on official record. Moreover, if the person on whose behalf Form CA is submitted is the same as the person identified as copyright claimant in the basic registration, the Copyright Office will place a note referring to the supplementary registration in its records of the basic registration.

PLEASE READ DETAILED INSTRUCTIONS ON REVERSE

Please read the following line-by-line instructions carefully and refer to them while completing Form CA.

# INSTRUCTIONS

## For Completing FORM CA (Supplementary Registration)

### PART A: BASIC INSTRUCTIONS

• **General Instructions:** The information in this part identifies the basic registration to be corrected or amplified. Each item must agree exactly with the information as it already appears in the basic registration (even if the purpose of filing Form CA is to change one of these items).

• **Title of Work:** Give the title as it appears in the basic registration, including previous or alternative titles if they appear.

• **Registration Number:** This is a series of numerical digits, pre- ceded by one or more letters. The registration number appears in the upper right hand corner of the certificate of registration.

• **Registration Date:** Give the year when the basic registration was completed.

• **Name(s) of Author(s) and Name(s) of Copyright Claim- ant(s):** Give all of the names as they appear in the basic registra- tion.

### PART B: CORRECTION

• **General Instructions:** Complete this part **only** if information in the basic registration was incorrect at the time that basic registration was made. Leave this part blank and complete Part C, instead, if your purpose is to add, update, or clarify information rather than to rectify an actual error.

• **Location and Nature of Incorrect Information:** Give the line number and the heading or description of the space in the basic registration where the error occurs (for example: "Line number 3 . . . Citizenship of author").

• **Incorrect Information as It Appears in Basic Registration:** Transcribe the erroneous statement exactly as it appears in the basic registration.

• **Corrected Information:** Give the statement as it should have ap- peared.

• **Explanation of Correction (Optional):** If you wish, you may add an explanation of the error or its correction.

## PART C: AMPLIFICATION

• **General Instructions:** Complete this part if you want to provide any of the following: (1) additional information that could have been given but was omitted at the time of basic registration; (2) changes in facts, such as changes of title or address of claimant, that have occurred since the basic registration; or (3) explanations clarifying information in the basic registration.

• **Location and Nature of Information to be Amplified:** Give the line number and the heading or description of the space in the basic registration where the information to be amplified appears.

• **Amplified Information:** Give a statement of the added, updated, or explanatory information as clearly and succinctly as possible.

• **Explanation of Amplification (Optional):** If you wish, you may add an explanation of the amplification.

## PARTS D, E, F, G: CONTINUATION, FEE, MAILING INSTRUCTIONS AND CERTIFICATION

• **Continuation (Part D):** Use this space if you do not have enough room in Parts B or C.

• **Deposit Account and Mailing Instructions (Part E):** If you maintain a Deposit Account in the Copyright Office, identify it in Part E. Otherwise, you will need to send the non-refundable filing fee of $10 with your form. The space headed "Correspondence" should contain the name and address of the person to be consulted if correspondence about the form becomes necessary.

• **Certification (Part F):** The application is not acceptable unless it bears the handwritten signature of the author, or other copyright claimant, or of the owner of exclusive right(s), or of the duly authorized agent of such author, claimant, or owner.

• **Address for Return of Certificate (Part G):** The address box must be completed legibly, since the certificate will be returned in a window envelope.

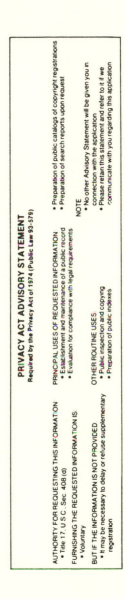

# FORM CA

UNITED STATES COPYRIGHT OFFICE

REGISTRATION NUMBER

| TX | TXU | PA | PAU | VA | VAU | SR | SRU | RE |
|----|-----|----|-----|----|-----|----|-----|-----|

Effective Date of Supplementary Registration

........... ........... ...........
MONTH         DAY          YEAR

---

DO NOT WRITE ABOVE THIS LINE. FOR COPYRIGHT OFFICE USE ONLY

**A**
Basic Instructions

**TITLE OF WORK:**

**REGISTRATION NUMBER OF BASIC REGISTRATION:**

**YEAR OF BASIC REGISTRATION:**

**NAME(S) OF AUTHOR(S):**

**NAME(S) OF COPYRIGHT CLAIMANT(S):**

**B**
Correction

**LOCATION AND NATURE OF INCORRECT INFORMATION IN BASIC REGISTRATION:**

Line Number .......... Line Heading or Description ..........

**INCORRECT INFORMATION AS IT APPEARS IN BASIC REGISTRATION:**

CORRECTED INFORMATION:

EXPLANATION OF CORRECTION: (Optional)

**C** Amplification

**LOCATION AND NATURE OF INFORMATION IN BASIC REGISTRATION TO BE AMPLIFIED:**

Line Number . . . . . . . . . . Line Heading or Description . . . . . . . . . . . . . . . . . . . . .

AMPLIFIED INFORMATION:

EXPLANATION OF AMPLIFIED INFORMATION: (Optional)

241

FORM CA RECEIVED:

FOR
COPYRIGHT
OFFICE
USE
ONLY

EXAMINED BY: ................

CHECKED BY: ................

CORRESPONDENCE:
☐ YES

REMITTANCE NUMBER AND DATE:

REFERENCE TO THIS REGISTRATION
ADDED TO BASIC REGISTRATION:
☐ YES ☐ NO

DEPOSIT ACCOUNT FUNDS USED: ☐

**DO NOT WRITE ABOVE THIS LINE.  FOR COPYRIGHT OFFICE USE ONLY**

**CONTINUATION OF:** (Check which)  ☐ PART B  OR  ☐ PART C

**(D)** Continuation

**DEPOSIT ACCOUNT:** If the registration fee is to be charged to a Deposit Account established in the Copyright Office, give name and number of Account:

Name .................... Account Number ....................

**(E)** Deposit
Account and
Mailing
Instructions

**CORRESPONDENCE:** Give name and address to which correspondence should be sent:

Name . . . . . . . . . . . . . . . . . . . . . . . . . . . . . . . . . . . . . . . . . . . . Apt. No. . . . . . . . .

Address . . . . . . . . . . . . . . . . . . . . . . . . . . . . . . . . . . . . . . . . . . . . . . . . . . . . . . . . . . .

         (Number and Street)         (City)         (State)         (ZIP Code)

**(F)**

---

**CERTIFICATION ✱** I, the undersigned, hereby certify that I am the: (Check one)

☐ author ☐ other copyright claimant ☐ owner of exclusive right(s) ☐ authorized agent of: . . . . . . . . . . . . . . . . . . . . . . . . . . . . . . . . . . . . . . . .

                                           (Name of author or other copyright claimant, or owner of exclusive right(s))

of the work identified in this application and that the statements made by me in this application are correct to the best of my knowledge.

Handwritten signature: (X) . . . . . . . . . . . . . . . . . . . . . . . . . . . . . . . . . . . . . . . . . . . . . .

Typed or printed name . . . . . . . . . . . . . . . . . . . . . . . . . . . . . . . . . . . . . . . . . . . . .

Date: . . . . . . . . . . . . . . . . . . . . . . . . . . . . . . . . . . . . . . . . . . . . . . . . . . . . . . . . . .

✱ 17 USC §506(e) FALSE REPRESENTATION – Any person who knowingly makes a false representation of a material fact in the application for copyright registration provided for by section 409 or in any written statement filed in connection with the application, shall be fined not more than $2,500.

**Certification (Application must be signed)**

---

**(G)**

**MAIL CERTIFICATE TO**

**(Certificate will be mailed in window envelope)**

. . . . . . . . . . . . . . . . . . . . . . . . . . . . . . . . . .

. . . . . . . . . . . . . . . . . . . . . . . . . . . . . . . . . .
         (Name)

. . . . . . . . . . . . . . . . . . . . . . . . . . . . . . . . . .
(Number, Street and Apartment Number)

. . . . . . . . . . . . . . . . . . . . . . . . . . . . . . . . . .
   (City)         (State)         (ZIP code)

**Address for Return of Certificate**

---

April 1988—15,000

☆ U.S. GOVERNMENT PRINTING OFFICE: 1988—202-133 60,014

# Appendix B

## Labor Organizations and Associations

### NEW YORK CITY

Actors Equity Association
165 West 46 Street
New York, N.Y. 10036
(212) 869 8530

American Federation for Television and Radio Artists (AFTRA)
260 Madison Avenue
New York, N.Y. 10016
(212) 532 0800

American Federation of Musicians (AFM)
1501 Broadway
New York, N.Y. 10036
(212) 869 1330

American Society of Composers, Authors and Publishers (ASCAP)
1 Lincoln Plaza
New York, N.Y. 10023
(212) 595 3050

Broadcast Music, Inc. (BMI)
320 West 57 Street
New York, N.Y. 10019
(212) 586 2000

Directors Guild of America (DGA)
110 West 57 Street
New York, N.Y. 10019
(212) 581 0370

International Alliance of Theatrical Stage Employees (IATSE)
1515 Broadway
New York, N.Y. 10016
(212) 730 1770

National Association of Broadcast Employees & Technicians (NABET)
322 Eighth Avenue
New York, N.Y. 10001
(212) 633 9292

Screen Actors Guild (SAG)
1515 Broadway
New York, N.Y. 10036
(212) 944 1030

Writers Guild of America (WGA)
555 West 57 Street
New York, N.Y. 10019
(212) 245 6180

## LOS ANGELES

Actors Equity Association
6430 Sunset Blvd.
Los Angeles, CA 90028
(213) 462 2334

American Federation for Television and Radio Artists
6922 Hollywood Boulevard
Hollywood, CA 90028
(213) 461 8111

American Film Institute
2021 N. Western Ave.
Los Angeles, CA 90027
(213) 856 7600

American Society of Composers, Authors and Publishers
21550 Oxnard Ave.
Suite 590
Woodland Hills, CA 91367
(213) 466 7681

Broadcast Music, Inc.
8730 Sunset Blvd.
Los Angeles, CA 90069
(213) 659 9109

Directors Guild of America
7920 Sunset Blvd.
Los Angeles, CA 90046
(213) 289 2000

International Alliance of Theatrical Stage Employees
14724 Ventura Blvd.
Sherman Oaks, CA
(818) 905 8999

Screen Actors Guild
7765 Hollywood Blvd.
Hollywood, CA 90028
(213) 465 4600

Writers Guild of America
8955 Beverly Blvd.
Los Angeles, CA 90048
(213) 550 1000

# NOTES

The notes contained herein are intended for reference only, and are not intended to be inclusive or comprehensive.

## CHAPTER 1

1. *Trust Company (for estate of Stephens Mitchell) v. MGM/UA Entertainment Company,* 772 F.2d 740 (11th Cir. 1985). *Gone with the Wind* not to be expanded beyond the film as first made, despite strong public demand, because Margaret Mitchell resisted all attempts to write a sequel.

2. But see *Russell v. Price,* 448 F. Supp. 303 (C.D. Cal. 1977). "[E]ven though the derivative work may have fallen into the public domain, to the extent that it partakes of the original work it cannot be used without the consent of the proprieter of the underlying copyright."

3. *Goldsmith v. Commissioner of Internal Revenue,* 143 F.2d 466 (2d Cir. 1944) states that the "copyright owner can assign separately to whomsoever. [T]he assignee does not become the owner of the copyright itself and acquires only what lesser rights are granted by the term of the assignment."

4. *Hearst Corporation v. Shopping Center Network, Inc.,* 307 F. Supp. 551 (1969) states that "the mere registration and deposit of copies of the unpublished works with the Copyright Office constitutes the act of obtaining statutory copyright."

5. *Bartsch v. Metro-Goldwyn-Mayer Film Co.,* 391 F.2d 150 (2d Cir. 1968) holds that the copyright owner is unable to enjoin the assignee of the motion picture version from broadcasting picture on television.

6. *Seigel v. Merrick,* 441 F. Supp. 587 (S.D.N.Y. 1977). Dispute over turn-around provision, regarding play *Promises, Promises.*

7. But see *Granz v. Harris,* 198 F.2d 585 (2nd Cir. 1952), which states that relief can be granted to the author, if editing rights are clearly defined in the contract.

8. *Grove Press, Inc. v. Greenleaf Publishing Co.,* 247 F. Supp. 518 (E.D.N.Y. 1965), which states that the failure of the French author to copyright his English translation does not mean that the original French language work was now unprotected.

9. *Hempstead Theatre Corp. v. Metropolitan Playhouses, Inc.,* 6 N.Y.2d 311, 160 N.E.2d 604, 189 N.Y.S.2d 837 (1959) states that the distinction between gross receipts and net receipts are crucial to the outcome.

10. *Republic Pictures v. Roy Rogers,* 222 F.2d 950 (9th Cir. 1955) holds that the "only appellee has the right to use his name, picture or voice in advertisements except for advertisements of motion pictures."

11. See WGA basic agreement.

12. *Poe v. Michael Todd Co., Inc.,* 151 F. Supp. 801 (S.D.N.Y. 1957) held that the author was entitled to determination of damages for failure to give screen credits; however, to grant an injunction to stop the release of the film *Around the World in Eighty Days* would not be equitable to the considerate efforts already placed in the film production.

13. *Sunset Securities Co. v. Coward-McCann, Inc.,* 306 F.2d 777 (Cal. 1957) states that the failure to pay a specific sum results in the reversion of motion picture rights.

14. *Hearst Corporation v. Shopping Center Network, Inc.,* 307 F. Supp. 551 (1969) regarding *Yellow Submarine,* common law copyright remedies available, thus not limited to federal copyright law; however, using copyright statute means abandoning common law rights.


## CHAPTER 2

1. *Pryor v. Franklin,* Case No TAC 17 MP 114 Labor Commissioner, State of California, Division of Labor Standards Enforcement (C. G. Joseph, Special Hearing Officer, August 18, 1982), held that the manager holding himself out to third parties as agent, "procuring and attempting to procure employment [for Pryor] in various entertainment fields," was acting as an agent. He was unlicensed by the State of California and guilty of conflict of interest and blatant self-dealing.

2. *Article II, NY Gen. Bus. Law., Sec 170–190 and the CA Labor Code.*

3. *Pine v. Laine,* 321 NYS 2d 303 (1st Dept. 1971) defines the difference between the procurement of a recording contract (agent's function) and business managing.

4. *Gershunov v. Panov,* 430 NYS 2d 299 (1st Dept. 1980). A conflict of interest between managerial and agency status negates recovery.

5. *Mandel v. Liebman,* 100 N.E. 2d 149 (1951) holds that, where one side renders service to the other, it may not be said the contract was unconscionable.

6. *Croce v. Kurnit,* 565 F. Supp. 884 (S.D.N.Y. 1982) discusses breach of manager's fiduciary duty.

7. *In the Matter of the Arbitration Between Freddie Prinze aka Freddie Pruetzel v. David Jonas,* 381 N.Y.S. 2d 824, 38 N.Y. 2d 570 (1976) discussed contracts with minors. The arbitration clause within the contract was "not unreasonable" since arbitration is a standard practice in the entertainment industry. Also see *Buch-*

*wald v. Katz,* 62 Cal. Rptr. 364, 254 Cal. App.2d 347 (1967), which discusses validity of arbitration.

## CHAPTER 3

1. *Pryor v. Franklin,* TAC 17 MP 114, State of California Labor Commissioner, Division of Labor Standards Enforcement (Aug. 18, 1982). The manager, holding himself out to third parties as agent, was "procuring and attempting to procure employment [for Pryor] in various entertainment fields" was found to be acting as agent. He was unlicensed in California and was guilty of conflict of interest and blatant self-dealing.

2. *Pine v. Laine,* 321 N.Y.S.2d 303 (1st Dep't. 1971) citing Gen. Bus. Law. Sec. 171 (7), defines difference between the procurement of a recording contract (the agent's function) and business managing. See also *Gershunov v. Panov,* 430 N.Y.S.2d 299 (1st Dep't., 1980), conflict of interest between managerial and agency status negates recovery.

3. *Raquel Welch and Raquel Welch Productions, Inc. v. Metro-Goldwyn-Mayer Film Co.,* 254 Cal. Rptr. 645, 207 Cal. App. 3rd 164 (1989). Actor won her claim in support of pay or play clause. Damage to actor's reputation in the industry required substantial additional damages.

4. *Mandel v. Liebman,* 100 N.E.2d 149 (N.Y. 1951), defined unconscionability as that which no man in his senses and not under delusion would make on the one hand, and as that which no honest or fair man would accept on the other.

## CHAPTER 4

1. *Raquel Welch and Raquel Welch Productions, Inc. v. Metro-Goldwyn-Mayer Film Co.,* 254 Cal. Rptr. 645, 207 Cal. App. 3d 164 (1989) regarding success in pay or play suit.

2. *Warner Brothers Pictures Inc. v. James Bumgarner aka James Garner,* 17 Ca.1 Rptr. 171 (1962), where actor prevailed against producer's *force majeure* claim based on short-lived strike.

3. *In the Matter of the Arbitration Between Freddie Prinze aka Freddie Preutzel v. David Jonas,* 381 N.Y.S. 2d 824, 38 N.Y. 2d 570, 345 N.E. 2d 295 (1976), concerning validity of contracts with minors and the ruling that the arbitration clause within the contract between Prinze and personal manager Jonas was not unreasonable.

4. *Metro-Goldwyn-Mayer Film Co. v. Scheider,* 352 N.Y.S. 2d 205 (App. Div. 1st Dep't. 1974), regarding exercise of option to use actor for plot and series.

5. *Goudal v. Cecil B. De Mille Picture Corp.,* 5 F2d 432 (Ca. App. 1931) regarding validity of yearly options for pay increases after wrongful discharge.

6. *In the Matter of the Arbitration Between Freddie Prinze aka Freddie Pruetzel v. David Jonas,* 381 N.Y.S. 2d 824, 38 N.Y. 2d 570, 345 N.E. 2d 295 (1976), regarding validity of contract with minors.

7. *Warner Brothers Pictures Inc. v. Brodel,* 192 P.2d 949 (Cal. 1948). Minors within the entertainment industry are protected by statute and the courts, but

once protective provisions in the contract are adhered to, contracts are valid despite the age of the minor.

## CHAPTER 5

1. A copy of the WGA Theatrical and Television Basic Agreement (hereinafter referred to as WGA basic agreement) is available by contacting WGA East, 555 West 57 St., New York, N.Y. 10019, or WGA West, 8955 Beverly Blvd., Los Angeles, Calif. 90048.

2. See *17 U.S.C. sec. 101* (definitions) and *sec. 201 (b)*. "In the case of a work made for hire, the employer or other person for whom the work was prepared is considered the author for purposes of title, and, unless the parties have expressly agreed otherwise in a written instrument signed by them, owns all the rights comprised in the copyright."

3. See WGA basic agreement regarding guild membership requirements.

4. See WGA basic agreement regarding general provisions for location expenses.

5. *Stevens v. National Broadcasting Company,* 270 Ca. App. 2d 886, 76 Cal. Rptr. 106 (2d Dist., Div. 1 1969), regarding employer's ownership of items created by employees as part of their employment duties.

6. The Copyright Act of 1976 states that "(a) transfer of copyright ownership, other than by operation of law, is not valid unless an instrument of conveyance, or a note or memorandum of the transfer, is in writing and signed by the owner of the rights conveyed or such owner's duly authorized agent." *17 U.S.C. Sec. 201 (b)* states that a work made for hire creates an operation of law that transfers copyright ownership without requiring a written agreement. But, the presence of a written and signed transfer of copyright ownership from the screenwriter to the producer erases any doubt whatsoever.

7. *Gilliam v. American Broadcasting Companies,* 538 F.2d 14, 24 (2d Cir. 1976) defines moral rights as the "rights of the artist to have his work attributed to him in the form that he created it." But note *Seroff v. Simon & Schuster, Inc.,* 6 Misc. 2d, 383, 162 N.Y.S. 2d 770 (N.Y. Sup. Ct. 1957), *aff'd,* 12 A.D.2d 475 (1st Dept. 1960), which states that, without a specific contract provision, an American author does not have any specific moral rights. Moral rights may be created, transferred, or surrendered by contract.

8. *Warner Brothers Pictures, Inc. v. James Bumgarner, aka James Garner,* 17 Cal. Rptr. 171 (1962). A writer's strike was held not to activate the *force majeure* clause in a contract with the leading actor in a television series. See also WGA basic agreement regarding *force majeure.*

9. See WGA basic agreement regarding theatrical compensation.

10. See WGA basic agreement regarding accrual of rights to compensation and credit upon termination.

11. See WGA basic agreement regarding disclosure of financial information by the production company.

12. See WGA basic agreement regarding warranties and indemnification.

13. See WGA basic agreement regarding the use of credits.

14. See WGA basic agreement regarding the inadvertent omission of a name in the writing credit.

15. See *17 U.S.C. sec. 101* (definitions) and *sec. 201 (b)*. "In the case of a work made for hire, the employer or other person for whom the work was prepared is considered the author for purposes of title, and, unless the parties have expressly agreed otherwise in a written instrument signed by them, owns all the rights comprised in the copyright."

## CHAPTER 6

1. *American Broadcasting Company, Inc. v. Wolf,* 430 N.Y.S. 2d 275 (App. Div. 1980), where broadcaster breached good faith negotiation and first refusal provisions of contract with ABC, but injunctive relief was not warranted because ABC waived its claim for injunctive relief.

2. *Raquel Welch and Raquel Welch Productions, Inc. v. Metro-Goldwyn-Mayer Film Co.,* 254 Cal. Rptr. 645, 207 Cal. App.3rd 164 (1989) affirms validity of pay or play provision.

3. *Gilliam v. American Broadcasting Companies,* 538 F.2d 14 (2d Cir. 1976) discusses the right of editing the owner's work. Owner failed in claim for injunctive relief and was awarded a disclaimer to be broadcast with airing.

4. *Rosemont Enterprises, Inc. v. Random House, Inc.,* 294 N.Y.S. 2d 122 (Sup. Ct. N.Y. Co. 1968) discusses "sole and exclusive world-wide rights to exploit commercially in any manner the name, personality, likeness or life story or incidents in the life of Howard Hughes."

5. *Warner Brothers Pictures, Inc. v. James Bumgarner, aka James Garner,* 17 Cal. Rptr. 171 (1962). Denied *force majeure* claim based on short-lived strike that did not impair production seriously enough.

## CHAPTER 7

1. *Raquel Welch & Raquel Welch Productions, Inc. v. Metro-Goldwyn-Mayer Film Co.,* 254 Cal. Rptr. 645, 207 Cal. App. 164 (1988) discusses Raquel Welch Productions' agreement to loan out Welch's services to MGM for production of *Cannery Row.*

2. *Raquel Welch & Raquel Welch Productions, Inc. v. Metro-Goldwyn-Mayer Film Co.,* 254 Cal. Rptr. 645, 207 Cal. App. 164 (1988) discusses validity of the pay or play provision and studio's obligation to pay actor full value of the original agreement.

3. D. E. Buderman, R. C. Berry, E. P. Pierson, M. E. Silfin and J. A. Glasser, *Law and Business of the Entertainment Industries* (1987), states that "uniqueness of a performer's talents is central in obtaining an injunction. A showing of great difficulty and inconvenience in finding a substitute of similar talents may be sufficient."

4. *Warner Brothers Pictures, Inc. v. James Bumgarner aka James Garner,* 17 Cal. Rptr. 171 (1962), regarding failure of *force majeure* claim based on short-lived strike.

## CHAPTER 8

1. See *17 U.S.C.*
2. See *17 U.S.C. sec. 101* and *sec. 201(b)*. "In the case of a work made for hire, the employer or other person for whom the work was prepared is considered the author for purposes of this title, unless the parties have expressly agreed otherwise in a written instrument, signed by them, owns all the rights comprised in the copyright."

## CHAPTER 9

1. *Burnett v. Warner Brothers Pictures*, 493 N.Y.S. 2d App. Div., 1st Dept. (1985), regarding the assignment of rights.
2. *United States v. Paramount Pictures Inc.*, 334 U.S. 131 (1948). In a suit citing Section 4 of the Sherman Act, The United States alleged that the five major film producers monopolized the film industry by producing, distributing, and exhibiting films through their own theaters to the exclusion and deteriment of interstate commerce.
3. *Gilliam v. American Broadcasting Companies Inc.*, 538 F.2d 14 (2nd Cir. 1976) discusses the right to edit owner's work.
4. *Burnett v. Warner Brothers Pictures*, 493 N.Y.S. 2d App. Div., 1st Dept. (1985) regarding the assignment of rights.
5. *Midas Productions, Inc. v. Baer*, 437 F.Supp. 1388 (C.D. CAL. 1977) and *Smith v. Weinstein*, 578 F.Supp. 1297 (S.D.N.Y., 1984). The completed film alone may be copyrighted; the idea that gave birth to the film remains unprotected. See also *17 U.S.C. sec. 102(b)*.
6. *Burnett v. Warner Brothers Pictures*, 493 N.Y.S. 2d App. Div., 1st Dept. (1985).
7. *Poe v. Michael Todd Company Inc.*, 151 F. Supp. 801 (S.D.N.Y., 1957) and *Paramount Pictures, Inc. v. Smith*, 91 F.2nd 863 (9th Cir. 1937). Failure to announce credit within the production for work performed may result in damages to the offended party.

## CHAPTER 10

1. *Preminger v. Columbia Pictures Corp.*, 267 N.Y.S. 2d 594 (Sup. Ct. 1966). Absent specific contractual provision, producer prevented from editing for television and commercial breaks.
2. *Goudal v. Cecil B. DeMille Pictures Corp.*, 5 P.2d 432 (Ca. App. 1931), regarding validity of options after wrongful discharge.
3. *CBS Inc. v. Merrick*, 716 F. 2d 1292 (9th Cir. 1983), regarding breach of contract based on failure to deliver motion picture on schedule.
4. *Smithers v. Metro-Goldwyn-Mayer Film Co.*, 139 Cal.App. 3d 643 (1983). Failure to grant bargained for credits was breach of contract.
5. *Warner Brothers Pictures Inc. v. James Bumgarner aka James Garner*, 17 Cal. Rptr. 171 (1962). Loss of *force majeure* claim based on short-lived strike.

## CHAPTER 11

1. *HBO v. Federal Communications Commission,* 587 F.1248 (D.C.C. 1978) states that there is "nothing novel or startling about a contract granting the exclusive right to publish or broadcast."

2. *Buffalo Broadcasting Company, Inc. v. ASCAP,* 744 F.2d 917 (2nd Cir. 1984), which discusses the means by which television stations can obtain use of protected music.

3. See *17 U.S.C. sec. 401(b).*

4. *United Artists v. Strand Productions,* 216 F.2d 305 (9th Cir. 1954), which states that proper construction of contract provisions are important in anticipating future developments in the growth of television.

5. *Sony Corporation of America et al. v. Universal City Studios,* 464 U.S. 417 (1984) discusses current developments in the private use of video machines.

6. *Autry v. Republic Productions,* 213 F.2d 667 (9th Cir. 1954). Implicit in the grant of television rights is the privilege to cut and edit.

7. *In Re Complaint by Massachusetts Media Association v. Station WCVB-TV, Concerning Fairness Doctrine,* 53 F.C.C. 2d 281 (1975), which states that the FCC is "specifically prohibited by Section 326 of the Communications Act from censoring broadcast material, but the Commission is authorized to impose administrative sanctions for violation of Section 1464 of the United States Criminal Code which prohibits uttering any obscene, indecent or profane language by means of radio communications."

8. *HBO v. Federal Communications Commission,* 587 F.1248 (D.C.C. 1978) defined length of exclusive broadcast availability contracts.

9. *Restatement, Second, Contracts Sec. 27, (1979)* states the importance of drafting a contract as clearly as possible since, despite what may have been confirmed during negotiations of a contract, "the subsequent written document may make a binding modification of the terms previously agreed to."

10. SAG basic agreement states that the "producer will include a provision prohibiting the licensee from eliminating or changing the billing as it appears on the positive prints of the motion picture."

11. Calamari and Perillo, *The Law of Contracts* (1987) Sec. 11–18, states "if the breach is material, the aggrieved party may cancel the contract. . . . If the breach is immaterial, the aggrieved party may not cancel the contract but may sue for partial breach."

## CHAPTER 12

1. *Mel Hardman Productions Inc. v. Robinson,* 604 F.2d 913 (Utah 1979), regarding disagreement as to terms regarding financing party's desire for production to be done to its satisfaction.

2. *Burnett v. Warner Brothers Pictures, Inc.,* 493 N.Y.S. 2d App. Div. 1st Dept. (1985). Assignment of all rights to Warner Brothers for *Everyone Comes to Rick's* meant that Warner Brothers could use it in all forms of media.

3. *Warner Brothers Pictures Inc. v. James Bumgarner aka James Garner,* 17 Cal. Rptr. 171 (1962), where actor prevailed against production company's *force majeure* claim based on short-lived strike.

## CHAPTER 14

1. *In Re Miller,* 447 A.2d 549 (N.J. 1982), involving the interpretation of a contract granting interest in certain royalty payments accruing from the sale of Glenn Miller Orchestra recordings following terminated agreement.

2. *Goudal v. Cecil B. De Mille Picture Corp.,* 5 P 2d 432 (Ca. App 1931), regarding validity of option in employment contract.

3. *Loew's Inc. v. Cole,* 185 F.2d 641 (9th Cir. 1950), regarding attempted dismissal based on morals clause (dispute prompted by House Un-American Activities Committee).

4. *Stephano v. New Group Publications, Inc.,* 485 N.Y.S. 2d 220 (Ct. App. 1984), regarding photographer's use of a model's likeness in several advertisements without consent, permission, or commercial benefit.

5. *Raquel Welch and Raquel Welch Productions Inc. v. Metro-Goldwyn-Mayer Film Co.,* 254 Cal. Rptr. 645 (1988), regarding validity of pay or play clause.

6. *Warner Brothers Pictures Inc. v. James Bumgarner aka James Garner,* 17 Cal. Rptr. 171 (1962), regarding denial of *force majeure* claim based on limited strike.

7. *DeLaurentis v. Cinematografica de Las Americas,* 215 N.Y.S. 2d 60, 9 N.Y. 2d 503 (1961), regarding validity of resolving dispute by arbitration in New York City under the rules and regulations of the AAA.

8. *DeLaurentis v. Cinematografica de Las Americas,* 215 N.Y.S. 2d 60, 9 N.Y. 2d 503 (1961).

9. *Wilhelmina Models, Inc. v. Abdulmajid,* 413 N.Y.S. 2d 21 (1979). Court reversed order for preliminary injunction on the basis that plaintiff had not shown clearly irreparable harm had been done.

## CHAPTER 16

1. *O'Sullivan v. Management Agency and Music, Ltd.,* 3 W.L.R. (Court of Appeals [UK]) August 10, 1984. Unfair bargaining position regarding artist's position relative to management agency.

2. *Croce v. Kurnit,* 565 F. Supp. 884 (S.D.N.Y. 1982). Attorney who represented the client as personal manager breached fiduciary duty by failing to advise client to seek independent counsel.

# BIBLIOGRAPHY

American Law Institute. *Restatement of the Law of Contracts.* Philadelphia: 1932.

American Law Institute. *Restatement (Second) of the Law of Contracts.* Philadelphia: 1981.

Ball, Horace. *The Law of Copyright and Literary Property.* New York: Bank & Co., 1944.

Biederman, Donald E., Berry, Robert C., Pierson, Edward P., Silfen, Martin E. and Glasser, Jeanne A. *Law and Business of the Entertainment Industries.* Dedham, Mass.: Auburn House, 1987.

Breglio, John F. *Negotiating Contracts in the Entertainment Industry.* Law Journal Seminars-Press, a Division of New York Law Publishing Co., 1986.

Corbin, Arthur L. *Corbin's Text on Contracts.* Chicago: West Publishing Co., 1952.

Farber, Donald C. *Entertainment Industry Contracts: Negotiating and Drafting Guide.* 4 vols. Matthew Bender & Co. Los Angeles: Times Mirror Books, 1987.

Farber, Donald C. *Forming Collaboration Agreements,* New York Law Journal, (Feb. 27, 1987), p.5, col.1.

Farnsworth, E. Allen. *Contracts.* Little, Brown & Co., 1982.

Friedman, Leon. *TV Financing Pacts,* New York Law Journal, (May 8, 1988), p.5, col.1.

Goldstein, Paul, *Copyright, Principles, Law and Practice.* Boston: Little, Brown & Co., 1989.

Goodale, James C. *Communication Law 1989.* New York: Practicing Law Institute, 1989.

Goodale, James C. *All About Cable.* Law Journal Seminars-Press, a Division of New York Law Publishing Co., 1981.

Goodrich. *The Story of the American Law Institute,* Wash. U.L.Q. 283, 1951.

Henn, Harry G. *Copyright Law: A Practitioner's Guide.* New York: Practicing Law Institute, 1988.

Holmes, Oliver Wendel. *The Common Law.* Boston: Little, Brown and Co., 1881.

Holsinger, Ralph L. *Media Law.* New York: Random House, 1981.

Horwitz, Lester and Horwitz, Ethan. *Intellectual Property Counseling and Litigation.* Matthew Bender Co. Los Angeles: Times Mirror Books, 1988.

Lindey, Alexander. *Lindey on Entertainment, Publishing and the Arts.* New York: Clark Boardman and Co., Ltd., 1980.

Loss, Louis. *Fundamentals of Securities Regulations* (with 1985 supplement). Boston: Little, Brown and Company, 1983.

Matthew Bender & Co. *Bender's Uniform Commercial Code Service.* Los Angeles: Times Mirror Books.

Nelson, Harold L., Teeter, Dwight T. and Le Duc, Don R. *Law of Mass Communication.* 6th Ed. Mineola, N.Y.: The Foundation Press, 1989.

Nimmer, Melville B., and Geller, Paul Edward. *International Copyright Law and Practice.* Matthew Bender & Co. Los Angeles: Times Mirror Books, 1988.

Nimmer, Melville B. *Nimmer on Copyright.* Matthew Bender & Co. Los Angeles: Times Mirror Books, 1963.

Pember, Don R. *Mass Media Law.* Dubuque, IA: Wm. C. Brown, 1987.

Rosden, George Eric and Rosden, Peter Eric. *The Law of Advertising.* Matthew Bender and Co. Los Angeles: Times Mirror Books, 1973.

Rudell, Michael I. *Highlights of New Production Contracts,* New York Law Journal (July 28, 1985), p.1., col.1.

Selz, Thomas D. and Simensky, Melvin. *Entertainment Law, Legal Concepts and Business Practices.* 3 vols. Colorado Springs, CO: Shephard's/McGraw Hill, 1983.

Silfin, Martin E. *Counseling Clients in the Entertainment Industry.* New York: Practicing Law Institute, 1983.

Simensky, Melvin. *Defining "Entertainment Law:" A Merger of Business and Legal Considerations,* New York Law Journal (September 27, 1985), p.5, col.1.

Simensky, Melvin. *Protecting Entertainment Rights,* New York Law Journal (July 27, 1984), p.4, col.4.

Simensky, Melvin. *Defining Entertainment Law.* The Entertainment and Sports Lawyer, Winter/Spring, p.13., 1986.

Stein, Ira C. *Cable Television Handbook and Forms.* Colorado Springs, CO: Shephard's/McGraw Hill, 1985.

Taubman, Joseph. *Performing Arts Management and Law.* New York: Law-Arts Publishers, 1972.

Ward, Peter C. *Federal Trade Commission, Law Practice and Procedure.* Law Journal Seminars-Press, a division of New York Law Publishing Co., 1986.

# INDEX

Above the line (budget), 52, 69, 70, 71, 84, 172

Accountant (CPA), 19, 28, 30, 77, 117, 151, 185–86

Actor agreement, 33–51

Advertising, 112; campaigns, 156; as component of the entertainment industry, 17; right to, 39, 43, 118, 130–31; of talent, 16

Agent, 10, 12; agreement, 21–32; responsibility of, 22; versus personal manager, 13

American Arbitration Association (AAA), 20, 42, 168–69, 184

American Federation of Musicians (AFM), 45, 112, 166

American Federation of Television and Radio Artists (AFTRA), 163, 166

American Society of Composers, Authors and Publishers (ASCAP), 105

Annuity clause, 17

Assignment: of actor's agreement, 46; of option, 5; of territorial rights, 15; of underlying rights by producer, 66

Attorney, 16, 183–85

Attorney-in-fact. *See* Power of attorney

Below the line costs, 52, 69, 70, 84, 172

Blue sky, 177

Bona fide, 27, 29, 30, 104, 123, 133, 140

Breach of contract, 38, 81, 98–99, 125–26, 136; material, 81, 99, 136, 170–71; suit, 17

Broadcast Music Inc. (BMI), 105

Cable television system, 106, 116

Cameraman, 86

Casting director, 71, 86

Censorship, 34, 122, 150

Community Antenna Television (CATV), 122

Compensation: for actor's services, 35–36; for agent's services, 24–28; definition of, 27–28; development fee as an advance of, 67; for director's services, 90; by distributor, 109; for exercise of option, 7; for home video rights, 148; for personal manager's services, 12, 16–17; for producer's services, 75; for retakes, 37; for screen writer's services, 57–59; for talent's services, 13, 17, 164–66; for television syndication rights, 133; upon termination, 75

Completion bond, 138–39, 180–82
Confidentiality, 61
Conversion, to master video record-
    ings, 149–50
Coproduction, international, 137–45
Copyright, 2, 8–9, 40, 55, 63, 75, 95,
    100, 109, 116, 139–40, 143, 144,
    147, 153, 154; assignment of, 61;
    clarification of ownership by, 3, 9;
    fair use of, 101; foreign registration,
    151; length of protection, 100–101;
    and moral rights, 40; notice, 75,
    101, 139; transfer of, 101
Copyright Act, 53, 100
Costume designer, 71
Covenants, negative, 42–43, 80, 97,
    169
Creative control, 6, 14, 66, 69–71,
    84–85, 139, 150, 162

Dailies, 72, 83, 107
Darth Vader, 113
Debt financing, 178–79; bridge loan,
    179; credit line, 179
Development fee, 67
Director agreement, 82–99
Director of photography, 68, 71, 86
Director's cut, 83
Directors Guild of America (DGA),
    89, 92, 112, 156
Distributor: as producer, 83; producer
    retained by, 65–81; relating to home
    video license agreement, in general,
    146–56; relating to license to televi-
    sion syndication, in general,
    127–36; relating to pay-per-view
    agreements, in general, 115–26;
    rights of, 106–9; versus producer,
    106
Distributor's gross, 76–77
*Droit moral,* 7, 40, 55, 65, 95, 155
Dubbing, 35, 122, 131, 156

Editor, 72, 83, 86
Employee for hire, 52, 53, 55; em-
    ployee who creates a work for hire,
    111
Endorsement, 119
Entertainment, definition of, 12, 17

Escape clause, 29
Exhibitor: motion picture, 113–14
Expenses, 18–19, 43, 54, 78, 95–96,
    161

Federal Communications Commission
    (FCC), 131
Final cut, 74, 84, 107–8, 122
Financial reports, 178; Form 10-K,
    178; Form 10-Q, 178
First assistant director, 71, 86
*Force majeure,* 41, 51, 56, 80–81,
    97–98, 126, 145, 167
Four wall, 114

Good faith, 89
Gross profits, 36–37, 43–44, 92–93
Gross revenues, 16–17

Holdback, 155
Home video license agreement,
    146–56
House nut, 145

Incapacity: of director, 98; of talent,
    170
Incorporation, by talent, 20, 31, 42,
    168
Indemnification, 105, 121, 144–45
Independent contractor, 20, 32
Injunction, 62, 97, 169
Insurance: mandatory, 141; require-
    ment of, 46, 63, 76, 90, 163–64
Internal Revenue Service (IRS), 185
International Alliance of Theatrical
    and Stage Employees (IATSE), 74,
    112

Jurisdiction, over disputes, 20, 168

Key person clause, 11–12, 23

Laboratory, 123, 133; access letter,
    123, 133; access to, 140
Library of Congress, 2
License: of agent, 10–11, 21–22; of
    motion picture for television syndi-
    cation, in general, 127–36; of mo-
    tion picture to U.S. network, 142;

period, 118; of sequel rights, 76; to subdistributor, 125
License fees, pay-per-view, 116–17
Lighting director, 71, 86
Loan out, 33, 52, 69, 83
Logo, 125

Master Antenna Television (MATV), 122
Master tape, 123
Merchandising: of actor's character, 46, 162–63; based on motion picture characters, 112–13; by home video distributor, 154; of products derived from a motion picture, 6; retained by producer from director, 95; secured by producer's employment agreement, 65, 75–76; secured by producer under employee for hire agreement, 55
Mickey Mouse, 113
Minor: requirement for judicial approval, 49; unique under the Law, 49
Moral rights, 7, 40, 55
Morals clause, 160–61
Motion Picture Association of America (MPAA), 73, 107, 110–11, 116, 121, 130; ratings of, 73
Motion Picture Export Association of America (MPEAA), 116
Motion picture rights, acquisition of, 1–9
Music composer, 72, 86, 100, 101, 124, 134
Music soundtrack, 100

Negative cost, 110
Negotiations, third party, 5
Net Profits, 36–37, 43–44, 110
Networks: ABC, 127; CBS, 127; Fox, 127; NBC, 127
Notice: exercise of option, 4
Novel, 1, 2; right to novelize, 6, 63

Option: acquisition of motion picture, 1–9; in endorsement agreements, 158; exercise of motion picture, 4; to extend endorsement agreement,

164; to obtain additional territories, 122–23, 132–33; producer's, 65; regarding commissions following termination of a personal management contract, 18; renewal of agent's agreement by exercise of, 28–29; renewal of personal manager's agreement by exercise of, 14–15; transfer of, by producer to distributor, 65–66
Overhead, 72

Package of motion pictures, 124, 134–35
Packaging entity, 17
Paramount Pictures, 44, 77
Pay or play, 24, 36, 47, 60, 67, 91–92, 166
Pay-per-view, 93, 107, 113–26, 172, 180
Performance criteria, 22–23
Personal manager, 10–20
Postproduction, 35, 37, 54, 64, 69, 73, 74, 85, 87–88
Power of attorney, 4, 15–16, 31
Preproduction, 35, 38, 39, 65, 74, 85, 87–88
Presale: financing, 179–80
Private placement, 172, 173, 174; memorandum of, 174
Producer's employment agreement, 64–81
Producer's net, 59–60
Production manager, 71
Public domain, 3, 9
Public offering, 177–78
Public relations: agency, 13; for the actor, 45
Publisher: literary, 2; music, 100, 101, 103

Rambo, 113
Registration, securities, 173; exemptions from, 173–77
Regulation A, 176–77
Regulation D, 173–76; Rule 501, 175; Rule 504, 176; Rule 505, 176; Rule 506, 176
Release window, 149

Reversion of option, 8
Rights: acquisition of underlying, 1,
    65; ancillary, 142–43; of approval in
    endorsement agreements, 160;
    assignment of underlying, 66;
    audio-visual, 104; clearance of mu-
    sic, 102; to cure, 56–57, 63, 126; to
    distribute on free television, 128; to
    enter agreement, 95; of first negoti-
    ations, 88; forfeit of, by producer,
    78; granted for television syndica-
    tion, 128; incidental, 119; music
    rights granted, 102, 108; nontheatri-
    cal media, 104; privacy, 3, 119; of
    producer on home video, 151–52;
    television, 104; theater, 104; trailer,
    104; warranty of ownership of, 111
Rooney, Mickey, 48

Satellite, 44
Satellite Master Antenna Television
    (SMATV), 122
Screen Actor's Guild (SAG), 45, 47,
    112, 156, 163
Screen credits, 8, 39, 53, 61–62, 79,
    96–97, 113, 125, 135
Screen writer, 52–63
Securities Act of 1933, Section 4 (2),
    173
Security and Exchange Commission
    (SEC), 173, 176, 177, 178
Society of European Stage Authors
    and Composers (SESAC), 105
Sound editor, 71, 86
Sound engineer, 71, 86
Sound track, 6, 75, 100, 108, 113
Special effects director, 71
Subtitling, 132

Suspension clause 19, 30
Synchronization license, 108, 120,
    130
Synchronization rights, 102, 103, 104;
    for free television, 105

Television: rights of, 5; syndication
    agreement, 127–36
Television Receiver Only (TVRO), 122
Temple, Shirley, 44
Term, 14, 22, 103, 164
Territory, 15, 102–3, 115–16, 141,
    147; for endorsement agreement,
    158
Trust, monies held in, 45, 78, 94
Turnaround, 5, 67–68
Twentieth Century Fox, 44, 77

Unconscionability, 31–32
Unenforceability: of a single clause in
    agreement, 19–20, 30–31, 51, 168;
    of an unconscionable term, 14
Unit manager, 71
Universal Copyright Convention, 9

VCR, 156
Venture capital, 179
Video cassette: as component of the
    entertainment industry, 17; rights
    of, 5, 41, 44, 56, 93, 146, 147, 149,
    150

Warner Brothers, 44, 77
Warranties, 2, 42, 61, 78; of original-
    ity of created material, 94–95,
    104–5, 111, 119–21, 128–30, 166–67
Writers Guild of America (WGA),
    52–53, 54, 59, 60, 61, 62, 112, 156

**About the Author**

PETER MULLER is an attorney in the entertainment industry. He is president of M.E.G., an entertainment company, the past president of ACA Joe, and has extensive experience in the business of motion picture production.